CLIFF RAILWAYS

CLIFF RAILWAYS
~ AN HISTORIC SURVEY ~

• PETER JOHNSON •

PEN & SWORD
TRANSPORT
AN IMPRINT OF PEN & SWORD BOOKS LTD.
YORKSHIRE – PHILADELPHIA

Title page image: Opened in 1884, the cliff railway on the Yorkshire Coast at Saltburn is now the oldest water-balanced system in Britain. It was photographed on 12 May 2021. (Steve Sedgwick)

Reverse of title page: The first cliff railway at Scarborough's South Bay still provides a public service. It appears to be the backdrop for a religious or politcal gathering in this photograph.

Jacket, front image: The Lynton & Lynmouth Lift is the only British cliff railway to serve two places. This is the Lynmouth terminus.

Jacket, rear, upper image: The North Cliff Railway at Scarborough in happier times, opened in 1930, closed in 1997.

Jacket, rear, lower image: The West Hill lift at Hastings in the summer of 2024.

First published in Great Britain in 2025 by
Pen and Sword Transport
An imprint of
Pen & Sword Books Ltd.
Yorkshire - Philadelphia

Copyright © Peter Johnson, 2025

ISBN 978 1 39904 830 9

The right of Peter Johnson to be identified as author of this work has been asserted by him in accordance with the Copyright, Designs and Patents Act 1988.

A CIP catalogue record for this book is available from the British Library.

All rights reserved. No part of this book may be reproduced, transmitted, downloaded, decompiled or reverse engineered in any form or by any means, electronic or mechanical including photocopying, recording or by any information storage and retrieval system, without permission from the Publisher in writing. NO AI TRAINING: Without in any way limiting the Author's and Publisher's exclusive rights under copyright, any use of this publication to "train" generative artificial intelligence (AI) technologies to generate text is expressly prohibited. The Author and Publisher reserve all rights to license uses of this work for generative AI training and development of machine learning language models.

Typeset in Palatino 11/13 by SJmagic DESIGN SERVICES, India.

The Publisher's authorised representative in the EU for product safety is Authorised Rep Compliance Ltd., Ground Floor, 71 Lower Baggot Street, Dublin D02 P593, Ireland.
www.arccompliance.com

For a complete list of Pen & Sword titles please contact

PEN & SWORD BOOKS LIMITED
George House, Beevor Street, Off Pontefract Road, Hoyle Mill, Barnsley, South Yorkshire, England, S71 1HN.
E-mail: enquiries@pen-and-sword.co.uk
Website: www.pen-and-sword.co.uk

or

PEN AND SWORD BOOKS
1950 Lawrence Rd, Havertown, PA 19083, USA
E-mail: uspen-and-sword@casematepublishers.com
Website: www.penandswordbooks.com

CONTENTS

Preface 6
Acknowledgements and Sources 8

Chapter 1   1875 South Cliff Tramway, Scarborough 9
Chapter 2   1878 Queen's Parade Tramway, Scarborough 20
Chapter 3   1881 Central Tramway, Scarborough 24
Chapter 4   1884 Paston Place, Brighton 34
Chapter 5   1884 Saltburn Incline Tramway 36
Chapter 6   1884 Falcon Cliff Hotel Lift I, Douglas 45
Chapter 7   1885/1890 Folkestone Cliff Tramway, the Leas 47
Chapter 8   1890 Lynton & Lynmouth Lift 60
Chapter 9   1890 Browside Tramway, Isle of Man 77
Chapter 10   1891 Hastings, West Hill Lift 80
Chapter 11   1892 Bridgnorth, Castle Hill Railway 92
Chapter 12   1893 Clifton Rocks Railway 103
Chapter 13   1896 Folkestone, Sandgate Hill Lift 110
Chapter 14   1896 Aberystwyth, Constitutional Hill Lift 115
Chapter 15   1898 Port Soderick Lift 127
Chapter 16   1900 Douglas Head Incline Railway 130
Chapter 17   1902 Hastings East Hill Lift 133
Chapter 18   1904 Folkestone Metropole Lift 144
Chapter 19   1908 Bournemouth, East Lift 147
Chapter 20   1908 Bournemouth, West Lift 152
Chapter 21   1910 Broadstairs Lift 156
Chapter 22   1912 Cliftonville Lift 160
Chapter 23   1912 Southend-on-Sea Lift 162
Chapter 24   1926 Babbacombe Cliff Light Railway 170
Chapter 25   1927 Falcon Cliff Hotel Lift II, Douglas 185
Chapter 26   1929 Scarborough, St Nicholas Lift 188
Chapter 27   1930 Scarborough, North Bay Lift 193
Chapter 28   1935 Bournemouth, Southbourne (Fisherman's Walk) Lift 196
Chapter 29   1979 Llechwedd Slate Caverns 200
Chapter 30   1992 Centre for Alternative Technology Lift, Llwyngwern 203

APPENDICES

Appendix 1   Unbuilt Cliff Railways 208
Appendix 2   Babbacombe Cliff Light Railway Estimate of Expenses 1923 210
Appendix 3   Cable Tramways 212
Appendix 4   Electric Stairways 215
Appendix 5   Steep-Grade Railways 216
Appendix 6   Automated People Movers 221
Appendix 7   Vertical Lifts 222
Appendix 8   Other Lifts 231
Photographic Addendum 233
Bibliography 237
Index 238

PREFACE

There is something about a cliff railway, its tiny car or cars gliding quietly up and down a cliffside, carrying a small number of passengers to their destination. Their usual antique appearance only adds to their charm.

In 1950 there were eighteen cliff railways operating in Britain or being prepared for operation following wartime closure. At the time of writing, in 2024, there are thirteen, two of which did not exist in 1950. One more is the subject of a lottery fund-supported restoration, another awaits repairs to storm damage, and a third is subject to a survey to determine the requirements, and cost, of returning it to service. Before 1950, another eight cliff railways had existed for varying periods of time.

These fascinating contrivances, similar yet so different, are short rope-worked railways that run up and down steep gradients, mostly at seaside resorts. There have been seven in Kent, five in Yorkshire and five on the Isle of Man. There are now three in Wales, although Aberystwyth was the solitary example there until 1979, and remains the only one at a seaside location, and the future of one of them is uncertain.

The first cliff railways made use of mining technology and were water balanced, the water often being free and plentiful. Where it was not so cheap or plentiful the addition of an oil engine enabled it to be recycled. Later installations used oil engines, and then diesel engines and/or electric motors, for haulage.

Most of these railways were built using local authority planning powers but exceptionally an Act of Parliament authorised the Lynton & Lynmouth line, and gave it the distinction of creating a statutory company to run it, and a Light Railway Order sanctioned that at Babbacombe. Folkestone Corporation also obtained a Light Railway Order to authorise its ownership and operation of the Leas railway.

Until 1902 the railways were built by private capital but shareholder pressure for dividends influenced outcomes to varying extents and reserves often failed to match the demands of renewals, which led to several lines being taken over by local authorities. It is to their owners' credit that three railways are thriving in the ownership of their founding company. Some authorities also took on the challenge of building and operating their own railways, finding different ways of dealing with the challenges imposed upon them by the recent years of austerity insofar as they affected their railways.

Three particular names are associated with the promotion and construction of British cliff railways. The forerunner, in terms of volume of work and number of lines, is R. Waygood & Company, a business founded by Richard Waygood (1806–79) in Beaminster, Dorset, in 1833. Active in general engineering and the manufacture of hot water apparatus and stoves, the enterprise moved to London in 1840 and took an interest in lifts after Henry Claude Walker (1852–1939) joined the firm in 1865. Waygood retired in 1872 and the business was continued after his death. Walker became a partner and then chairman, a post that he retained after the Waygood company was registered in 1900. The company became pre-eminent for the supply of lifts in Britain, being awarded warrants for installations in royal residences. It later became a part of the US Otis lift company.

George Newnes, a newspaper magnate, and George Croydon Marks, an engineer who then specialised in hydraulic engineering, worked together on three cliff railways between 1890 and 1893, first at

Lynton, then on the Castle Hill Railway, Bridgnorth, and the Clifton Rocks Railway. Newnes provided the capital while Marks provided the engineering know-how. From 1895 Marks was involved with the Constitution Hill Railway, Aberystwyth, and other developments in the Welsh resort.

Cliff railways, using vehicles with flanged wheels on running rails, are often referred to as cliff lifts, which is not so surprising, as many of them were supplied by lift companies, and sometimes they are known as funiculars, which the *New Oxford English Dictionary* defines as 'of a railway, especially one on a mountainside operating by cable with ascending and descending cars counterbalanced', which means that single-car systems are not funiculars, although some may disagree, as they are still counterbalanced. For many the terms are interchangeable. Incidentally, cliff railways located overseas are usually referred to as funiculars.

For the cliff railways that are members of the Heritage Railways Association a 'rail-mounted cableway group' was formed to enable them to share items of common interest, and to present a united front in dealings with the Health & Safety Executive's mines inspectorate, which regulates their operations to ensure compliance with the Lifting Operations Equipment and Lift Regulations 1998.

It should be noted that the use of cliff railways is not just a British phenomenon, and they are to be found in many countries overseas, including Austria, Brazil, Canada, France, Germany, Hong Kong, Italy, Malaysia, Norway, Spain, Sweden, Switzerland, Ukraine and the US.

As an interest in cliff railways often leads to an interest in other installations that had operating features in common or that serve or served a similar purpose, details of some of these are given in the appendices.

Humour on a cliff railway. The Lynmouth line appears to be the only one honoured with such a postcard. (Rupert Besley/J. Arthur Dixon)

ACKNOWLEDGEMENTS AND SOURCES

Sometime in the 1970s I came across a copy of Geoffrey Body's and Richard L. Eastleigh's small book *Cliff Railways* (David & Charles, 1964). Long superseded, it got me, and many others, interested in the subject. I started collecting postcards and over the years the collection grew to include original albumen prints as well as lantern slides and other photographic formats.

When the concept of this book was first floated, it was to have been a book that concentrated on the illustrations. The volume of information available about some of the railways has made it very different. And while some of the histories are quite extensive, others are quite short because there is very little information available about them.

Most of the information contained herein has been extracted from digitised newspapers accessed from the British Newspaper Archive (www.britishnewspaperarchive.co.uk), along with some obtained from the Board of Trade and Ministry of Transport files in the National Archive at Kew. The titles listed in the bibliography helped to fill in some of the gaps that remained, and I particularly acknowledge the works of Keith Turner and Martin Easdown in this respect.

It will be seen that in many of the older cliff railway photographs the railways are incidental to the image, and that where the railway is the subject of an image the resolution is insufficient to reveal as much detail as might be desired, rendering it impossible to track known changes from photographs. It is also true that many changes that show on photographs were not recorded contemporaneously so might not be dateable.

The illustrations mostly came from my collection or were of my own taking. Alan Bowler, Barry Edwards, Jon Knowles, Steve Sedgwick and the Online Transport Archive (via secretary Peter Waller) also kindly made photographs available.

Many thanks are due to Ashley Clarke and his staff at the Lynton & Lynmouth Lift for a pleasant afternoon seeing the lift in operation at close quarters and for answering questions.

Peter Johnson
Leicester
SEPTEMBER 2025

CHAPTER 1

1875 SOUTH CLIFF TRAMWAY, SCARBOROUGH

Opened 6 July 1875, 4ft 8½in gauge, double track, 286ft long, gradient 1 in 1.75, hydraulic, water balance, operational.
Scarborough is the home of the first British cliff railway, which was followed by four more, although one of them was very short lived and only two survive.

In the 1870s, the town was an expanding resort on the east coast, with visitors attracted to beaches on the north and south bays. The town itself was originally developed as a small fishing port before the advancement of tourism, aided by the arrival of the York & North Midland Railway in 1845, led to its expansion on the clifftop of the south bay, followed by further growth towards the north bay.

On the south bay, the older development to the north was separated from later expansion southwards by a deep gully, which was bridged by the Cliff Bridge Company in 1827 to access the Spa that the company was developing. It was the Spa, and its location beneath the clifftop, that provided the incentive for constructing the first cliff railway.

The Scarborough South Cliff Tramway Company was registered in April 1873, its £4,500 capital comprising 1,500 £3 shares. A prospectus published in the *Yorkshire Post* on 3 June named five local men as directors and William Harrington Lucas (1837–1902) as engineer. The rapid increase in the South Cliff suburb's population, it was claimed, had directed attention to the inconvenience of the existing communication with the Spa Terrace and the South Sands, some 170ft elevation apart.

An 'incline tramway' was therefore proposed to connect the two locations, using hydraulic power to work the cars on the tramway, which would be constructed on the principle used successfully on mining inclines and improved recently to ensure its safety and convenience. The undertaking would obtain its water from the sea and an agreement had been made with the Cliff Bridge Company that gave it an option to purchase the tramway at a future date on agreed terms.

On 7 June the *Whitby Gazette* reported that most of the shares had been allotted and forecast an early start to construction. However, the latter turned out to be rather optimistic for Stewart & Bury, Architects, did not advertise for tenders until 30 September (*Yorkshire Post*) and construction did not start for some time.

The *Sheffield Daily Telegraph*'s 'erratic correspondent', who signed himself Arcturus, adopted a whimsical approach when he commented on the works, suggesting that the 'curious wooden framework' erected on the cliff face was a salmon ladder and disbelieving the workman who had told him that it was a tramway (15 August 1874). The earliest 'normal' report on the subject was that of the *Driffield Times* on 28 November 1874, which merely said that construction was progressing.

On 31 May 1875, though, the *York Herald* said that the tramway was 300ft long on a 33-degree incline. Two handsome carriages, it said, delivered by the Metropolitan Carriage Company of Saltley, had been designed to carry fourteen persons each. The rope had a breaking strain of 20 tons, while the maximum load would not exceed 2 tons. The contractor was a local man, William Jowsey (1834–1905), and Crossley Brothers of Manchester had installed two gas engines to pump sea water to the top

The photograph is the earliest of the tramway yet found by the author, showing both stations and the water tanks at the top and the line apparently in operation. An elevated walkway from the Spa enters the photo from the right and a canvas-covered canopy has been erected by the bottom station to shelter patrons from the elements. Another footpath from the Spa passes through the stonework that supports the line above the lower station. Where it emerges, on the left of the tramway, is a pile of detritus, including lengths of rail, probably surplus from construction but whether it enables the photo to be dated to the 1870s is unclear. There is more clutter to the left of the lower station, too, and it is notable that there are no signs or notices on the building. The Prince of Wales Hotel dominates the skyline. It would be interesting to know the nature of the discussion about the fish in the foreground.

station; Scarborough being a spa town, there was a demand for sea water for bathing.

The tramway was opened without ceremony on 6 July, the *York Herald* (7 July) saying that a formal unveiling would be at a later date. The paper described how director Richard Hunt (1812–77) frequently rode up and down during the day. Of the passengers, it said 'a certain degree of timidity is apparent in almost every one', none of them had ever seen or experienced anything like it before, after all, and told how its reporter had heard one woman say to her friend that they should have 'a pennyworth of fright'.

An advertisement announcing the tramway's opening in the *York Herald* on 7 July 1875 called it the 'new inclined carriage way' and several newspaper reports used the same term. It also said that a bucket of fresh salt water could be obtained from the top station for one penny.

The salt water was of interest to the newly established South Cliff Baths Company, which in 1876 obtained permission to lay a pipe under the road from the tramway's upper station to its premises then under construction in Ramsdale [now Ramshill] Road (*York Herald*, 11 April).

The tramway had also been mentioned when the town council had met in August 1875, councillors discussing whether beach users caught by the tide had any right to free access to the Cliff Bridge Company's grounds. One councillor reported hearing about a group that had descended by the tramway and had been allowed entrance while another said that others had been refused admission without payment. The consensus was that anyone 'fairly' caught by the tide should have free access (*York Herald*, 10 August). On 26 August the same paper said of the tramway that 'a trip is well worth the penny charged for a journey either up or down'.

Although the tramway was, in legal terms, a railway built on private land without powers, the directors knew that they would benefit from the kudos attached to undergoing a Board of Trade inspection. However, their attempts to obtain a satisfactory inspection and meet the Board's requirements were drawn out.

Following the company solicitor's 5 June 1875 enquiry about the procedure to be followed, saying that the company desired an inspection if practicable, the Board decided that the 1842 Regulation of Railways Act gave it the power to inspect and instructed Colonel Charles Scrope Hutchinson (1827-1912), who visited Scarborough on 22 June.

He found that the tramway was not ready for inspection, but he told the company what must be done before he could recommend its approval for the carriage of passengers and asked for the Board to be notified when the works had been carried out, in order that he might make a formal inspection. Hearing that the line had been opened and deciding that responsibility for any accident would lie with the company, on 30 August the Board asked if the changes had been made.

The company did not reply until 9 October, when it said that while provision had been made for restraining the upper carriage when not in use, to relieve the strain on the ropes, its engineer had advised that there were practical difficulties in providing a drop hook on each carriage, to restrain the car in the event of a wire breaking. He added that not only did the wire rope have a breaking strain of 28 tons

A view looking generally northwards, with the tramway running diagonally across the picture, the top station and the roof of the lower station visible. Prominent are the Prince of Wales Hotel and the Esplanade on the left, the Grand Hotel on the right, with the Spa bridge to its left, and the Spa in the centre. Part of the Spa complex was designed by Joseph Paxton, better known for designing the 1851 Great Exhibition's Crystal Palace.

The drawing of the 'powerful hook' provided to the Board of Trade in 1875. (National Archives)

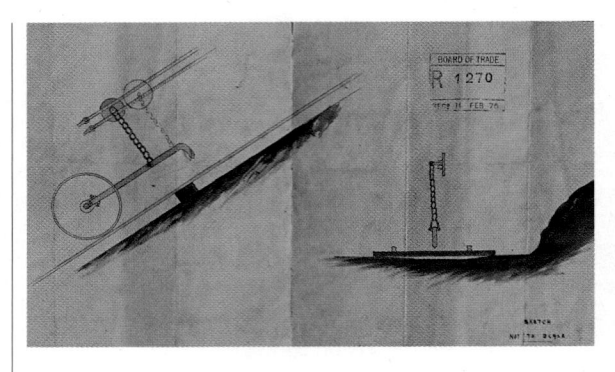

and the weight of the carriage never exceed 3 tons, but a second rope had been installed. On 14 October the Board replied that until a satisfactory self-acting arrangement for stopping a car from running back down the tramway in the event of a rope breaking had been provided, the works would not be authorised.

Capitulation was immediate and on 26 October a sketch of a proposed drop hook was submitted to the Board. This was rejected by Hutchinson, though, who thought the hook would not catch on the sleepers as intended, resulting in a second sketch, illustrated, being submitted in February 1876, which he also rejected. The company, therefore, adopted the original design and the matter was left until 31 July 1877, when it reported that Hutchinson's requirements had been met and requesting an inspection.

Hutchinson, who had retired from the Royal Engineers on full pay and with the honorary rank of major general on 30 December 1876, reported from Manchester on 21 August 1877. Describing the tramway, he said that the rails, sleepers and longitudinal timbers were of a substantial character and appeared to be well maintained since his June 1875 visit. At length, he reported, a device to stop the cars running away if the rope broke had been provided, in the shape of a 'powerful hook' attached to the upper end of each car. The greatest possible care would be required to be taken in working the tramway, with frequent and thorough inspections of the ropes and their renewal from time to time, before they wore out. 'As yet no accident of any kind has … taken place.' He recommended that the Board need not object to the use of the tramway.

At the company meeting held on 7 February 1876 shareholders were told that results had been much better than anticipated, the directors recommending a 10% dividend from the £427 7s 4d surplus that remained from the £616 1s 4d income after £427 7s 4d costs had been deducted. On the capital account the situation did not look quite so rosy, capital having been increased to £6,750, £4,886 1s 1d spent, £4,632 5s issued and £2,200 required to discharge liabilities, including the cost of increasing the capacity of the water tanks that had been found to be necessary.

Director Richard Hunt, proprietor of the Prince of Wales Hotel, and who had been described as the driving force behind the tramway's inception in the local media, died on 27 February 1877, aged 65. His obituary in the *York Herald* (2 March) said that he had been originally in York before moving to Scarborough and had been a musician before moving into hotel management, conducting local musical groups until shortly before his death. He was also, said the paper, proud of his mechanical skills and had invented a life raft that used rollers at the same time that the music publisher J.A. Novello had invented a similar device. The most important of his inventions, the paper continued, was the incline carriageway, now in use at the South Cliff, for which he had obtained a patent.

The provisional specification for Hunt's patent, for the invention of 'improvements in the means of facilitating transit of steep inclines, and in the apparatus and carriages to be used therefor' had been submitted on 11 November 1875 and the final specification approved on 11 May 1876.

Briefly, the key features were grooved balance wheels at each end, around which passed duplicate steel ropes connecting the two cars, the upper wheel being equipped with a brake. The carriages had under tanks with their lower surfaces having the same inclination as the incline and used to contain water used as the 'gravitating power', and upper compartments for passengers. The steel ropes were attached to the cars by sprung draw rods, and clutches and a drop hook attached to the draw rods combined to act as a safety measure.

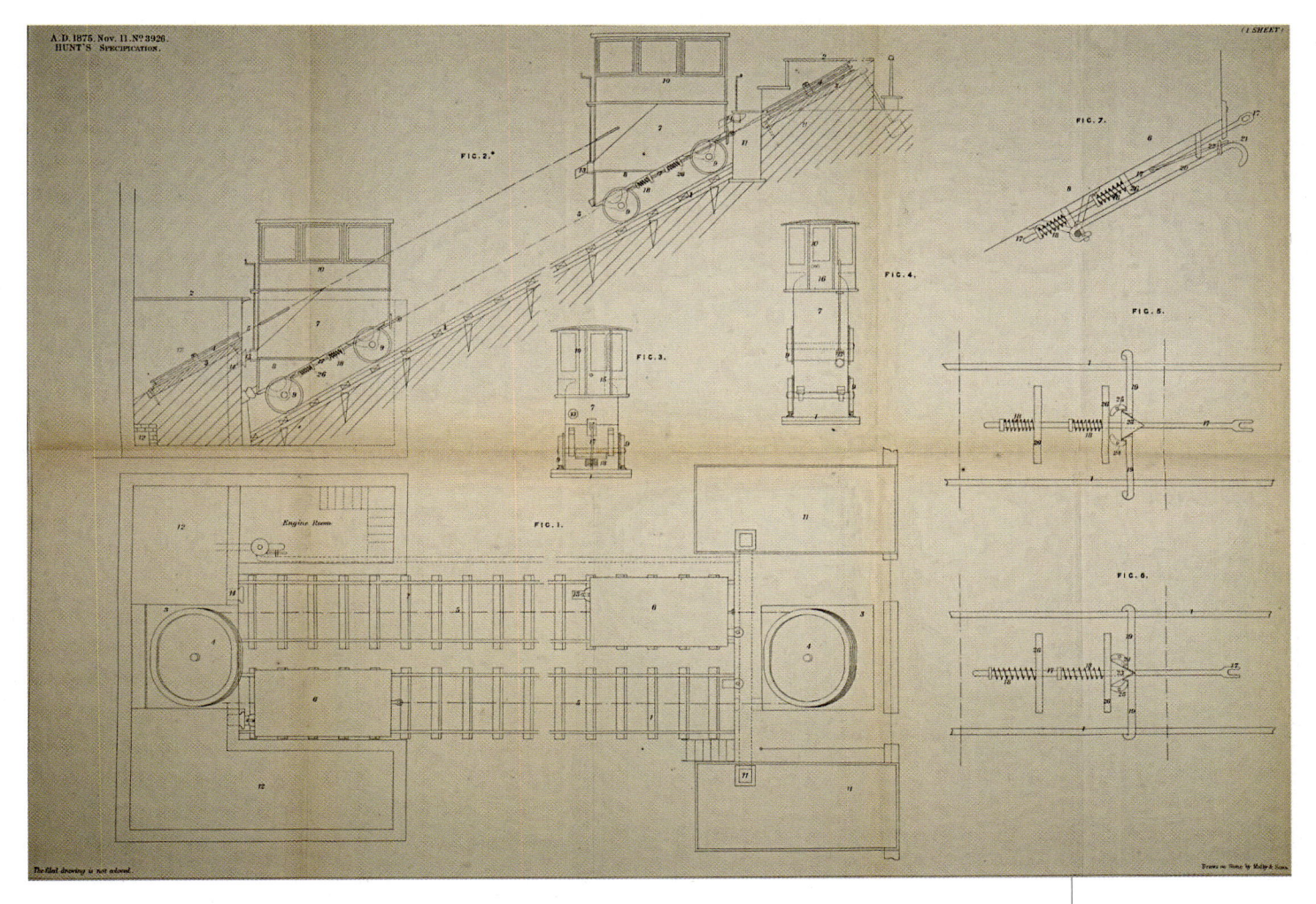

The patent was not mentioned in the prospectus and the author has found no evidence that anyone made use of it, although its features are shared by other water-balanced cliff railways. Any differences will merely fine tune the details worked out by Hunt.

Following Hutchinson's inspection, the company appointed Henry Percy Holt (1849–1903), who was also dealing with the Queen's Parade tramway, as its consulting engineer. His first move was to have the tramway, including the cars, overhauled, during the 1877–78 winter closure period. The ropes and drawbars were also replaced (*York Herald*, 29 January / 16 April 1878).

After one of the drop hooks fell without reason and stopped the cars, he had the company ask the Board of Trade for approval to remove them. On 12 October Hutchinson reported that improper maintenance of the catch that held the hook had allowed it to drop and said that he had no objection to the hooks being replaced by an alternative safety device. Thereafter the Board of Trade files are silent on the operation of the South Cliff Tramway.

Also in 1878, the directors decided that not only should dogs be charged for but that staff should have the right to refuse to carry wet and dirty animals. Regular users could also buy 14 tickets for 1s. A total of 400,000 passengers were carried during the year (*Newcastle Courant*, 8 August 1879).

In 1877 the Cliff Bridge Company appointed a committee to see whether

Richard Hunt's cliff railway patent application diagram, 1875.

1875 SOUTH CLIFF TRAMWAY, SCARBOROUGH • 13

From at least 1877 the beach at the foot of the tramway was known as the 'children's corner', which presumably meant that they would not be rebuked for digging holes in the same. This circa 1900 postcard view shows that the tramway has lost its large promotion board and flagpole, presumably due to the weather. The station building, extended to its left to accommodate the gas engine in the 1880s, has also been extended at the front. The stone wall in front of the station and the curved wave wall alongside it were built following storm damage in 1882. The cliffside building has been lost in, or destroyed by, the boscage. (Queen Series)

SCARBOROUGH - SOUTH CLIFF TRAMWAY

it should exercise its right to purchase the tramway, but the committee decided that the responsibility was too much and deemed it inexpedient for the company to exercise its right (*York Herald*, 23 October).

The tramway's management was streamlined by the appointment of Gabriel Gordon Cleather (1847–1908) as secretary and manager in 1881. Previously the company's solicitor had acted as secretary and the tramway's operation had been managed by Robert Mitchell (born 1842), an accountant. Cleather, secretary of the Scarborough & Whitby Railway from 1873 until 1877, appears to have been an ambitious individual. After the Whitby Railway had ceased operations for lack of funds in 1877, he had obtained the same position with Scarborough's marine aquarium, taking the manager's position in 1878, which required the incumbent to be discharged. He was a founding director of the new Central Tramway, becoming its managing director when it opened later in 1881, both positions that he retained while working for the South Cliff Company.

One of the things he had to deal with on the South Cliff was a landslip that caused the tramway to be closed for a few hours on 25 September, following a period of heavy rainfall (*Yorkshire Post*, 27 September 1881).

Reporting to the shareholders in February 1882, the directors were impressed with Cleather's first year in office, for he had reduced the working expenses by £217 3s 6d while the fare income, affected by poor weather and the landslip, had only fallen by £97 18s, enabling them to declare a 5% dividend. He gave up his appointments in Scarborough, however, in September 1882, when he left for London to manage the Crystal Palace. He was replaced by Valentine Fowler (1849–1918), an auctioneer and estate agent.

More storms in March 1883 also destroyed the walkway from the Spa and damaged the steps to the beach (*York Herald*, 7/12 March). Unreported damage was done to the lean-to structure on the left of the station building as well.

Elected a director in 1883, Richard Henry Butterworth (1939–22), a retired mechanical engineer, was appointed managing director and consulting engineer from 1 January 1885 (*York Herald*, 14 February 1883/*Yorkshire Gazette*, 24 January 1885). In 1889 he made modifications to the cars that enabled their water tanks to be filled and emptied automatically, saving much time in the tramway's operation (*Yorkshire Evening Post*, 15 January 1889).

Passenger numbers were reported in 1890, 285,427 passing the turnstiles, 185,497 ascending, enabling the company to pay a 6% dividend (*Yorkshire Post*, 24 January 1891). The 1890s were obviously good for the tramway, for the dividend reached 7½% in 1895 and a fund was started to redeem the debentures, enabling a lottery for the redemption of two of them to be held on 14 January 1895. The 1895 report included a breakdown of revenue by ticket type: Ordinary (single), £894 18s 3d; contract, £300 8s; children, £75 4s; annual, £29 10s, dog, £1 15s 3d. In the same year £200 was set aside for boiler repairs and renewals (*Morning Post*, 1 January 1895/*York Herald*, 12 January 1895/*York Herald*, 28 January 1896).

In 1901 the walkway bridge from the Spa was again destroyed during a storm and was replaced by 'iron girders' at a cost of £79 12s 2d the following year (*Sheffield Daily Telegraph*, 26 January 1903). More damage was done in 1903 and 1905 (*Sheffield Daily Telegraph*, 1 February 1904/10 January 1905).

With the tramway closed for maintenance during the winter, it had been customary to remove the car bodies from the frames and to chain the frames in position. On 5 December 1912 the chain holding the frame at the top station broke, the frame running away and colliding with the lower station buffers, destroying itself, the loose haulage rope connected to it being 'swirled round at a tremendous speed' and causing much damage to the top station. Two employees walking on the tramway managed to avoid the runaway and the swirling rope (*Leeds Mercury/Yorkshire Evening Post*, 6 December).

Nothing was said about the accident in the reports of the 1913 annual meeting, when the shareholders were told that it was time to renew the tramway, including electrifying the pumping and replacing the cars. The new cars had five windows each side instead of four and entered service during 1913 (*Sheffield Daily Telegraph/Leeds Mercury*, 27 January). At the 1914 meeting it was reported that £230 had been spent on new cars (of unknown origin) and that steam pumping had been replaced by electricity (*Sheffield Daily Telegraph*, 2 February).

Sunday services run in conjunction with events at the Spa ran at a loss in 1907 and were discontinued (*Sheffield Daily Telegraph/Yorkshire Post*, 3 February 1908).

There have been two fatal accidents on the tramway, one of an employee, the other of a passenger. The first occurred on 17 April 1925, when Arthur Fletcher, a 59-year-old retired postman, was oiling the track and was run down by an ascending car. Reviving sufficiently to admit responsibility, he died in hospital a few hours later. At the inquest a verdict of accidental death was recorded, with no negligence attributed to any party. Nowadays the company would be criticised, and probably prosecuted, for not having a safe system of work in place (*Leeds Mercury*, 18 April/*Yorkshire Post*, 25 April).

The second fatal accident occurred on 28 May 1952, when Mary Ellen Coward, a widow aged 78, boarded a car at the lower station and was thrown off balance into the pit below when it started to move before the doors closed. Sustaining severe injuries, she died in hospital on 2 June.

At the inquest it was said that the rules required a bell to be sounded to inform the driver that the doors were closed, and the cars were ready to move, but that at busy times the driver assumed that if he could draw power the doors were closed, and he could start the cars. The events of 28 May were attributed to a temporary fault; the deputy coroner, briefing the jury, saying that the fault was combined with carelessness to cause the accident. A verdict of accidental death was returned, with a rider that the 'irregular system adopted for signalling' had contributed to it (*Hull Daily Mail*, 29 May/11 June/*Yorkshire Post*, 11 June).

This 1988 scene shows the 1935 cars in operation. At this date it can be seen that the footpath 'tunnel' though the tramway from the Spa had been blocked up.

The upper station in 1982, when the fare was 7p. Scarborough Castle can be seen on the skyline.

The lift benefitted indirectly from a £7.158 million restoration of the adjacent 52-acre Spa gardens, now known as the South Cliff Gardens, completed in 2023, when access to the tramway tunnel was reinstated. This, and the following images, were taken in 2023.

16 • CLIFF RAILWAYS: AN HISTORIC SURVEY

An uncommon view of the lower station.

In 2007 the cars were modified to improve access for wheelchair users and prams and increasing capacity to twenty passengers, not all of whom can be seated despite the solicitation.

1875 SOUTH CLIFF TRAMWAY, SCARBOROUGH

The electronic control desk in 2024.

The tramway was rebuilt by the Leeds-based locomotive builder, Hudswell, Clarke, in 1935. The entire system was replaced, and the water-balanced arrangement replaced by electric winding. Construction of new car bodies, which reverted to four windows each side and seated twelve, was contracted out so their builder is unknown.

A fire broke out in the tramway's switch room on 2 February 1954. A fireman said that it originated in a tip-up seat, spread to floorboards and melted a gas pipe, leading to the gas igniting as well. The author considers that the most likely cause of a tip-up seat catching fire would be the careless disposal of smoking materials.

The company was wound up in 1968 and ownership passed to Jack Walker, who had been running the lift since it was re-opened after the war. He sold it to the council for £110,000 in 1993.

There were runaway incidents in 1997 and 1998, the first shortly after an electronic control panel had been installed and the second causing serious injuries to passengers. The company that did the work reduced its £167,000 bill by £50,000 but the injured passengers had to wait several years for their compensation.

Repairs, including replacing the head wheel and removing the cars and carriages to the council's Dean Road, had delayed the seasonal resumption of services in 1998.

The track was renewed in 2007, which might also be when the staircase was constructed alongside the south-side track, facilitating maintenance and emergency evacuation.

Despite these setbacks and the unbudgeted maintenance costs that the lift incurred, the council kept its faith in the lift, and it remains a testament to the authority and the original promoters that the first cliff railway still has a part to play in 21st Century Scarborough.

The top station in 2023, looking a lot smarter than it did in the 1980s. The ramp that enables wheelchair access was built in 2002.

A view of the south track car at the top station looking across the bay.

1875 SOUTH CLIFF TRAMWAY, SCARBOROUGH • 19

CHAPTER 2

1878 QUEEN'S PARADE TRAMWAY, SCARBOROUGH

Opened 11 October 1878, 4ft gauge, double track, 242ft long, gradient 1 in 23, hydraulic, gas engine, closed 1887.
Compared with the South Cliff, in the 1860s Scarborough's North Cliff was not at all well developed. Grand hotels and boarding houses were being built along Queen's Parade but there was nothing there to encourage visitors. With this in mind the promenade pier was opened in 1869 but access to it, and the beach, was not to the taste of Victorian visitors, despite the cliff being much shallower than the South Cliff.

With this, poor pier patronage and the immediate success of the South Cliff Tramway in mind, a North Cliff tramway was proposed to encourage visitors to the pier during 1877 (*York Herald*, 14 July).

A prospectus was issued to raise £3,500 capital in January 1878 and the Queen's Parade Tramway Company was registered on 4 March 1878 (*Midland & Northern Coal & Iron Trades Gazette*, 20 March) and Henry

The photograph shows the pier as built. The approximate position of the tramway is indicated. Also indicated is the location of the North Bay lift.

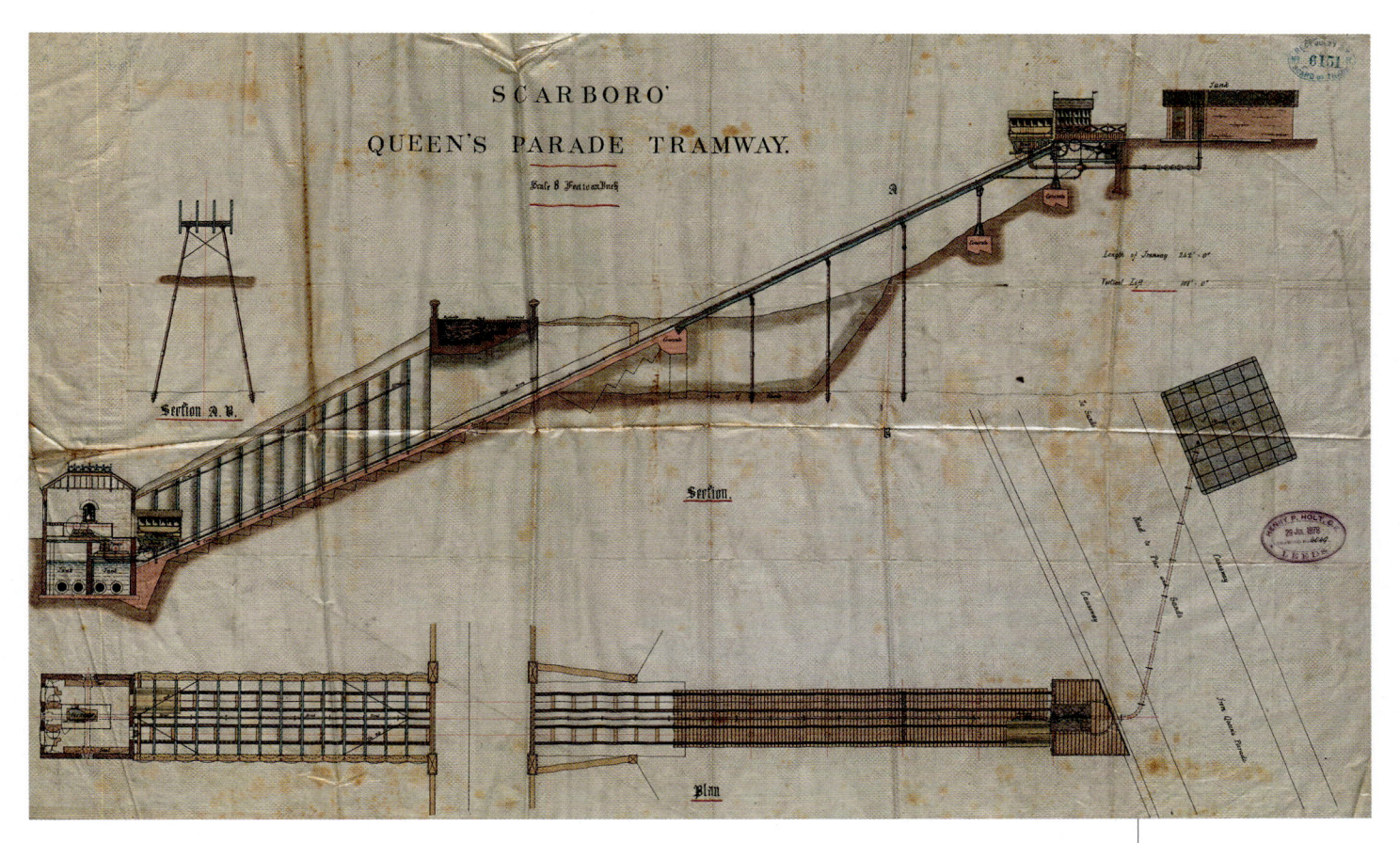

Percy Holt (1849–1903), born in Wakefield and working in Leeds, was appointed engineer. He had worked for the Yorkshire Engine Company, the Great Northern and Midland railways as well as several railways overseas before starting his own consultancy. The contract was let to Messrs Wade & Son of Leeds and work was started straight away (*York Herald*, 25 March).

The ground being quite easy, progress was quick and completion during August 1878 was anticipated. However, when one of the cars was being lowered into position on 8 August the rope broke, causing the car to run away about 30ft before it collided with the lower station, causing it considerable damage. In its report, the *York Herald* (9 August) noted that the work was still in the hands of the contractors, who would be responsible for making good.

Repairs were completed in time for the Board of Trade's Hutchinson to make his inspection on 10 October 1878. In his report he said that he had made an inspection on 10 August, 'when I found it incomplete', drawing a veil over the remnants of the mayhem that he must have seen. The tramway was, he wrote, not as steep as the South Cliff line, and 58ft shorter.

He required that through bolts should be used to secure the rail joints 'to the planks', that the sills of the cars should be widened, and that the retaining walls of the lower section should be protected. Hutchinson noted that no emergency brake had been provided to stop the cars in the event of the ropes breaking. He concluded that as the tramway would not be used during the winter, he had no objection to passengers being carried for the rest of the season and required that the works he specified be undertaken before the line was reopened in the spring of 1879. Passengers were carried from 11 October (*York Herald*, 12 October).

Hutchinson's remark that the tramway was similar to the South Cliff line is the closest that exists to a contemporary report on it. However, on 30 March 1881, Holt, the engineer, submitted a reference to Messrs

Submitted to the Board of Trade when the tramway was nearly complete, Holt's drawing shows its layout and the nature of its foundations. The water tank is detached from the upper station by the road to the beach.

The upper part of the tramway, showing the arch of the bridge that crossed it and one of the cars at the station. In a report of a visit to Scarborough published in the *Sheffield Independent* on 7 September 1878, the writer said that they had seen 'highly painted and varnished tramcars, of peculiar construction' when they arrived 'from Birmingham', presumably from the works of the Metropolitan Railway Carriage & Wagon Company at Saltley. They were lettered 'Queen Parade Tramway' (sic) on the side panels.

Crossley Brothers in Manchester lauding the quality of the 3½hp 'Otto' gas engine that the company had supplied to the tramway in June 1878, saying that it ran up to fourteen hours a day during the season without repairs, lifting water 130ft at a cost of only 1d per thirty passengers. On the other tramway that he acted for, the South Cliff, which used steam, the cost was nearly three times greater (*New Zealand Herald*, 3 February 1882).

On 21 May 1879 Holt informed the Board of Trade that it was intended to operate the tramway from 31 May and asked if it would be convenient for Hutchinson to visit on that date. It was not convenient, but Hutchinson made his inspection some three weeks later, reporting on 20 June that his requirements had been met and that an emergency brake had been provided, but now that the backs of the retaining walls had been filled in, a fence was required to prevent the public from falling on to the tramway. Subject to it being erected without delay, then he recommended that the Board of Trade should issue its certificate authorising the tramway to be opened for public traffic.

No reports concerning the tramway or its business have been found until 1882, when at the annual meeting, one of the directors commented on the efficiency with which the tracks had been relaid (*York Herald*, 25 February). Too soon to have been the result of natural wear and tear, this might have been the consequence of storm damage exacerbated by the absence of sea defences.

In 1885 the line was relaid again, due to the cliff slipping (*York Herald*, 27 February 1886), and further work was required on the track and at the top station in 1886 that exhausted the surplus (*Yorkshire Post*, 23 February 1887). After two years without a dividend, and realising that the only way to improve the situation would be to invest in strengthening the tramway's formation, the shareholders were ready to accept

Seen beyond the castle, the image shows the tramway and the pier before the fence required by Hutchinson in 1879 had been erected. The castle site has been in occupation since the Iron Age and the stone structure dates from the tenth century. In front of the lower station is the entrance to the pier and beyond it is the Breakwater Hotel. Built to capitalise on the tramway and the pier, when an escaped prisoner was apprehended at the hotel in 1883 the location was described as being remote (*Yorkshire Post*, 27 March 1883). (J. Valentine)

the council's offer to sell the undertaking for £1,500, the council having refused the company's £2,000 counter-offer. In little more than ten years the shareholders had lost more than 50% of their investment.

The council had been developing plans to develop the cliffs as a park (Clarence Gardens) and to build a road along the beach since 1882, and work had started in 1887 (*Leeds Mercury*, 2 July). There was no delay in taking possession of its purchase and the *Yorkshire Post* reported that the lift had been removed in its 23 August 1888 edition.

The pier lasted until January 1905, when it was washed away by a 'huge tidal wave'. The pavilion, which had been repurposed as a miniature theatre, was destroyed by the waves of two high tides a few months later (*Yorkshire Evening Press*, 2 October 1905).

CHAPTER 3

1881 CENTRAL TRAMWAY, SCARBOROUGH

Opened 1 August 1881, 4ft 8½in gauge, double track, 234ft long, gradient 1 in 2.82, steam, electric from 1920, operational. This is Scarborough's third cliff railway, located to the north of the Grand Hotel. The first intimation of it came in an advertisement encouraging applications for copies of the prospectus promoting £5 shares in the £10,000 capital (*Yorkshire Herald*, 22 January 1881). In its memorandum of association, the company gave itself wide-ranging powers, not just to build and operate the proposed lift, but to build other railways and lifts within 30 miles of Scarborough and to acquire, build and operate hotels, dramshops, refreshment rooms, photographic galleries, shops and houses, docks and wharves, and to obtain, store and sell sea water.

There was no delay in starting work, the *York Herald* reporting activity on the site in its 5 February issue, although the council did not give its approval until March (*Yorkshire Herald*, 15 March). The contractor was George Wood of Hull, who had the tramway ready to be opened on 1 August, when the directors and some shareholders made a return journey from the top station before the chairman, John Woodall Woodall (1832–1905), declared the line open (*York Herald*, 2 August). Some 1,000 passengers were carried in the two hours following (*Sheffield Daily Telegraph*, 6 August). One of the directors, G. G. Cleather, who is mentioned in relation to the South Cliff Tramway, was appointed managing director.

The supply of engines had been contracted to the Tangye company in Birmingham but when it became clear that the contract was not going to be honoured, Robey & Company of Lincoln was persuaded to supply one of its existing designs modified with a Morton condenser fitted to avoid visitors seeing steam emitted on the cliff. The engines and condensers were tested satisfactorily by their makers, but Wood and Thomas Morgan (contractor and engineer respectively) decided that the condensers were ineffective and did not pay for them. The matter went to court in July 1883, when Robey sued Wood for the £161 outstanding balance, Wood having paid £53 19s into court. After two days of evidence, and the judge declaring that it was 'one of the most undefended cases' that he had heard, the jury found in Robey's favour and awarded £182 in addition to the sum already paid into court (*Lincolnshire Chronicle*, 20 July).

The engineer Thomas Feaster Morgan (1846–1924) had been born in nearby Sleights (*Yorkshire Post*, 30 September). He devised the patent automatic brakes that were to meet with official approval when the undertaking was inspected. No further information about his career has been found.

At the 1886 annual meeting the chairman, trying to get support for the creation of a reserve fund, said that the tramway had not been built honestly; the report said that the directors were continually feeling the effects of the defective and negligent construction of the undertaking (*Yorkshire Post*, 19 February / *York Herald*, 27 February). Even allowing for the lack of great earthworks, it had been built at great haste.

Major General C. S. Hutchinson inspected the tramway on 29 September, saying that the 'patent brake arrangements' had been incomplete when he had visited on 11 August. Unlike the existing tramways, he reported, this line was not water balanced; haulage being provided by a steam engine, of which two were installed, connected to a flat steel rope. The brake arrangements had been carried out with much skill, he added, having been commissioned 'yesterday' and when the rope was broken the cars stopped in about 10ft. Tramways of this kind, he concluded, depended upon brake arrangements, permanent way and engines being kept in a thoroughly efficient state, and provided this was done he could recommend that the Board of Trade did not object to the tramway being used for public traffic.

Although the tramway had been operated for over a year, by the time of the 1883 general meeting some shareholders were concerned about the company's position, the capital account being overdrawn by nearly £2,000, which had been covered by borrowing. At the meeting the chairman started by saying that a 'stupid' error in the accounts made the company's position look better than it was, adding that he thought the directors had made a mistake in paying a (2½%) dividend the year before, when they should have husbanded their resources, and had been unwise to close the tramway during the 1881–82 winter, speaking as though he was not one of their number. The winter closure decision had been rectified for 1882–83, he said, and receipts to date had covered expenses. Although his proposal to adopt the accounts was seconded, he agreed with a shareholder's proposal that should they not be received, a committee of investigation be appointed, and the meeting be adjourned for two weeks (*York Herald*, 9 March).

When the meeting resumed the committee blamed the company's promotion for the overspend and called for the resignations of the directors, the secretary, the manager and the auditor. While the directors present said they were prepared to resign, the chairman said that the matter would have to be dealt with at a special meeting, of which no report has been found.

The tramway was not operating when the photograph was taken, and the cars are stabled at the midway point. Its proximity to the Grand Hotel and its lower station can be seen. On the left is the Spa toll bridge, which led to the South Cliff tramway. With 365 rooms when it opened in 1867, the Grand Hotel claimed to be the largest hotel in Europe. It is now Grade II* listed. At the 2023 election for York & North Yorkshire Mayor one of the candidates campaigned to take the building into public ownership.

The chairman remained in place at the 1884 meeting, though, when he had to deal with motions proposed by four members of the investigation committee. One of these, the dismissal of Henry Oswald Wellburn (1849–1901), the company's solicitor and manager, probably arose from the investigation the year before, when they had been able to examine the company's books and saw how much he had claimed for work undertaken.

Wellburn had owed his position as solicitor to being named as such in the company's articles; he had also been appointed manager when G. G. Cleather had left to join the Crystal Palace in 1882. At the meeting he said that he intended to stand down at the end of the quarter, 31 March, but would not be forced out before. The shareholders were apparently annoyed about his level of billing in 1881–82, when his workload for the company could be expected to be increased by the company's formation and the tramway's construction. The chairman observed that the motions were invalid and that the issues should be resolved amicably, adding that the position of the director named would be resolved by time – either he would resign, or his term would expire; in any event, he had not attended any meetings. The motions were withdrawn and Wellburn's position was not clarified in the *York Herald's* 7 March report.

There were two incidents of note on the tramway during 1884. On 22 March the northernmost car was found to have fallen from its stabling point and collided with the lower station, obviously damaging both. The previous night the rope had been detached for adjustment and the car wedged in position, but tramway staff were unable to say whether the accident had been caused by vandalism or by the weight of the car overcoming the wedges (*York Herald*, 24 March).

The second incident demonstrated that the car doors were not locked when the cars were in motion, with potentially fatal consequences. In August a child boarded the car, which started to move before her mother had boarded. Attempting to re-join her parent, the child fell between the rails and rolled halfway down the tramway before coming to a stop, sustaining only bruises and scratches. The incident prompted the directors to close the tramway for a complete overhaul; it reopened on 1 September (*Yorkshire Gazette*, 16 August/2 September).

Sometime around 1887, Samuel Aspin, a plumber and gasfitter, was appointed manager. He remained with the company, from 1905 also serving as a director, until his death in 1927, aged 72.

On 4 August 1890 the tramway carried a record 8,400 passengers, benefitting during the year by a prolonged visit to the bay of the Channel Fleet and a visit by 6,500 of Bass & Company's employees from Burton-on-Trent to the town on 15 August, which between them contributed to the directors' ability to declared a 5½% dividend for the first time (*York Herald*, 6 August/15 August/*Yorkshire Evening Press*, 15 November/*York Herald*, 11 November 1891). The Bass employees travelled on thirteen trains, which arrived between 7.30 and 9.30 am.

The year 1895 was another record year, aided by the opening of the nearby Fishery & Marine Exhibition, and 350,000 passengers were carried. The financial position was so good that the company was able to make its lease payments, previously one year in arrears, up to date. Recommending a 6s per share dividend for the year ending 31 October, the directors said that during the forthcoming winter the boilers would be retubed (*York Herald*, 16/27 November). The freehold was purchased for £3,000 in 1898, funded by the issue of debentures.

High levels of traffic continued during the 1890s. In 1899 the directors reported that the cars had been replaced at a cost of £150 each; the maker is unknown. At the annual meeting the chairman told the shareholders that 220,734 passengers had travelled up and 60,320 had travelled down during the previous year and that costs would be reduced if the number travelling down could be increased. Rising costs had

This photograph is significant for being the only one known of the original cars and showing the upper station from the east side. The tower belonged to the Marine Parade. (Central Tramway Ltd)

Seen from the upper station, the 1899 cars in use. The lower station has been signed to remind passengers where they were.

1881 CENTRAL TRAMWAY, SCARBOROUGH • 27

Very few photographs exist of the cars with the Plaxton bodies that entered service in the 1930s. This postcard view from the 1960s shows that an attempt had been made to apply a similar livery to the cars and the station building. (Dennis Productions)

affected wages, coal, coke and firewood (*York Herald*, 17/23 November).

The tramway began the 1900s in a good position. Not only had the cars been replaced but during 1900–01 the track was renewed and the top station remodelled and reconstructed, the latter in response to the council's development of St Nicholas Park on former St Nicholas estate land. In 1901, though, the chairman closed the annual meeting by saying that he did not know what effect the forthcoming street tramways (in Scarborough) would have on the undertaking, which turned out to be rather prescient (*Sheffield Daily Telegraph*, 21 November 1901).

The 3ft 6in gauge street tramways opened on 6 May 1904 and one route passed the tramway's lower station. In November the company reported that the year's revenue had fallen to £680, £517 less than in 1903 (*Yorkshire Post*, 19 November 1904).

In 1905 the company's financial woes were worsened by having to pay £161 10s plus costs for a compensation claim made in respect of an accident that had occurred in 1904; the details are unknown. The directors decided to insure both passengers and employees (*Yorkshire Post*, 30 November 1905).

This was a wise precaution but probably of no benefit when Percy Henry Askham, a 32-year-old coal merchant, was knocked into the boiler house coal store by a moving car on 24 October 1908. Sustaining a fractured skull and a broken neck, he died in hospital the following 8 January. His death certificate records the cause of death as 'injury to spinal cord caused by being hit by tram car on Central Tramway and knocked into coke house when delivering coke'. With the boiler house located under the tramway, the coal chute was obviously accessed from above. No contemporary reports of the accident, Askham's death or the inquest and its adjournment have been found in local newspapers (*Diss Express*, 30 October 1908 / *Leeds Mercury*, 11 January 1909).

Following five years of declining receipts, in 1909 they started to increase again, improving each year until August 1914, when the prospect of war must have affected tourist numbers. The promise of the end of hostilities brought a big increase in 1918 and in 1919 revenue was more than doubled. A total of £500 was set aside to redeem debentures and £100 for a new rope. A 10% dividend was paid in 1920, and in 1925, when 454,759 passengers were carried, shareholders received not only a 10% dividend but a 2% bonus. The lowest dividend in the 1920s was 8%, in 1928. No reports for the following years have been found (*Sheffield Daily Telegraph*, 25 November 1909/26 November 1918/*Yorkshire Post*, 4 December 1919/23 November 1920/25 November 1925/*Halifax Evening Courier*, 3 December 1925/4 December 1928).

In 1920, one of the tramway's porters appeared in court for making a false representation about his earnings to enhance his old age pension. Overpaid £44, Thomas McCourt (1848–1929) was fined £5. One of the directors gave him a reference, saying that he had worked for the company for thirty-three years and had offended 'more in ignorance than wilfully' (*Driffield Times*, 23 November).

The steam engines were disposed of in 1920 and replaced by a 500v DC electric motor powered by the town's tramway system. When that closed in 1932 Hudswell, Clarke of Leeds was commissioned to renew the entire tramway, supplying and installing a 400v three-phase 60hp motor and an interlocked braking system, relaying the tracks and supplying new cars with bodies made by local company F. W. Plaxton Ltd, better known among transport enthusiasts for its bus bodies. With five windows on each side, the cars had room for thirty passengers, ten of them standing.

In 1959 the company was subject to a takeover bid by the South Cliff Tramway, which circulated the shareholders, offering to buy their £5 shares for £7 10s each. The directors said they could find no merit in the offer and advised them to ignore it, which seems to have been the end of the matter. In 1967, however, the company came under the control of a Rotherham-based family, which has focused on developing the tramway.

Concrete foundations were built to support the lower section of the track in 1967 and the remainder received the same treatment in 1981. Following damage caused by a fire at the Olympia Centre on 29 July 1975, new cars made by George Neville Truck Equipment Ltd of Kirkby in Ashfield were commissioned in 1976. When subsequent pile driving on the Olympia site damaged the track and closed the tramway for a year, the company was successful in its claim against the contractor for the repairs and lost revenue.

This photograph of one of the new cars at the upper station was taken on 12 June 1976. Unlike the Plaxton-bodied cars they have a flat roof and only three windows on each side. (J. H. Meredith)

Right: Work in progress on the upper section of the tramway on 3 October 1981. (J. H. Meredith)

Far right: This 1982 view of the tramway shows the concrete trackbed. The cars and upper station buildings were painted green by 1991. A flight of steps built alongside the left-hand side of tramway between 1984 and 1991 is known as the 'McBean Steps', named after William McBean (1816-91) who had been a prominent Scarborough businessman and politician. They give pedestrian access to the Marine Parade site from the foreshore.

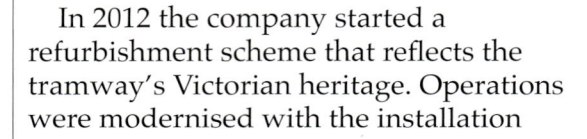

In 2012 the company started a refurbishment scheme that reflects the tramway's Victorian heritage. Operations were modernised with the installation of an automated control system that accompanied the installation of a new 60hp motor in 2009 and in 2016 a Twiflex hydraulic disc brake was fitted. The control

The interior of the upper station, showing a glimpse of one of the car interiors and the control booth with its electronic panel in 2012. (Steve Sedgwick)

30 • CLIFF RAILWAYS: AN HISTORIC SURVEY

The lower station with wall art and a twenty-first-century take on Victorian signage seen on 29 May 2023.

The upper station in 2023. The directors never developed the empire permitted by the company's articles but the upper station was provided with space that could be let out. John Inskip (1833–1911) had relocated his established fine art and photography business there by 7 October 1882 (*York Herald*) and the dining room, 'doing a respectable good business', was available to let for £200 on 2 November (*Sheffield Daily Telegraph*, 2 November). In recent years it has accommodated a bar and café.

system and brake were replaced during the winter of 2019–20.

The cars received further attention in 2022, when Wheel Sets (UK) Ltd of Rotherham replaced the carriages with galvanised steel structures, refurbished the bodies and fitted spring-loaded emergency brakes integrated with the control system. A seven-coat polyurethane paint system that should better withstand the weather was applied.

The company made a profit of £120,202 in 2021. It also benefits from the income from a property portfolio that has been built up since 1993.

1881 CENTRAL TRAMWAY, SCARBOROUGH • 31

As the afternoon sun catches the side of the car, the photograph shows the relationship between the tramway and the harbour.

The entrance to the upper station on 23 June 2024. In common with most cliff railways, payments are handled at one station only, in this case ascending passengers pay after travelling.

32 • CLIFF RAILWAYS: AN HISTORIC SURVEY

The camera's zoom lens compresses the image and gives a deceptive impression of the cars passing close to the upper station, also on 23 June 2024. In 1993 the company had reached agreement to purchase the South Cliff Tramway but was blocked by the council's refusal to transfer a wayleave for a right of access over Spa land.

CHAPTER 4

1884 PASTON PLACE, BRIGHTON

Opened April 1884 ?. Gauge, gradient, method of operation, unknown. Closed and removed May 1884 ?.

Magnus Volk's (1851–1937) lift at Paston Place, Brighton, is the most ephemeral and least recorded of all the British cliff railways and lifts. It was built to connect his newly extended electric railway, opened on 5 April 1884, with Madeira Place. The *West Sussex Journal* (8 April 1884) reported that the 'electric lift' was unfinished and was expected to be working in 'another fortnight'.

The lift had been erected on the western of two flights of steps at Paston Place,

When Magnus Volk extended his electric railway to Paston Place in 1884 he also erected some sort of lift on the left-hand (western) staircase from Marine Parade. Despite undertaking to relocate it on to the eastern staircase when residents complained about the extra distance required for non-lift users to walk towards the Palace pier, the level of complaint was sufficient to persuade him to dismantle it completely. (Pan-Aero Pictures)

34 • CLIFF RAILWAYS: AN HISTORIC SURVEY

The staircases as seen 140 years later. The western staircase being closed to the public, it has not been possible to examine for signs of a lift being erected upon it. From 1884 the railway was run from the right-hand arch, which contained Volks' workshop and the railway's substation on the ground floor and his office on the first floor. In 1983 the author was with a party shown the mercury arc rectifier then still in use, as part of a railway centenary tour.

which was just one of the factors that caused an outbreak of outrage in Brighton when the extended railway and lift were opened. There had been no reported complaints when the council had given its approval to the proposal in 1883. Unwilling to ride out the storm of complaint, Volk capitulated and removed the lift. His decision was announced to the works committee on 9 May.

So passed the cliff railway with the briefest existence of them all. No action was taken in response to Volk's proposal, later in 1884, to take advantage of that year's Brighton Improvement Act to build another lift at Paston Place (*Southern Weekly News*, 3 November 1883/*Brighton Gazette*, 17 May 1884).

Although the newspaper quoted states that the lift was powered by electricity, Volk's biography (Conrad Volk, *Magnus Volk of Brighton*: Phillimore, 1971) describes a water-balanced installation, with two cars, 7ft × 4ft each, made of pitch pine, seating five, but the source for this information is not given. As the steps are only slightly more than 5ft wide and, after a cursory examination, show no sign of alteration, the erection of a double-track lift seems unlikely, while a single-track electric lift with a 4ft wide car would have been possible, although the author is left wondering where the motor and head wheel went, and how it could have left no obvious evidence of its existence. Unfortunately, there is at present no public access to the relevant staircase.

CHAPTER 5
1884 SALTBURN INCLINE TRAMWAY

Opened 2 June 1884, 3ft 9in gauge, 4ft 2½in from 1921, double track, 207ft long, gradient 1 in 1.4, water balance, operational.

Saltburn-by-the-Sea, to give it its full name, is located on the north Yorkshire coast, 8 miles east of Middlesbrough. Joseph Pease (1799–1872), one of the Quaker bankers who played an important role in the development of railways in the North East, initiated its development as a resort following a visit to the site in 1858. The Saltburn Improvement Company, incorporated in 1860, bought Marske and Upleatham estate land from the Earl of Zetland and sold building plots, resulting in a town with wide streets and substantial houses, many of them with sea views.

Before moving on to the story of the town's cliff railway, a digression to the development of the pier is required. To encourage tourism the Saltburn Pier Company was established by self-made engineer, contractor and developer John Anderson (1805–78) in 1867 and the 1,500ft-long pier was opened in July 1869. To overcome any reluctance by visitors to make the journey down and up the cliff to reach the pier, the pier company had ordered the construction of a vertical lift that was still being built when the pier opened. However, on 16 October the incomplete structure was destroyed in a storm (*Newcastle Daily Chronicle*, 5 July 1869/*Shields Daily Gazette*, 20 October 1869).

Construction of the lift had been resumed by the date of the pier company's annual meeting in February 1870 and it was opened on 28 June. Some 120ft high and using water to provide traction, its 8ft square cage could carry twenty passengers. During its construction the *Newcastle Daily Chronicle* (5 July 1869) had deplored its use of timber, saying that the structure looked more like coal staithes and that public works in 'beautiful places' like Saltburn should be ornamental (*Northern Echo*, 28 February 1870/*Middlesbrough Daily Gazette*, 28 June).

The pier was not the great commercial success anticipated by its promoters. In 1875 its length was reduced by 100 yards during a storm (*Middlesbrough Daily Gazette*, 16 October). Rather than replacing the missing section, the company decided to retain the same promenading area by widening the existing structure at the sea end and to build a new landing stage (*Middlesbrough Daily Gazette*, 16 April 1876). But barely had the repairs been completed, when, on 21 December 1876, another storm took another 40 yards. Repairs were again undertaken and the pier strengthened but the future of the company was in doubt (*Northern Echo*, 23 December 1876/*Middlesbrough Daily Gazette*, 9 April 1877).

Only minor damage was sustained in the next two years and in the spring of 1879 the hoist was overhauled in anticipation of a good season. However, it was not to be, because by the end of the company's financial year, on 30 September, earning had been insufficient to pay the loan interest. On 5 December a winding-up order was obtained and on 28 January 1880 John Christopher Simpson (1841–1900) was appointed liquidator (*Middlesbrough Daily Gazette*, 29 April/6 December 1879/*York Herald*, 1 November/*Daily Gazette*, 24 February 1880).

The pier and hoist, and the company's other assets, failed to reach the reserve when offered for sale by auction on 18 August 1880 and Simpson continued to run the enterprise in liquidation, raising sufficient to repair the hoist again in 1882, and apparently waiting for 'something to turn up' (*Yorkshire Gazette*, 21 August 1880 / *Loftus Advertiser*, 3 June 1882).

Something did turn up in 1883, when the Middlesbrough [Estate] Owners, three members of the Pease family, took over the Improvement Company. The town was in a poor state, with properties abandoned, when visitor numbers fell in line with a depression in the iron trade. Apart from restoring derelict houses and repairing roads, the new owners undertook to construct a promenade along the beach and to landscape the cliff with walks, shelters and seating areas. In May, they also bought the pier company and announced that they would replace the hoist with 'an inclined railway' like those at Scarborough (*Middlesbrough Daily Gazette*, 6 February / 2 June 1883).

The contract for installation of the water balanced tramway was placed with Tangye & Company, of Birmingham, whose leading hydraulics draughtsman in 1882–83 had been George Croydon Marks (1858–1938), who will appear several times more in this book. His biography (see Bibliography) connects him with this contract but according to his 1884 application for membership of the Institution of Civil Engineers, from July 1883 he had worked for Ross & Walpole in Dublin, so any connection with Saltburn can only have been slight.

Saltburn's hoist. The lift was built on the same site.

This 1884 photograph not only shows the new lift but also the new paths and promenade as well as the original pier fencing and kiosks. (J. Valentine)

Tangye subcontracted manufacture of the car bodies to the Metropolitan Railway Carriage & Wagon Company and obtained a 6hp Otto gas engine from Crossley Brothers to pump the water.

The opening was announced to take place on 15 June 1884 (*Truth*, 7 June) and in its account of the start of the Saltburn 'season' the *Northern Echo* (2 July) said that the new incline tramway 'is daily growing more popular' and that the saloon cars were 'so neatly finished as to be of attraction themselves'. Traditionally, the trams have not operated during the winter but in recent years they have operated Friday to Monday in December and the first weekend in January.

From 1884 the lift and the pier had quiet existences, with no reported incidents until 8 May 1924, when the schooner *Ovenberg*, carrying china clay from Fowey to Leith, ran aground alongside the pier, and successive tides used the ship to drive a hole some 70 yards long in it. It was a double blow for the Middlesbrough Owners, happening at the start of the season and a year after the pier had been re-decked (*Newcastle Daily Chronicle*, 10 May).

The incident caused the Owners to re-assess their commitment to Saltburn, though. Having sold nearly all their development land, it was less important to them to maintain the attractions, the pier, the tramway and the ornate gardens, so they offered them to the town council for £15,000, leaving it to the council to have the pier repaired. The council, however, was constrained in its ability to respond by the town's low permanent population of 4,000 residents, and low rateable value, £25,000, which limited its borrowing powers. As it was already committed to borrowing to fund a sewerage scheme, the matter was put to the electorate to decide by means of a referendum, which on 6 October rejected the motion to buy the property (*Yorkshire Post*, 26 August/30 September/7 October 1924).

The Middlesbrough Owners therefore took action against the ship's owners for negligence and damages. Giving judgment in their favour, the judge was very critical of the captain's performance, saying that he had been warned of the risk of colliding with the pier, his soundings, if he took any, were inadequate, and he had not anchored the vessel when he got into shallow water. Notwithstanding the judgment, the pier was not repaired until 1930 (*Newcastle Daily Chronicle*, 16 June 1925/*Cleveland Standard*, 15 February 1930).

In the meantime, the Otto engine had been replaced by electric pumps in 1913 and the track replaced during the winter of 1921–22, the gauge being widened to 4ft 2½in at the same time.

There was no change in the status of the Saltburn attractions until 1937, when they were offered to Saltburn & Marske Urban District Council for £12,000. This time the (enlarged) council agreed to take them on, obtaining an Act of Parliament in 1938 for that purpose.

The tramway and pier were closed during the war and the pier was not reopened until 1952. In 1955 the cars were rebodied, retaining the profile of the originals but losing their stained-glass windows and plush seats.

In 1980 the railway resumed service after the winter closure with the cars clad in aluminium. Stained glass windows designed by local artist Cloe Buck were installed in 1991 (*East Cleveland Herald*, 20 February 1991). The move to restore Victorian features started when the pier buildings were Victorianised in 1979. The lift was awarded a Grade II* listing on 26 February 1999.

Over the winter of 2010–11 the cars were restored at the Haltwhistle works of Stanegate Restorations and Replicas, although the timber components of one of them were not reuseable. Victorian features applied included a bi-coloured internal roof, bench seats and external matchboard panelling. The 1991 glazing was retained (BBC, 22 April 2011).

The lift received a thorough mechanical overhaul in 2018. It reopened in 2019 but then the Coronavirus pandemic caused it to be closed in 2020 and 2021, reopening in time for the late Queen's platinum jubilee celebrations in 2022 (BBC, 19 May 2018/ *Teesside News*, 18 March 2020/14 July 2021/6 May 2022).

This garish postcard view shows almost the entire tramway undertaking. It can also be seen that the tramway and the pier shared the same architect. (Phoenix Series)

One of the 1955 cars seen at the top station on 10 July 1960, decorated simply and with the local authority's crest on the side. While the bodyside detailing is simpler, the window profile is similar to that of the original cars. Doors with round tops have been replaced by a simpler rectangular pattern and the undercarriages were probably partially enclosed with steel plate at the same time. (C. H. A. Townley)

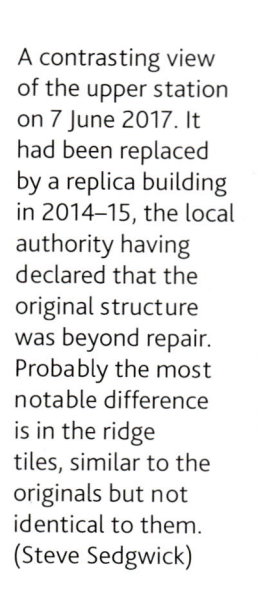

A contrasting view of the upper station on 7 June 2017. It had been replaced by a replica building in 2014–15, the local authority having declared that the original structure was beyond repair. Probably the most notable difference is in the ridge tiles, similar to the originals but not identical to them. (Steve Sedgwick)

40 • CLIFF RAILWAYS: AN HISTORIC SURVEY

Closed for maintenance on 9 January 2024, reopening was deferred by an electrical fire in the pump room at the lower station building on 15 January. Fortunately, there was no structural damage, but the lift was not reopened until 27 September 2024.

Far left: From 2006 the pier and lift have been floodlit at night, as seen here in 2022, when the photographer realised that a combination of high tide and little wind would enhance the effect (BBC, October 2005). (Steve Sedgwick)

Left: The upper station and its keeper on 17 June 2017. There is no undercover accommodation for waiting passengers. (Steve Sedgwick)

In 2023 a family enjoys a ride on the tramway, a view that illustrates the interior created by Stanegate Restorations in Haltwhistle.

One of the cars seen with the tank filler in action on 18 July 2023.

Looking down the tramway in 2023. Admission to the pier is now free.

42 • CLIFF RAILWAYS: AN HISTORIC SURVEY

A glimpse of the machine room at the lower station, showing the electric motor and pump. The January 2024 fire started in the upper cupboard on the right-hand wall.

The passenger side of the bottom station. The Transport Trust's 'red wheel' was awarded in 2015, recording the tramway's status as the oldest operational water-balanced lift in the UK.

A queue for the lift at the lower station in 2016. The pump room is on the left. (Steve Sedgwick)

The cars stabled on the cliffside while the fire damage sustained at the lower station is repaired, 23 June 2014.

44 • CLIFF RAILWAYS: AN HISTORIC SURVEY

CHAPTER 6

1884 FALCON CLIFF HOTEL LIFT I, DOUGLAS

Opened 14 July 1884, 4ft gauge, double track, 218ft long, gradient 1 in 1.98, hydraulic, closed 1897.

The first of four lifts to be built on the Isle of Man was constructed for the Falcon Cliff Castle Hotel Company, which acquired the property on the cliff on what was then the northern edge of Douglas, the island's capital, in 1883.

A prospectus, issued with the objective of raising £12,000 to fund the development, explained that the promoters took their inspiration from Manchester's Belle Vue Zoo in providing attractions for visitors in addition to improving the hotel. They also wished to improve access by installing a lift, 'similar to those so well-known at Scarborough' from 'Sea Road', now Queens Promenade, and the grounds (*Isle of Man Times*, 19 May 1883).

The water-balanced lift was tested on 7–8 July 1884 and entered service on 14 July. The contractor had been Salmon, Barnes & Company of Ulverston and its engineer was Lewis Llewellyn Vulliamy (1838–99). Vulliamy described how he had tested the safety brake by replacing the wire rope with a hemp one and cutting it 'suddenly'. The car stopped instantly (*Isle of Man Times*, 12 July 1884).

When the company's shareholders met on 4 November, they were told that the lift and veranda had cost £636 9s 10d and during its brief operating period had earned £98 10s and had cost £1 per week to run (*Isle of Man Times*, 8 November 1884).

It transpired that the water supply was inadequate to keep the lift running at peak times so in June 1886 an Otto gas engine was installed by William Knox & Son, the manufacturer's local agent, who also made a modification to the braking system (*Isle of Man Times*, 29 May / 12 June 1886).

On 8 October an accident occurred that could have had fatal consequences when the upper car was being prepared for lowering

A view along the front at Douglas, with the Falcon Cliff complex prominent on the skyline. The entrance to the lift's lower station is indicated. The rails of Thomas Lightfoot's Douglas horse tram, opened in 1876, can be seen in the road. (Hudson's Series)

to the bottom for the winter. A temporary winch had been placed near the upper station for the purpose when the chocks securing it became dislodged, causing the winch handle to revolve at speed and hitting 26-year-old George Stephen Popplewell's arm. Fortunately, it was not broken but he was off work for at least two weeks. In December Knox sued the hotel company for non-payment of the £313 10s bill but the case was settled for £270 (*Isle of Man Times*, 9 October/18 December 1886/21 May 1887). Popplewell died in 1914 and was buried in Onchan cemetery.

The quest to operate the lift more quickly resulted in a fatal accident on 31 May 1887. Local company Thomas Cain & Sons was employed to make the necessary alterations, but the Falcon company insisted on the efficacy of the brake being demonstrated. During the tests the car at the top ran away and the wire rope, which had been detached from the bottom car, lashed out and killed 24-year-old Alfred Walker Cain, one of Thomas Cain's sons. This is a condensed version of the account published in the *Isle of Man Times* (4 June). An inquest was held but the certified cause of death was 'Injuries received to his head and internal injuries from being struck by recoil of steel rope detached from tram carriage on lift to Falcon Cliff but how the carriage escaped there is not sufficient evidence to satisfactorily account for it.' Cain was also buried in Onchan cemetery. Lift operation resumed on 30 July or 1 August. Security of operation was enhanced by the installation of a second rope in 1888 (*Isle of Man Times*, 4/11/18 June/30 July/12 May 1888).

Competition from other attractions in Douglas affected the company's original prosperity and in 1896 the directors tried to sell the business as a going concern, with no success. Not having the resources to continue, a liquidator was appointed and in March 1897 the property was sold for £9,000. The new owners reopened for business immediately, including the lift, but in November the lift was sold to Thomas Forrester at Port Soderick and dismantled. The owners' intention of replacing it with a vertical lift was not put into effect (*The Era*, 9 May/*Sheffield Daily Telegraph*, 4 August 1896/*Isle of Man Times*, 13 March/20 November 1897).

The Falcon Cliff Hotel, its lift and the imposing entrance to the lower station.

CHAPTER 7

1885/1890 FOLKESTONE CLIFF TRAMWAY, THE LEAS

Opened 21 September 1885, 5ft 10in gauge, double track, 164ft long, gradient 1 in 1.58, water balance, not operated since 2016.

Opened 4 August 1890, 5ft gauge, double track, 155ft long, gradient 1 in 1.49, water balance, closed 1966.

Folkestone is a south coast seaside resort and harbour in Kent that came to prominence during the nineteenth century, but which declined somewhat following the advent of overseas package holidays. Thirty miles from Calais, the entrance to the Channel Tunnel lies to its east. Three cliff railways were built here and the first, and last survivor, is the subject of a major restoration scheme at the time of writing.

Schemes for a lift on the Leas here had apparently been mooted since the 1860s but the only one known to have made much progress was that of the Folkestone Promenade & Pier Company, which obtained Board of Trade Orders for a pier and lift in 1878 and 1881 and an Act of Parliament in 1884. By including compulsory purchase powers, the last was an attempt to overcome the difficulties of dealing with the town's primary landowner, the Earl of Radnor. When the Folkestone Cliff Tramway Company announced its intention to build a lift in May 1885, the pier company focused its attention on the pier.

The lift company said that it was influenced by those at Scarborough. A £5 a year, fifty-year lease on Radnor land also included the exclusive right to build other lifts on his lordship's seafront land at Folkestone for twenty years and the right to counter any other proposal during the following thirty years. The capital sought was £2,000 of the £3,000 authorised, much less than the £15,000 [sic] one of the Scarborough lifts required, noted the *Folkestone Express* on 2 May, adding that the Folkestone lift would be 50ft shorter and that the company did not have to purchase the land freehold.

By the time the company's prospectus was issued on 8 June construction had already been started. The architect was Reginald [John] Pope (1851–1931) and R. Waygood & Company was commissioned to supply the lift. The latter appointed a local builder, John Newman (1832–1915), to build the formation and construct the buildings and to lay the track. To protect the view from the Leas, the upper station was to be out of sight and no buildings were to be provided. In contrast, the lower station building was to include waiting, reading and refreshment rooms as well as toilets (*Folkestone Express*, 13 June 1885).

The Board of Trade sent General Hutchinson to inspect the lift on 7 September 1885. He spent an hour examining the equipment before he was entertained to lunch at the Pavilion Hotel, during which he asked for the emergency brake to be tested. One of the cars moved less than an inch when positioned about 6ft from the lower station and a hemp rope, which had replaced the wire one, securing it was cut with an axe (*Folkestone Express*, 12 September).

Hutchinson's report was dated 9 September. It was, he wrote, similar to the South Cliff lift at Scarborough. Its length was 164ft and inclined at 40 degrees. Flat bottom rail weighing 28lb to the yard was fixed to 11in square longitudinals

An early view of the 1885 lift. Very few photographs are known of it before the 1890 lift was positioned to its right. From this angle it can be seen that the passenger access to the cars is from the side.

bedded in concrete. The 5ft 10in gauge was maintained by transoms fitted between the longitudinals at 5ft intervals. A 6in square oak longitudinal beam fixed to the transoms was a part of the braking system.

Designed for fifteen passengers, the 12 ft × 7ft 6in car bodies rested on an iron tank nearly triangular in section. The cables were attached to the lower axle, along with a double set of spring-loaded toothed cams that would grip on the oak longitudinals if the cable broke. A governor was to be fitted, otherwise the speed would be totally controlled by the brakesman.

While regretting the lack of covered accommodation at the top station, Hutchinson thought that the arrangements for the lift had been carefully considered and ably carried out. He required that a step should be fitted below the doors of the cars to reduce the gap to the platforms, that more bolts should be used to hold the cars to the tanks, that some shelter should be provided for the brakesman, at the top station, and that the speed should not exceed 4mph. He also recommended that the condition of the steel rope should be subject to regular review, that one or more should be kept in reserve, and that the safety arrangements should be tested occasionally.

With completion of Hutchinson's requirements still outstanding, the lift was opened temporarily on 16 September, 'Regatta Day', when 2,389 paying passengers were carried. With his requirements met, the lift opened on 21 September and carried between 1,400 and 1,500 passengers each day during the first week. On 19 September the company entertained the engineer's and contractor's workforce to supper at the Bathing Establishment (*Folkestone Express*, 26 September/17 October).

When the shareholders met on 16 October, they were told that £2,957 18s 7d had been spent on the capital account, that 14,947 passengers carried on seventeen operating days, excluding Sundays, had earned the company £62 5s 7d. Only two men were employed, one to work the brakes and the other to collect the fares. Water was obtained from the Folkestone Waterworks Company at the rate of 1s per 1,000 gallons. If this proved to be unsustainable then a pump could be installed to return used water to the top level (*Folkestone Express*, 17 October 1885).

Meeting next on 14 October 1886, after a full season's operations, the shareholders were informed that 237,645 passengers had earned the company £986 0s 5d, and that the balance on the revenue account was sufficient for a 15% dividend, very satisfactory results. The highest number carried on one day had been 5,600, while the average had been 600 a day. The capital account was £352 4s 8d overdrawn, explained the chairman, and rather than borrowing the money to clear it and paying interest, or issuing shares that would qualify for dividend payments, it was cheaper to pay the overdraft interest, especially after the company's revenue, and bank balance, developed during the season. An agreement had been reached with the water company to supply water on payment of a toll of 20% of the gross takings (*Folkestone Express*, 16 October 1886).

At the 1887 meeting the highlights were that passenger numbers and revenue were reduced slightly, a consequence of a big exhibition in the town that had boosted numbers the year before, and that the dividend would be 'only' 12%. Expenditure on a further safety feature had brought the outstanding capital to £502 18s, so £600 of new £5 shares would be issued to existing shareholders on a one for five basis (*Folkestone Express*, 22 October).

With over two years' wear, Waygood & Company inspected the lift in March 1888, reporting that rope, [winding] wheel, shaft and bearings showed very little sign of wear. The brake wheel having reduced in diameter by ⅛in because the brake had been held on constantly during every journey, the brake spring was changed for one with fewer coils. The governor was in good order. The safety gear worked on one of the cars, dropping only 1¾in, despite the cams being clogged with pitch and the [chain] links with rust and sand. Owing to a defect in the testing regime, the gear on the other car had not worked but when serviced and cleaned both cars stopped instantly, dropping only 1in. The report was ended by complimenting the brakesman for the way in which he had looked after the lift (*Folkestone Express*, 10 March 1888).

During 1889 several issues came to a head that affected the lift's future. Over the short period that it had been in operation it had become an essential part of Folkestone's transport infrastructure, used by residents as well as visitors, producing complaints when the lift was closed for two periods totalling thirty-two days for essential maintenance. Then at peak times the water company could not supply the water required to keep the cars running as frequently as the traffic demanded. Despite these setbacks, traffic and revenue were both higher than in 1888.

When the shareholders met on 18 October, they voted to increase capital by £1,800 to pay for 20,000-gallon tanks to be constructed at both stations and the installation of pumps at the lower station. They were told that in a few years it would be necessary to build a second lift and the tanks and pumps would have the capacity to supply both. They were also told that the company would appeal against a rating assessment made on the basis of its income instead of the property cost or value like every other business. The original £150 had been increased to £386. It seems that the assessment committee thought that the £5 annual lease with Lord Radnor was too much of a good bargain. The outcome of the appeal was not reported (*Folkestone Express*, 19/23 October 1889).

Notwithstanding the shareholders' decision to approve the additional capital for the water and engines, by February 1890 construction of a second lift to the east of the first was in progress. The *Folkestone Chronicle* (22 February) explained that the work was being carried out under the supervision of the company's engineer, John Collins (1860–1922), with builder John Newman undertaking the works as agent for Charles Edward Robinson (1845–1912), the main contractor. No report has been found of the special shareholders' meeting that must have been held to increase the capital by £4,500 to pay for the works.

The *Chronicle*'s report explained that the new lift was intended to be used most, with the original one retained for use at peak times. Experience with the 1885 lift had suggested several changes, including changing the shape of the water tank and adopting a stepped arrangement for the seats, which would lower the centre of gravity, and which necessitated a steeper gradient, which the directors hoped would eliminate the oscillation experienced on the older lift.

Despatch of the new lift's sixteen-seat cars from Edward Hills & Sons, coachbuilders, from Dover on 8 July and delivery to Folkestone the next day naturally attracted attention. The *Folkestone Chronicle* (12 July) anticipated complaints from less nimble users, too (*Dover Express*, 11 July).

Hutchinson returned on 30 July. The lift's length, he reported, was 155ft, and it was inclined at 42 degrees. The gauge was 5ft, the cars 12ft × 6ft with access at each end and a central gangway. Two 4½in wire ropes had a breaking strain of 40 tons. The brakesman was provided with a shelter. With additional facilities also provided at the bottom station, public operation started on 4 August (*Folkestone Express*, 2/6 August/6 September).

By the time the shareholders met on 22 October, 309,306 passengers had been

Both lifts in use simultaneously. The building added on the right in 1890 is the pump room.

50 • CLIFF RAILWAYS: AN HISTORIC SURVEY

The upper station circa 1910, the 1895 lift in action.

carried and £1,268 15s 6d earned, so there was enough cash surplus to pay a 10% dividend. Responding to a question about revenue protection, the secretary explained that originally turnstiles were used but they could not count dogs and prams so the counters had been removed and connected to a bell that the brakesman rang once for every passenger, recording the numbers on a dial that had to reconcile with the cash; the bell must have been going constantly at peak times (*Folkestone Express*, 25 October 1890).

With no business lost to equipment failures, it was good news all round at the 1891 shareholders' meeting; 339,857 passengers, 30,000 more than in 1890, having earned the company £1,411 1s 5d and sufficient surplus for a 10% dividend. The shareholders were invited to inspect the pumps and other apparatus (*Folkestone Express*, 28 October 1891).

After four years' service, the new lift was overhauled, an exercise that was completed by testing the emergency brake in front of the directors (*Folkestone Express*, 9 May 1894).

John Henry Frederick Wessell (1852–1916), the assistant engineer, experienced a life-changing injury when his clothing was caught in the gas engine while he was cleaning it on 2 May 1896. While prompt attention ensured that he did not die on the spot, an arm had to be amputated. Joining the company as a brakesman by 1891, he was obviously well liked; a public appeal raised more than £40 for him but by 1911 he was working as a street musician. He had been born either in Hamburg or at sea and is buried in an unmarked plot in Folkestone's Cheriton Road cemetery (*Folkestone Express*, 9/16/23 May/19 September).

The lifts continued running during the First World War, and a minor accident was reported when they overran and caused some slight damage. A passenger fell over and knocked his head, broken glass scratching his hand. The *Folkestone Herald* (27 February 1915) noted that while one of the lifts was being repaired, the other remained in operation. After the war traffic increased considerably, 9,918 passengers being carried on the August bank holiday. (*Folkestone Herald*, 6 August 1921).

The two 1890 cars after the accident on 20 January 1930.

A 1960s postcard view with the 1890 lift in action. The fare was advertised at the upper station. (Photo Precision)

The second lift was involved in an accident on 20 January 1930, when one of the cars became detached during maintenance and ran away. Superficially, little damage was done to the car, only the windows were broken, but both cars were replaced. The *Folkestone Herald* (25 January) reported that the car was jammed into the station, destroying the wall and smashing the doors.

The only other matter concerning the lifts that interested the *Folkestone Herald* during the inter-war years was the renewal of the flag that was flown to indicate that the lift was open (30 May 1931).

The rapid decline of traffic after the outbreak of war in 1939 caused the directors to close the lifts in August 1940. The army lowered the cars at the top station to the bottom to remove any motivation for an invading force to cut the cables and the lower station became a Home Guard post. The undertaking was derequisitioned in 1945 but it took until 1948 to repair the lifts and reopen them to the public. In 1949 traffic was the best in the company's history.

British resorts and attractions experienced a boom in the 1950s and '60s but the arrival of cheap package holidays and guaranteed sunshine meant that it did not last. In Folkestone, the lift company had been a good investment for its shareholders – a 12½% dividend was paid as late as 1959 – but reserves failed to keep up with inflation and inadequate resources were available when major expenditure was required, which must have been brought home to the company after an accident on the 1885 lift on 4 June 1963. Two Territorials received the Queen's Commendation for brave conduct for their actions in protecting children from broken glass, but no contemporary reports have been found (*Liverpool Daily Post*, 31 August 1963).

This, and an accident on 30 June 1966 on the 1890 lift, when an inexperienced brakesman was held responsible for the cars colliding with the stations, inflicting bruises and shock on eleven passengers, are probably indicative of

One of the 1885 cars at the upper station. It has the company's name, fares and frequency painted above the rear windows.

the employment of inadequately trained seasonal labour; before the war it is quite likely that even seasonal staff had years of experience with the company (*Birmingham Daily Post*, 1 July).

Following the second accident the company's insurance provider advised that its cover would be terminated unless some device was installed that would automatically override any error on the part of the brakesman. Unable to fund the expenditure itself, the company informed the council that it would only continue operations if it received an annual grant, which resulted in the council offering to buy the lifts for a nominal £1.

The town clerk advised the council that it required legal authority to operate the lifts, despite the existence of other authority-owned and operated lifts that ran without specific legal authority, at Bournemouth, for example, and in January 1967 he enquired of the Ministry of Transport about obtaining a Light Railway Order. The Ministry was puzzled because it could not see how an order could be used to transfer a non-statutory railway.

In April the council's intentions were made clear. The order would be used to enable the council to acquire and operate the lifts, but in the meantime the council would use its existing powers to make a grant to the company to enable the new safety device to be fitted before the start of the summer season, and to cover any losses incurred in operating the lifts before the order had been made and the council enabled to taken them over.

The estimated costs of the safety device and the losses were £1,800 and £1,075 respectively. The Light Railway Order was made on 12 October 1967, giving the council power to make agreements providing for the transfer of the lifts from the lift company and for the operation of the lifts as a light railway. The 1890 lift was not run under the new regime, its stepped design possibly mitigating against it being chosen to be equipped with the safety device; it had not been run since 27 October 1966. The company's liquidation was completed in 1970 (*London Gazette*, 17 September 1970).

Initially, the lift was profitable for the council but by the time Shepway Council,

After the council had taken over, the 1885 lift seen in operation while the 1890 cars have been taken out of action. The operational cars and the station buildings were painted white. (J. H. Price)

Folkestone's post-1974 successor, was looking for assets to sell to raise funds, it was loss-making, so it was included in a list of leases and properties offered for sale by auction in April 1987. Even though the lease had less than two years to run, farmer Joseph Copeland bid £50,000 for it. Obliged to maintain the lift in its present form and not to remove it, he declared that he would run it at a profit (*Folkestone Herald*, 13/27 March, 3/10 April 1987).

The sale to Copeland was not completed, however, and the lift remained in Shepway's ownership. Services continued and a substantial restoration was carried out in 1985, when the 1890 lift was also dismantled. A further £21,000 of work carried out in 1992 included fitting a door interlock. In 2009, however, the council announced that it could no longer sustain the lift's losses. Passenger numbers had declined since a popular Sunday market held on the seafront had ended and costs had increased. Attempts to secure sponsorship had not succeeded. The lift ran for the last time on 30 June and the lease was surrendered to the Radnor estate (*Folkestone Herald*, 23 October 1992/BBC, 27 March/30 June 2009).

During the council's tenure, in 1989 Historic England awarded the complete installation of the lift, its buildings and its equipment a grade II* listing, citing its rarity, engineering and structural interest, its reciprocating pumps, working band brake, automatic hydraulic remote-control system and the architectural merit of its buildings.

In the council's stead, on 27 May 2010 a residents' group, the Folkestone Leas Lift Community Interest Company, was incorporated to run the lift, resuming operations on 26 July 2010. Small profits in 2010–12 were overturned by losses in 2013 and 2014. They enjoyed a good year in 2015, with a profit of £9,981, but this was wiped out by a £10,428 loss in 2016 (BBC, 26 July 2010).

While the accounts were being completed, the directors' confidence was struck another blow, because, following an inspection, the Health & Safety Executive served an improvement notice on the company, saying that the braking system was 'unreliable and prone to failure'. Unable to raise the £80,000 required for a new braking system, the lift was not

54 • CLIFF RAILWAYS: AN HISTORIC SURVEY

reopened for 2017 and on 4 May the company applied to be struck off the companies register.

That was not the end for the Leas lift, however, for another residents' group was formed, determined to raise the funds required to reopen the lift. It was incorporated as the Folkestone Leas Lift Community Interest Company on 11 January 2018 and changed its status

A temporary compound was erected to restore the 1885 car bodies, seen on 3 June 1985. They had lost their clerestory roofs during the 1970s.

While the 1885 lift was being renovated, the 1890 lift was dismantled, its winding wheel and band brake exposed in the process when photographed on 3 June 1985.

1885/1890 FOLKESTONE CLIFF TRAMWAY, THE LEAS • 55

An unknown photographer took the opportunity to record the interior of one of the 1890 cars after it had been removed.

The 1885 lift in action in June 2013. (Steve Sedgwick)

to that of a charitable incorporated organisation on 14 December 2020. The company's intervention was timely, as in 2019 Historic England had placed the lift on the heritage at-risk register.

After several false alarms, during which the lift deteriorated from being left unused and unmaintained, increasing costs further, in November 2023 completion of funding needed for a £6.6 million restoration was announced with a £4.8 million contribution from the National Lottery Heritage Fund, nearly £1 million of Section 106 funding from the Folkestone Harbour & Seafront Development Company, £660,000 from trusts and foundations plus £136,000 from the community. In 2024 Historic England contributed £200,000 when it was found that the original head wheel was irreparable. Including creating a visitor centre at the lower station and building a café to the west of it, work is scheduled, at the time of writing, to be completed in 2025 (BBC, 4 November 2023/*KentLive*, 15 May 2024).

56 • CLIFF RAILWAYS: AN HISTORIC SURVEY

In the meantime, the company had generated an income by leasing the lower station buildings as a café and by incorporating a subsidiary company to operate an 'escape room' in 2020 (*KentOnline*, 4 September / 16 October 2020).

A view inside the pump house in 2013. (Steve Sedgwick)

The lower station and the stabled cars in June 2019. (Joseph Brennan)

1885/1890 FOLKESTONE CLIFF TRAMWAY, THE LEAS • 57

A view of the interior, with the café located in the waiting room. The presence of the café eliminated vandalism as well as providing an income for the present lift company while it raised funds for restoration. This and the following photographs were taken on 8 June 2023.

A close-up of the upper station seen from below.

58 • CLIFF RAILWAYS: AN HISTORIC SURVEY

Among the first works undertaken when restoration started in 2024 was the removal of the winding wheel for assessment for repair. Manufacturing faults in the casting, however, made it irreparable and it will be replaced. A contractor was appointed in November 2024 and work started to clear the vegetation in January 2025. Solar panels will be installed on the disused 1890 formation. (Folkestone Leas Lift Company CIO)

CHAPTER 8

1890 LYNTON & LYNMOUTH LIFT

Opened 9 April 1890, 3ft 9in gauge, double track, 862ft long, gradient 1 in 1.75, water balance, operational.

During the nineteenth century the area of the north Devon coast around the confluence of the East and West Lyn rivers and the twin villages of Lynton and Lynmouth had not only become popular with tourists but also with wealthy visitors who holidayed there and bought, or had built, holiday homes. It had attracted the soubriquet 'England's Switzerland'. But 20 miles distant by horse-drawn carriage from each of the nearest commercial centres, Barnstaple, Ilfracombe and Minehead, as the century grew to a close visitors started to show a preference for places that were more easily accessible, in particular those that had railways.

While they tried to attract a railway, the Lynton/Lynmouth area's property owners and gentry determined to ensure that the area maintained its attraction to visitors. The cliff railway had its origins in an unfulfilled ambition to provide Lynmouth with a pier. Proposals in 1871 and 1876 had failed to progress but a third scheme in 1885 was different, because as well as the promenade required to access the pier, it included provision for 'A lift or hoist in connection therewith for the convenience of persons using the pier or landing place, and of others.'

The promoters were Thomas Hewitt (1838–1923) and John Heywood (1848–96), local residents with connections. The former was a barrister who secured the required Lynmouth Pier Order for a 'mere' £80 in 1886. He was to become a director of the lift company and of the Lynton & Barnstaple Railway. Heywood was a hotelier who ran Lynton's Valley of Rocks Hotel for a while. There had been no objections to the order but there had been no public meetings to explain the plans, either, and it is quite likely that few residents had any idea of what was intended.

Hewitt and Heywood transferred their rights in the order to the Lynton & Lynmouth Pier & Promenade Company, a company they had registered with £10,000 capital, and on 26 January 1887 the Lynton Local Board applied its seal to an agreement whereby it took over responsibility to build the 500ft-long promenade. It was alleged that the rateable value of the lift, when built, would cover the cost of the loan required but this expectation was not mentioned after the promenade was opened on 20 September 1887.

Construction had been started by local contractor Messrs Jones Brothers, a firm led by Bob Jones (1849–1921), in May 1887. It started by the village's distinctive Rhenish tower and extended to the point just past the subsequent cliff railway's lower station where the car park now starts. It was extended by another 1,000ft, its current extent, in 1895–96. In September 1887 the company accepted the Jones' offer to construct the lift and run it at their own risk (*Exeter & Plymouth Gazette*, 28 January/ *Ilfracombe Chronicle*, 21 May/*North Devon Herald*, 15 September/*North Devon Journal*, 29 September 1887/18 April/22 August 1895/26 March 1896).

One of Hewitt's guests at the opening was George Newnes, an MP and publisher who had found wealth and fame by publishing the magazine *Tit Bits*. Hewitt introduced Newnes to Bob Jones.

The outcome was that Newnes became an enthusiast for this area of north Devon, having Jones build a large house for him in Lynton and becoming a substantial benefactor of the locality. He also agreed to contribute substantially towards the lift. The pier was not built, incidentally, because Newnes declined to fund it when the landowner insisted on being paid for the required ground. The esplanade extension was opened without ceremony (*Western Morning News*, 19 May 1892).

Many thousands of tons of stone were excavated from the railway site during 1887, and, remarkably, considering the nature of the work to cut a steep slot in the rock, only one accident was reported, an unnamed man falling off the work platform and breaking his leg (*Ilfracombe Chronicle*, 3 December 1887).

It has been said that objections to the lift were the cause of the decision to seek Parliamentary powers, but none were reported. More likely, the promoters were influenced by a desire to secure the lift's water supply, unmentioned in the pier order. Whatever the reason, a Bill deposited in Parliament was enacted as the Lynton & Lynmouth Lift Act on 5 July 1888, making this the only lift authorised by Parliament.

Capital was £10,000 in £1 shares plus borrowing powers of £2,500. The Act was concerned with the incorporation and functioning of the company, the works, the use of water, tolls and the carriage of mail. Apart from taking power from the Tramways Act of 1870 governing the conduct of the company with regard to street works and the road authority, no railway or tramway Acts were incorporated, and no provision was made for any interaction with the Board of Trade. Concern that there might be errors in the deposited plans or book of reference might explain an unusual clause that authorised the company to apply for court orders to obtain certificates identifying errors and overriding them in carrying out the work. The Act nominated George Newnes and Bob Jones and one other person to be nominated by them to be the first directors.

Jones had signed the £6,047 5s estimate as engineer. The chief feature of the statutory lift was its division at North Walk, estimated to cost £3,718 5s for the lower section, £909 for the upper. The approach road at Lynton was estimated at £600, five overbridges at £320, three stations at £100 each and the conduits and aqueduct at £820. There were

The plan deposited in Parliament showing the route of the railway, its access road at Lynton and the limits of deviation. (Parliamentary Archives)

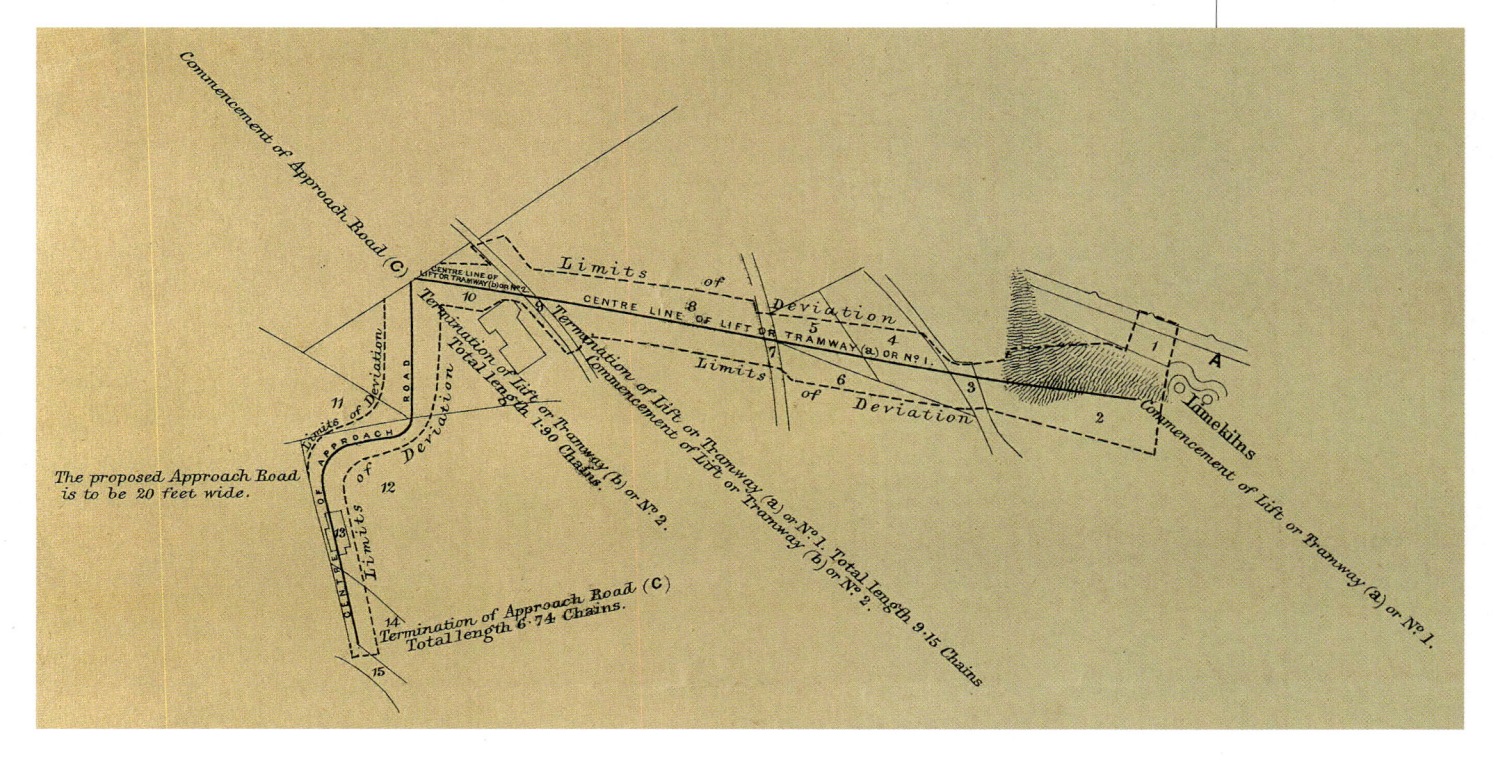

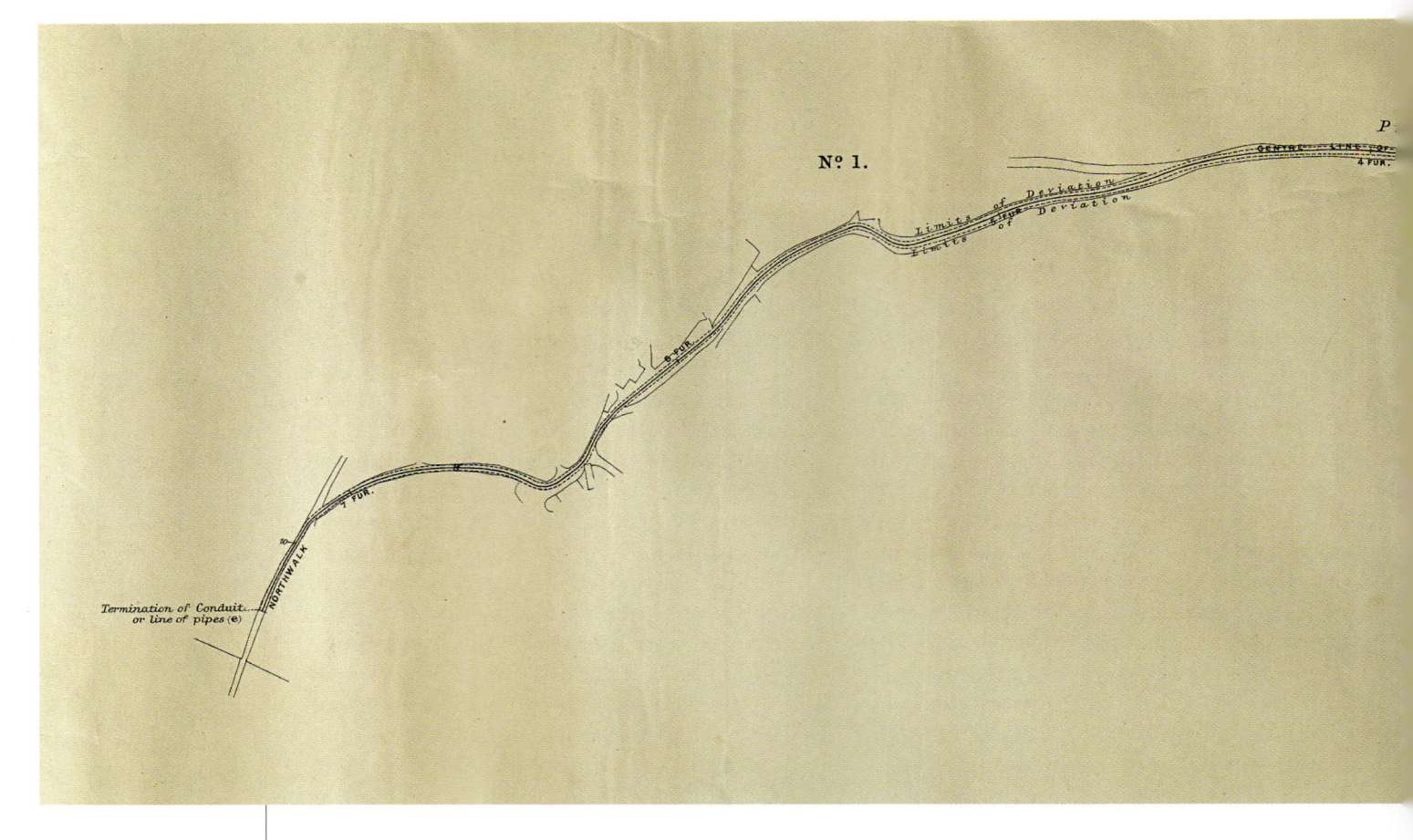

The authorised route of the pipeline from North Walk to the West Lyn River. (Parliamentary Archives)

two bridges at North Walk, where there was also a station. The location of the intended fifth bridge is unknown; it was not shown on the plan.

Construction of the lift continued throughout 1888 but suffered a setback on 20 November, when one of the North Walk bridge abutments was washed out during a storm. Fortunately, the newly appointed consulting engineer, G. C. Marks, the hydraulic engineer who had worked for Tangye, had arrived in Lynton the previous day and was able to offer advice on the remedial action required. Marks was, incidentally, related to Jones via his (Marks') maternal grandmother (*Western Morning News*, 29 August/*North Devon Journal*, 22 November 1888).

Marks also acted as a patent agent, which became the main focus of his career, and in June 1888 he had registered a patent for the improvements of hydraulic lifts on behalf of himself, Jones and Newnes. The features were that the track was single, except for the passing place in the middle; the passenger compartment was 'furnished with wheels', so the carriage could be used for luggage; and the provision of three independent brakes.

Engineering (12 April 1889) reported that the railway was expected to be opened in July, but no explanation was offered for it being delayed until Easter 1890. Reports published on 20 August 1889 attributed the delay to 'unforeseen circumstances' (*Bideford Weekly Gazette*) and that the ceremony was 'postponed for a few weeks' (*Exeter & Plymouth Gazette*). The blame was probably due to the three braking systems, more complex than those used elsewhere.

Despite the Act of Parliament not including any requirement for the Board of Trade's involvement in the lift, it was informed of its construction, for on 19 September 1889 Major Phillip Cardew (1851–1910), in the area to inspect the area's new electric light installation, saw the works in progress and thought it was his duty to inform the Board. C. S. Hutchinson was consulted, though, and minuted that no action was necessary.

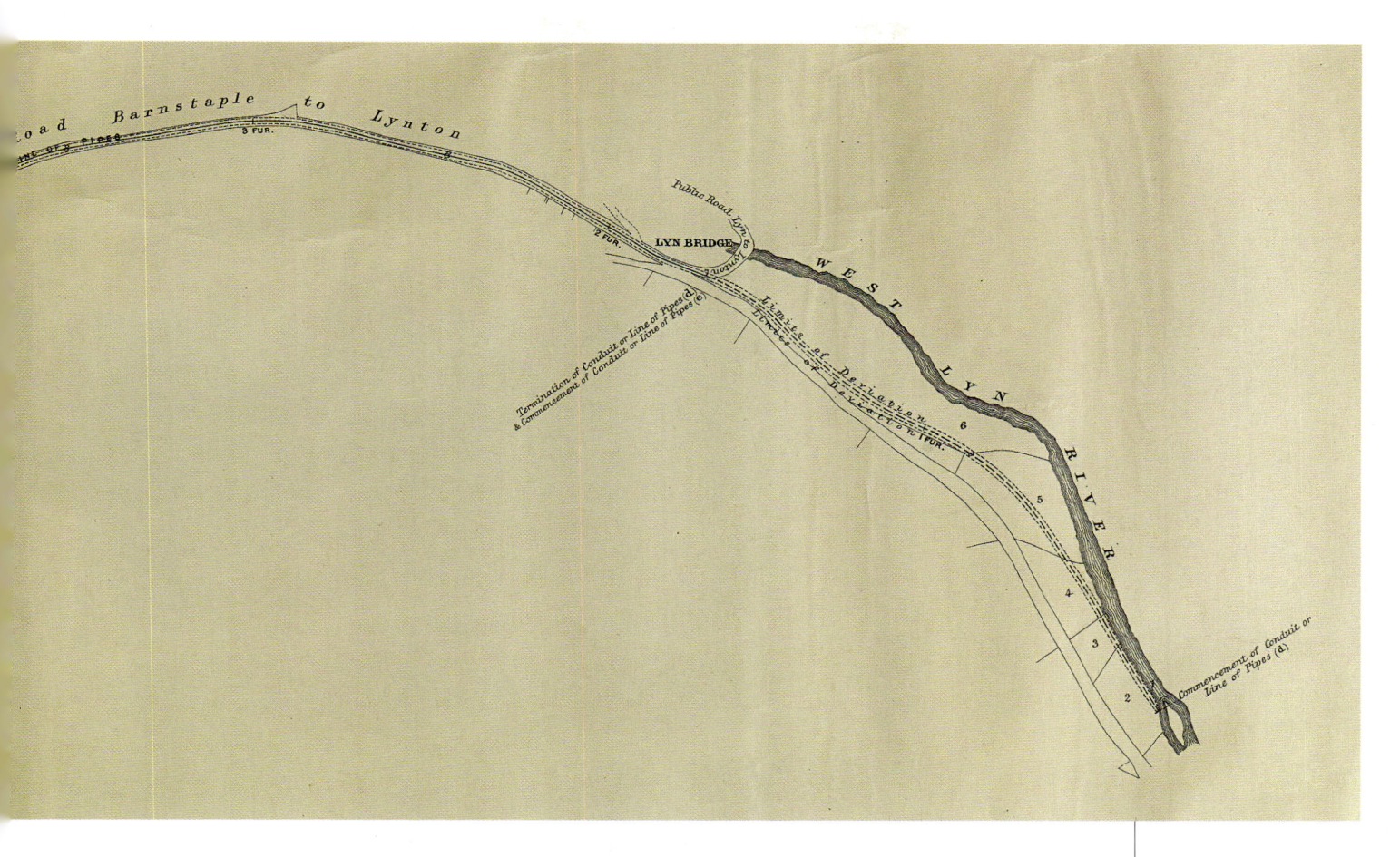

The company itself subsequently enquired about the requirements for an inspection in February 1890 and was told that it would be responsible for any expenses incurred. Hutchinson was appointed but the directors seem to have lost interest in the idea and no inspection was made.

The first reported sightings of the lift in operation were during February 1890, when Jones Brothers had used it to transport 5 tons of cement, which had taken five hours (*Ilfracombe Chronicle*, 1 March 1890).

On opening day, 7 April 1890, the twin villages were *en fête*, with decorations and banners throughout. Ada Medland Jeune (1860–1952), wife of the lord of the manor, declared the railway open at Lynton station, despatching a group of journalists to Lynmouth. The official party then

A pre-opening run with contractor Bob Jones and George Newnes on the platform. Notice how the edge of the platform has been battered by Jones's construction traffic. (Christopher Vickery)

Lynton station before the line was opened. The building was extended in the 1920s and survives as a part of the café. (Lynton & Lynmouth Lift Company)

The upper station on a quiet day in the early years. The car's suspension and wheels can be seen, and the driver's unprotected platform is loaded with luggage, for which the company made a charge. (Lynton & Lynmouth Lift Company)

64 • CLIFF RAILWAYS: AN HISTORIC SURVEY

adjourned to the adjacent Valley of Rocks Hotel for lunch.

In construction, the lift, usually referred to as a cliff railway from its opening, complied with the patent, having the ability to remove the car bodies to enable the carriage of goods and carts and the tracks close together except where the cars passed, which had enabled a small reduction in the land required and the volume of stone to be removed during construction. An intermediate platform was provided where the railway crossed North Walk for the benefit of visitors proceeding to Castle Hotel or the Valley of Rocks. Communication between the stations was by telephone. A pipeline a mile long supplied water from the river West Lyn to Lynton station. The carriages, probably made in Jones Brothers' workshop, were said to seat fourteen to sixteen passengers. An open platform at the downhill end provided for the brakesman was also used for light goods and passengers (*North Devon Herald*, 10 April 1890).

The railway was an immediate success. One week in August 9,000 passengers were carried and a week later it was recorded that 80,000 passengers, and 'an almost incredible number of tons of goods', had been carried since the line had opened. There was so much traffic that consideration was being given to replacing the line or doubling it, according to the papers. There was less traffic in December, though, when the company discovered that water does not move very well when it is frozen. Traffic the following year included 45 tons of garden refuse that took five hours to carry, although the earlier report that it took five hours to carry 5 tons of cement suggests that one of these reports is incorrect (*Exeter & Plymouth Gazette*, 2 September 1890/17 April 1891/*North Devon Herald*, 11 September 1890/*Ilfracombe Chronicle*, 1 March/6 December 1890).

At the end of 1890 the *North Devon Herald* (4 December) announced that the company anticipated spending more than £600 on replacing the apparatus, and reports during 1891 indicate that the railway required fine tuning to ensure smooth operation. By August, a larger reservoir had been commissioned and water-handling capacity increased, and following a landslip that caused the railway to be closed for several weeks in October, the opportunity was taken to carry out a wide-ranging upgrade, replacing the equipment and cars. The brake arrangements were improved, and operating was now at a regular speed, a buffer being used to slow the cars on the approach to Lynmouth. New water tanks on the undercarriages were narrower and shorter than before, to make them lighter. Self-oiling rollers had been placed on the track to keep the ropes off the ground, and reduce friction wear (*Western Times*, 29 October/*North Devon Journal*, 3 December 1891).

Highlights of operations were noted in local newspapers. On 17 August 1892 the Lynmouth Cottage Garden & Horticultural Society's annual flower

A view of the railway that pre-dates the extension of the esplanade in 1895–96. The flagpole indicates the location of the lower station building. At this date the abandoned lime kilns and the building alongside them belonged to George Newnes. (Montague Cooper)

A view of Lynmouth that also pre-dates the esplanade extension and the construction of Newnes' Hollerday House on the hill above the railway; the latter was destroyed by fire on 4 August 1913, newspaper reports accusing Suffragists of arson.

The street access to the lower station, complete with rustic gates. The building still exists, albeit without its decorative roofing tiles and with the frontage concealed by a later stone-clad extension.

66 • CLIFF RAILWAYS: AN HISTORIC SURVEY

show drew 2,340 passengers to the lift, the daily average being 1,000–1,300. Traffic in February 1893 included tons of sand from the beach, blocks of freestone brought in by sea, as well as coal and other goods; very few passengers during the winter. The stone was for Newnes' house being built on Hollerday Hill. A total of 114,000 passengers were carried during the year. A severe frost in February–March 1894 caused several pipes to burst and closed the railway for six weeks (*North Devon Journal*, 2 September 1892/2 March 1893/4 April 1895/*Exeter & Plymouth Gazette*, 4 May 1894).

More changes were made towards the end of the decade. Over the winter of 1896–97 toilets were built at Lynton, the rope was changed for one with a 44-ton breaking strain and the balance chain was changed for wire, eliminating the noise that had accompanied operations. In 1898 changes to the plumbing enabled cars to be run every three minutes, which no doubt enabled 3,400 passengers to be carried on 17 August, the flower show day (*Exeter & Plymouth Gazette*, 22 May 1897/*North Devon Journal*, 25 August/15 September 1898).

On 21 May 1897 a passenger told the Board of Trade that he thought the railway was unsafe. It had been reopened the day before, he wrote, after the new ropes had been installed, but he could not return because the automatic brake had broken.

Goods in transit just below the passing place.

A brakesman looking dressed more for the Wild West than for North Devon dealing with a passenger. There are advertisements in the car, one that is legible being for cigars available from a chemist in Lynton. Two of the wheels that enable the car to be removed to facilitate the carriage of goods are visible.

He drew attention to the lack of any barrier around the platform, saying that 'they' sometimes put a garden seat on it for passenger use and used it to carry barrels. He thought that there should be a 3ft-high railing to protect passengers. Noting that the Board was not responsible for the railway, one of the officers suggested copying the letter to the company, pointing out that it was responsible for safe working. While it did not retain copies of any correspondence with the company, photographs show that a railing was installed, and that a wire mesh was added subsequently.

Reports in the first years of the twentieth century relate to winter closures for repairs but did not always say what they were, even when the closure was as long as six weeks, as in 1902, or three months, as in 1906–07. During the 1908 closure the head wheel was replaced, and larger water tanks

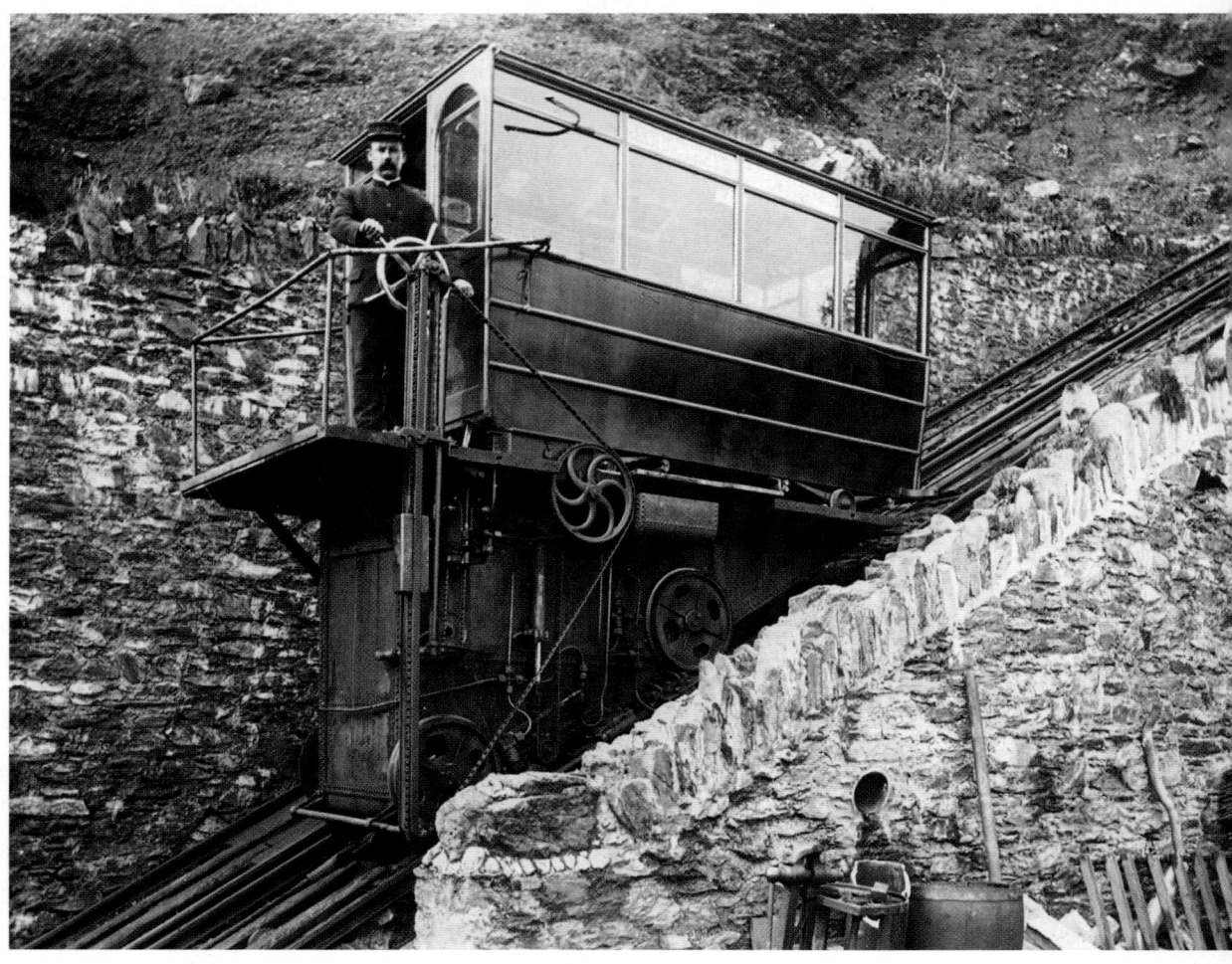

One of the cars near Lynmouth, showing the barrier erected after the complaint to the Board of Trade in 1897. Some idea of the complexity of the Jones/Marks braking systems may also be seen in this photograph.

68 • CLIFF RAILWAYS: AN HISTORIC SURVEY

were fitted, which presumably restored them to their original size, so that larger motor cars could be carried. The station approaches were widened to facilitate vehicular access, too; the 100 cars carried during the year fully justifying the effort (*North Devon Herald*, 28 May 1908/ *North Devon Journal*, 27 August 1908).

Although the railway was closed again on 21 November 1908, for the track to be renewed, the work carried out was extensive. Fifty tons of new, heavier rail was laid on concrete sleepers reinforced with pieces of the old rail. To reduce friction, the passing place was lengthened, which required some 3ft of rock to be removed from the cutting sides. A workshop equipped with lathe, grinding machine and other tools powered by an electric motor enabled the car underframes to be rebuilt to enable them to carry cars with a 12ft wheelbase. The wheelsets were also replaced. The railway was reopened on 17 May 1909 (*North Devon Herald*, 26 November 1908/28 January/18 March/29 April 1909, *Exeter & Plymouth Gazette*, 22 January/16 March 1909).

Just as this work was being started, a tragedy occurred at Lynton. At midday on 27 January Thomas Andrews, aged 45, a brakesman, was found drowned in the water tank. He had been employed on the railway since it opened and had previously served in the Army. Although the railway was closed for the track renewal, his duty that day was at Lynton station. Phoned twice from Lynmouth during the morning, no action had been taken when he had not answered. He was found by the gardener in the neighbouring property. At the inquest no explanation could be offered for

A view at North Walk, showing the wire mesh added to the platform barrier, the car framed between both of the North Walk bridges. (G. L. Gunn)

him going to the tank and it was concluded that he might have overbalanced when trying to check for ice and died from the shock of falling into near-frozen water. The verdict was accidental death. The company's insurance paid £226 13s 3d compensation, £100 held in trust for his 14-year-old daughter until she was 21 and the remainder for his widow (*North Devon Journal*, 28 January/4 February/11 March/ *Exeter & Plymouth Gazette*, 29 January 1909).

George Newnes, the publisher and politician who had taken up Bob Jones's idea for a cliff railway connecting Lynton with Lynmouth with enthusiasm, died on 9 June 1910, aged 59. Awarded a baronetcy for political services in 1900, he had been a great benefactor to the twin villages and, as will be seen, played a part in promoting other cliff railways, too. His son, Sir Frank Hillyard Newnes (1877–1955), replaced him as company chairman (*Western Times*, 10 June/28 October 1910).

On the railway, the regular programme of maintenance, renewals and improvements continued. The cars were provided with electric lighting in 1910 and when the rope was replaced in 1915 the buffers installed at Lynton in 1890 were changed for patent hydraulic devices (*North Devon Journal*, 10 March 1910/6 May 1915/*Exeter & Plymouth Gazette*, 2 September 1910).

A shock came in 1916 with the sudden death on 16 March of William Long, the mechanical engineer, at the age of 53. Born in Bath, he had moved to Lynton to work for Jones Brothers, playing a prominent role in the cliff railway's construction and remaining as engineer after it was completed.

Long's death left the company with only three employees – Albert Bevan (37), George Davie Blackford (36) and John Creek (30) – who were subject to enlistment for military service. The company appealed, on the basis that it was a statutory undertaking subject to Board of Trade rules and could not be run safely with fewer than three staff. The local tribunal claimed that the railway was a mere convenience, mainly for visitors. It heard that passenger numbers had fallen to 123,860 from 140,758 in 1914 and 185,492 in 1913, and only 150 tons of goods had been carried in 1915. An appeals tribunal in Barnstaple agreed that an exempt man could be trained in three months and gave Bevan a permanent exception, exempted Creek until 30 September, when another appeal could be made, and ordered Blackford to the colours at once. The Army representative objected but was refused leave to appeal (*North Devon Journal*, 25 May/*Western Times*, 22 June 1916).

By the time of another hearing the following February, Blackford had enlisted but Creek and Bevan were still being targeted, despite being graded C2 and B1 for health respectively. On this occasion the company's solicitor could not persuade the tribunal that the railway was of national importance and the men were told that they were expected to have joined the Army by 1 March. If Creek was not wanted as a combatant he could work in munitions, the chairman added. A total of 200,000 passengers had been carried in 2016. Blackford became a prisoner of war in March 1918 and died of his injuries in Lynton on 20 June 1919, 'another victim of German ill treatment' (*Exeter & Plymouth Gazette*, 2 January/*North Devon Journal*, 15 February 1917/30 May 1918/ *North Devon Herald*, 26 June 1919).

Only a man named Parker, presumably Blackford's replacement, remained working on the railway. The vacancies were filled by William Jordan (1872–1926), the Congregational minister, and John James Smith (1860–1919). With training by Witney Heywood Jones (1886–1960), Bob Jones's son, the railway was soon running again and continued throughout the war. In 1920 long queues were reported. (*North Devon Journal*, 8 March 1917/26 August 1920).

Bob Jones, who conceived and built the railway, died on 5 December 1921, aged 72. His brother, Tom, his partner in Jones Brothers, died on 21 September 1928. He had been a director and the company's secretary, the brothers' partnership having been responsible for managing the railway (*North Devon Journal*, 8 December 1921/27 September 1928).

Another attempt was made to increase the frequency of services in 1923, with the installation of a second 4in water main, and not stopping at the North Walk platform, but queues were still reported on busy days in August. Services were also run on Sundays and up to 9 pm on weekdays (*North Devon Journal*, 22 February/5 July/23 August).

In 1934 the company appealed against its £800 rating assessment, arguing that it should not exceed £650 and that it had been over-assessed for some time but that it had previously taken a line of least resistance. The 1928 valuation had been £540. After some debate about whether the cars and their tanks were part of the property, the company was awarded an assessment of £700 plus costs. During the hearing the company's solicitor mentioned that the capital was £8,000 and that for several years a 14% dividend had been paid.

John Creek, who had been forced to enlist in 1917, and served in Russia and Salonika, had returned to the railway after the war and became foreman. He died on 13 April 1940, aged 54; services were suspended while his funeral took place (*Exeter & Plymouth Gazette*, 19/26 April).

Compared with the First World War, during the Second the railway's news profile was very low, only generating two reports referring to its annual maintenance closure (*North Devon Journal*, 9 April 1942/4 March 1943).

From 1946 there were regular calls for the company to provide replacement transport during the maintenance closure. The education authority was also concerned about the inconvenience to school children. Southern National did run a service for three months from 20 December 1946 but subsequently told Lynton Urban District Council that it did not have the buses to run a permanent service and that the 1946–47 service had not covered the driver's wages (*North Devon Journal*, 3 October/24 December 1946/5/26 June 1947/29 January 1948/10 February/3 March/7 April 1949/2 February 1950).

Lynmouth station in 1921. The car has been painted in a lighter colour, the mouldings in a contrasting dark one. No platform awning is attached to the frame provided for it. The weighing machine was installed in 1890, the company's application to locate it on the esplanade being refused on the basis that it had enough space of its own. The ornate arch and bell were subsequently removed and reinstated. The similar arch and bell at Lynton are post-war installations. (J. Valentine)

An inter-war scene at Lynmouth. The station building had been extended on two sides and the flagpole has been removed. In 1909 Newnes had leased the lime kilns and the derelict building to the left of them to Lynton UDC for £1 a year. The kilns were adapted as toilets and a viewing platform, and a park was developed on the site of the other building. The park was replaced by the pavilion in 1932. The toilets were closed when the flood memorial building was opened in 1958 (*North Devon Journal*, 7 January 1909/5 February 1914/9 June 1932).

1890 LYNTON & LYNMOUTH LIFT • 71

A view of Lynton station, after the car bodies had been altered to permit side entry/exit at this station. Capacity is officially forty but in practice the limit is twenty, except, the author understands, in the case of school and similar parties. (R. J. Sellick)

On 28 November 1946 the stump of a fallen tree had fallen on to the railway, narrowly missing some passengers at Lynmouth and damaging the track, but in May 1948 the company lost its claim for £23 10s at Barnstaple County Court on a technicality, having claimed against the person on whose land the tree had first fallen, instead of the owner of the land where it had fallen from. Having to pay costs, the company appears to have made no further attempt to obtain compensation (*North Devon Journal*, 27 May 1948).

Passenger capacity was doubled in 1947, with the uphill end of the car bodies altered to provide a standing area; subsequently capacity was set at thirty, with twelve seated. Welded water tanks were installed in 1955–56.

The railway escaped being damaged by the storms that overwhelmed the East and West Lyn rivers and caused enormous damage around Lynmouth on 15 August

In this view of a car interior the lines and interior of the turtle-back roof may be seen. Given a constant programme of repair and renewal since 1890, the seats are probably the oldest parts of the cars to remain in use.

72 • CLIFF RAILWAYS: AN HISTORIC SURVEY

1952, killing thirty-four people in the rivers' catchment areas and destroying fifty-five buildings. It was able to contribute to the relief efforts by carrying cars until the roads were reopened, which it did again for a week in 1970 while the road was being resurfaced (BBC, 29 January 2018).

A landslip triggered by heavy rain on 30 October 1952 fractured the company's private water mains, ironically on a section of road traversed by the Duke of Edinburgh during his visit to see the flood damage and meet survivors the day before. With the Duke's party including company chairman George Herbert Laurence Easterbrook (1898–1973), it may be no surprise that he also travelled on the railway during his tour. Returning to Lynmouth on the occasion of the disaster's fiftieth anniversary in 2002, the Duke reprised his journey on the railway (*Torbay Express*, 29 October / *Western Morning News*, 1 November 1952 / *Torbay Express*, 15 January 1973).

A link with the railway's origins was broken on 18 April 1960, with the death of W. H. Jones, Bob Jones's son, aged 73. He had taken over the family's building business after the First World War and had been the railway's engineer in charge. One of his sons, Bob Heywood Benn Jones (1920–2000), became managing director and engineer (*Express & Echo*, 19 April).

After seventy years of incident-free operation, the descending car derailed about 15ft from Lynmouth station on 16 May 1960. With support from boatmen and hotel staff, an escape route was devised using tarpaulins and a ladder to get the passengers, mostly pensioners, to safety. Builders working nearby rigged ladders to rescue the passengers stranded 15ft from Lynton (*Express & Echo*, 17 May).

Services were stopped again on 17 August 1962, when a passenger riding on the platform dropped a camera as the car neared Lynton. It fell into the pit at the bottom and became jammed in the mechanism, and it was ninety minutes before the passengers could resume their journeys. Those in the upper car were reported to have sung songs to pass the time (*Guardian Journal*, 18 August 1962).

Collecting fares at Lynmouth in 1955. Fares are no longer the responsibility of the brakesman, passengers paying at the kiosk at Lynmouth.

At a time of price restraint, in 1975 the company obtained an order from the Department of the Environment authorising the increase of the 'up' fare from 3p to 4p. The inspector who considered the application said that with inflation, the 6d authorised in 1888 was the equivalent of 27p in 1974, so therefore the proposed 4p charge, with a maximum of 6d, was very reasonable. The inspector's report also revealed that the company had recently spent £4,026 plus VAT on replacing the rails and was planning to spend £1,118 to increase the load-bearing capacity of the North Walk bridge from 2 to 5 tons. It had also abandoned the practice of providing replacement taxis during the annual closure period as being impractical, 'in recent years', and was willing to undertake not to object to any application for a replacement bus service.

The railway's centenary was celebrated with free rides on 16 April 1990 and on 17 April 2015 the 125th anniversary was celebrated with a visit by HRH The Princess Royal. During the visit she was

A brief visit to Lynmouth on 22 December 2013 found the cars removed from their carriages and the railway's outdoor furniture under wraps.

A car arrives at the lower station on 27 July 2024. The following photographs were taken on the same occasion. The lighting in the terminal pit uses modern colour-changing LEDs that the company takes advantage of when it runs Halloween events.

introduced to descendants of Bob Jones (ITVX, 17 April 2015).

Unlike many other resorts and attractions, Lynmouth and Lynton, and their cliff railway, were not seriously affected by the adoption of overseas package holidays by the British public. Originally, the company was fortunate in having George Newnes as a majority shareholder and in his willingness to fund the modifications required to bring the railway to a condition of reliable operation. His enthusiasm for it has been fully justified as it has only spent £8,125 of its £10,000 authorised capital and has not only been able to finance its routine maintenance and improvements but to reward its shareholders. In the twenty-first century the absence of a convenient, easily graded, alternative pedestrian route avoiding the steep hill and the enthusiasm of its managers and staff ensures its continued success.

Only a small part of the queue waiting to ascend to Lynton is visible in this image. One of the plaques attached to the barrier is the National Transport Trust's Red Wheel award, which recognises the railway's status in the use of water power; it was presented on 9 June 2021. Also visible is the inner façade of the original station building, part of which, containing a museum display, is accessible to passengers. The block paving was installed during the 2023–24 winter closure.

Lynmouth station, and the company's electric van, seen from a descending car. The extensions to the original building are thought to have been made in the 1920s. The image also shows the viewing platform, now used to provide outdoor seating for the Pavilion, constructed on the lime kilns.

1890 LYNTON & LYNMOUTH LIFT • 75

Above left: The entrance to the company's private road at Lynmouth. From time to time, facilities are provided to the operators of markets and craft fairs.

Above right: Cars about to pass, seen from North Walk. The company's staff replaced the two footbridges in 1989. 'Emergency exits' provided at the bridges have been upgraded to bespoke walkways with handrails since 2019, the last one in 2023–24.

The approach to Lynton station seen from North Walk. Unusually, the head wheel is located above the tracks, protected from extreme weather by a Perspex sheet. The tank filler pipes can be seen either side of the tracks in front of the barrier.

76 • CLIFF RAILWAYS: AN HISTORIC SURVEY

CHAPTER 9

1890 BROWSIDE TRAMWAY, ISLE OF MAN

Opened 16 August 1890, 6ft gauge, double track, 390ft long, gradient 1 in 4, hydraulic, closed 1914.

The Browside Tramway at Laxey, Isle of Man, is one of the least known, least reported and among the least photographed of all the railways in this book. The second Manx cliff railway, it was built by a local company established to create and promote attractions in the vicinity of the 72ft Lady Isabella waterwheel in May 1890. Compared with the other lines in this book, its carriages were very basic. Opened without ceremony, the source of the opening date is not known. In 1891 it was being operated by John Callow, a Laxey man involved in various enterprises, who advertised, 'Save your wind and spare your limbs by taking the Browside Tram to the big wheel, Laxey.' The lower station was near Creer's mill (*Isle of Man Times*, 24 May 1890/13 June 1891).

Callow was injured on 15 July 1893 when the brakesman let go of the brake, causing the cars to run away. The empty up-bound car hit him when it collided with the platform where he was standing. The passengers in the down car were unhurt. Callow recovered (*Isle of Man Times*, 22 July 1893).

During a licensing application for the Laxey Wheel Café, next to the tramway's

Almost the entire route of the Browside Tramway can be seen in the splendid view of the Lady Isabella waterwheel.

upper terminus, in 1898, it was said that up to 1894 the average number of passengers was 45,000 a year (*Isle of Man Times*, 1898).

Those three paragraphs summarise the reporting on the tramway's existence. It might have been closed following a dispute over water charges with new mine owners in 1906, but it was certainly not reopened after the First World War.

A different view can just be had from above the wheel, where the location of one of the upper station platforms and cars are indicated. The lower part of the tramway survives as a footpath but the upper section had been obscured by a car park.

On the upper right of this photograph can also be seen the Snaefell Mountain Railway's Laxey car shed. (Frith)

78 • CLIFF RAILWAYS: AN HISTORIC SURVEY

The upper station of the tramway, smoke belching from the chimney acting as a reminder that the area was very industrial in years gone by.

1890 BROWSIDE TRAMWAY, ISLE OF MAN • 79

CHAPTER 10

1891 HASTINGS, WEST HILL LIFT

Opened 25 March 1891, 6ft gauge, double track, 500ft long, gradient 1 in 2.9, gas engine, electric from 1924, operational. Thirty miles from Folkestone, Hastings, on the English Channel coast of East Sussex, developed from being a coastal fishing village to being a popular resort with the advent of railways from 1851. As it grew, development took place to the north, separated from the coastal strip by the cliff-faced West Hill that rose above the town, which led to the construction of the first of two cliff railways.

In March 1889 two lift schemes were promoted. The promoters of the first had been working on it for two years and had secured the Albion Hotel's mews on George Street as a lower base. They intended to tunnel through the hill and erect a hydraulic lift like that at Folkestone, with the tunnel illuminated. To avoid disfiguring the area around the upper station, where the land had recently been bought by the council as a public open space, the promoters declared it would be below ground, the site surrounded by a balustrade 4ft 6in high that could be concealed by shrubbery if necessary. The 10,000 residents on the hill were expected to find the lift a great advantage, with visitors and a parcel carriage and delivery service providing additional revenue. A company would be formed to raise the £10,000 capital required.

The other scheme was for a vertical lift up the cliff face at Parade House, also on George Street, slightly to the west of the first. The promoters owned the land and said it would cost about £4,000 to build and that they would fund it themselves. They would need approval to build an iron bridge from the top of the lift to the hill or make some other arrangement to link the two. No further action was to be taken on this proposal (*Hastings Observer*, 23 March 1889).

The first scheme proceeded apace. A trial bore hole had been dug to a depth of 30ft before a public meeting was held on 13 May, when the key elements were described. Access to the top station would be by a flight of about twenty steps, a necessity because the corporation would not allow them to build above the hill. The station site, about 60ft × 20ft, would be surrounded by a balustrade. The cars would carry sixteen passengers each but because the system would be over-strong and not dependent on animal power they would carry as many as could be crammed in! The mews would be bought for £3,500 and part of them would be rented to the existing tenant. The work could be carried out for £12,000, they thought, so they intended to issue £10,000 in shares and to borrow £2,000.

Much was made of the comparisons with the Folkestone lift, where the season was only three months long, the population was a mere 25,000, and the lower station was 'nowhere in particular'. It was a pleasure lift, not a means of transport, yet it paid 12½%. In Hastings ten thousand residents lived on the West Hill, creating a year-round demand. At Folkestone £210 was paid annually for water, whereas in Hastings they would pay £50 for gas to pump the water up to the top (*Hastings Observer*, 11/18 May 1889).

The Hastings Lift Company issued its prospectus before the end of May. The five directors were local businessmen, and the engineers were a local partnership, the brothers Frederick (1837–1914) and John (1849–1896) Plowman, although they usually practised as architects. Hastings Corporation had agreed to a fifty-year lease for the West Hill land required for £20 per annum plus £10 per annum for every 1% earned over 5%. Some £3,000 of the £10,000 capital had already been applied for (*Hastings Observer*, 25 May 1889).

A delay in reaching agreement over the accommodation works required for the mews tenant meant that tenders were not invited until August. Five were received in September and the second lowest, from Holme & King for £5,418 12s 4d, against the engineers' £5,827 estimate, was accepted. In 1895–96 Holme & King were to build the Snowdon Mountain Railway. R. Waygood & Company, of London, tendered £1,800 to supply the machinery, carriages and rails, which was accepted (*Hastings Observer*, 17/24 August/21 September 1889).

Construction was started on 1 January 1890 and was expected to be completed by the end of June. There was much activity when a reporter visited in February. The preliminary heading extended some 90ft into the hill and temporary rails were being laid on which trucks carrying bricks and other materials upwards and spoil downwards would be hauled by a winch. On the hill, excavations had been made for the waiting and engine rooms and retaining walls were being made. The keystone of the lower arch was tapped into position on 26 February by the company chairman using a commemorative trowel presented to him by the contractors (*Hastings Observer*, 15 February/1 March 1890).

A labourer named Payne fell off scaffolding a distance of about 10ft on 2 April, sustaining injuries to his head, neck and torso. Although none were of a serious nature, reported the *Hastings Observer* (5 April 1890), he was taken to hospital. Two more men were hurt when removing formwork on 5 May. Both were taken to hospital, where one was discharged after a short time and the other, whose leg had been injured, was kept in (*Hastings Observer*, 10 May).

While Holme & King were making good progress on the tunnel, it was an anonymous letter to a local newspaper that undermined the company's future. Claiming to be a 'considerable' payer of rates, the writer, who fittingly signed his letter 'Ratepayer', claimed that the council's assent to the lift was an illegal act, placing the authority in breach of the covenants that it had accepted when it had bought the land. He hoped that the vendor would step in to insist on the covenants being honoured and insist on the removal of the 'last brick' above the ground.

Another letter in the same edition complained about Sunday working on the site, which attracted a response the following week from the contractor's engineer, George Hilder Libbis (1863–1948). He said that the contract forbad any Sunday work, except where necessary, and that he had never met a contractor who 'coveted the privilege of paying his men 50% extra for Sunday working', and that it was necessary to ensure the stability of the tunnel. On the following Sunday the work was finished by 1 pm and the workforce was immediately discharged (*Hastings Observer*, 26 April/5 May 1890).

The former landowner did complain to the council that the covenants had been

The stone installed by company chairman Edwin Smith (1833–1908). It is inscribed 'Keyed by Edwin Smith, chairman. February 26th, 1890. F. and J. Plowman, engineers. Holme and King, railway contractors'. Smith ran a furniture business and was prominent in town affairs. His obituary said that he was among those who encouraged the purchase of the East and West Hills for the town and that he 'lost a large sum of money' when the lift company failed (*Hastings Observer*, 29 August 1908).

breached, on two grounds: that spoil had been tipped in a gully and that the top station building was visible above ground level. On 30 July the council was informed that the building would be lowered while it agreed to remove the spoil, because the company refused (*Hastings Observer*, 2 August 1890).

Although no explanation has been found for these breaches, they have the appearance of being cost-cutting measures proposed by the contractor. A document entitled 'Plan of the proposed lift' preserved at the National Archives shows the upper station as built, with the stone balustrade and the cars accessed by a flight of steps, but during a site visit on 2 October, a journalist wrote that the waiting room, erected with the council's consent, had been demolished and would be replaced by taking a portion of the ladies' parlour. The engine room, he wrote, remained underground but the ladies' lavatories would not be provided. He added that it had been intended to hide the building by an earth mound planted with turf and shrubs. The spoil enabled an area to be levelled.

The visit was made at a stage where the pilot bore had been completed and some of the tunnel was completed. The party, which included the company chairman and its secretary, was pulled up the temporary track in two straw-lined tip wagons. On the return journey, the 'train' was stopped so that the party could climb ladders and examine the headings more closely. The line was expected to be opened in January 1891 (*Hastings Observer*, 4 October 1890).

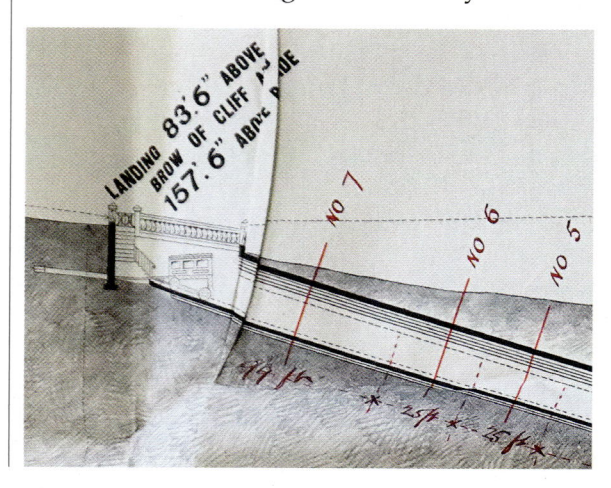

It was not only the top station works that had incurred extra expense but the ground through which the tunnel passes proved to be 'treacherous and unexpectedly difficult to support', shareholders were told in December. Only 1,004 £5 shares had been allotted, so a Mr Whiston had advanced to the company £2,000 on the Albion Mews at 4% and £3,000 on the lift at 4½%. The directors had each given £200 guarantees to the bank and had collectively guaranteed £2,500 to the contractors. To cover the borrowing, they intended to issue £6,000 of 6% preference shares. Supporting the company, the directors had said that they would not ask for any pay until it was paying 5%, the engineers had only taken £300 of the £400 in shares they were entitled to and would not claim any commission until 5% dividend had been paid, and the secretary had made no charges for his services after completing its registration (*Hastings Observer*, 20 December).

In the run-up to the opening on 25 March 1891, staff were recruited, the contractors' surplus plant and equipment was sold, the teak and ash carriages arrived from the Birmingham Carriage & Wagon Company, the George Street frontage was completed, and, on 23 March, C. S. Hutchinson made his inspection. The paper reported that he tested the brake and declared himself satisfied with the lift, but what it did not say was that because some (unspecified) aspects were incomplete the directors had asked him not to submit his report until they were. Consequently, his report was not submitted until 8 August 1892. He said that the gauge was 6ft 1in and that the track used 40lb flatbottom rail laid on 12in × 12in sleepers bedded in concrete (*Hastings Observer*, 7/14/28 March 1891/3 September 1892).

The opening was performed by the local MP, Wilson Noble (1855–1917). Describing the event, the *Hastings Observer* (28 March) said that the tunnel was 402ft long, 19ft wide and 18ft high. Some 1.75 million

Cross-section schematic of the upper station. (F. & J. Plowman)

OPENING OF THE WEST HILL LIFT, OLD TOWN, HASTINGS.

bricks had been used and 16,000 tons of stone and earth had been removed. In contradiction of Hutchinson's later report, it said that the gauge was 6ft. A 16hp Otto gas engine drove the equipment from the top station. The façade of the George Street entrance had been constructed by Elliott's Patent Stone Company in imitation red Mansfield stone. Receiving an inscribed silver carriage key, Noble declared the lift open and enjoyed a journey on the lift before the party adjourned to the Albion Hotel for lunch.

By 20 May 59,005 passengers had been carried, the peak day being Whit Monday, 18 May, when 5,711 were carried. On 3 August, a bank holiday, the number carried was 6,140. By 26 September 223,304 had been carried, earning £930 8s 8d. Outgoings were £11 a week. The directors were very happy, and in December recommended a 6% dividend (*Hastings Observer*, 8 August/10 October/12 December 1891).

A year later, however, they were very unhappy. Forty days' traffic had been lost while duplicate machinery had been installed and the bus service that had been run from the town's Albert memorial had lost more than £100, although it had served its purpose in promoting the lift. There had also been 'three or four' accidents of an unspecified nature. No dividend was recommended.

At the shareholders' meeting where these details were reported, one of them asked about opening on Sundays, to which the chairman replied that as it was not on

The lower station on the opening day, 25 March 1891. From this image it appears that the building did not get its roof until after operations had commenced.

A posed photograph of a car near the lower station. Holme & King's board remains in place above the tunnel.

the agenda no vote could be taken but that it could be discussed, adding that if Sunday opening was approved, he would resign from the board, a view shared by another director. It was a debate that continued for several years (*Hastings Observer*, 17 December 1892).

Another year on, and the directors were even more unhappy, for not only had the £450 interest payable almost cleared out the year's surplus, but on 27 September Whiston had called in the £5,000 loan, giving three months' notice. They had been unsuccessful in their attempts to borrow the money elsewhere in Hastings, they told the shareholders in December, and thought that the best way forward would be to issue £7,000 in 4½% debentures to enable the loan to be repaid and the overdraft to be cleared. They felt, however, that success would be dependent on the shareholders being prepared to advance the majority of the money themselves as an appeal to the public, at the present time, would not succeed. The alternative would be to

An early photograph of the lower station. The photographs that were taken during the opening ceremony do not appear to have survived.

84 • CLIFF RAILWAYS: AN HISTORIC SURVEY

liquidate the company and to form a new one with a smaller capital to take over the lift as a going concern.

By the time the shareholders met on 4 December, Holme & King, the contractors, had also made a claim for the £2,000 owed to them. Their proposal that they should be issued with debentures for the amount was refused as it would give them priority over other creditors. The motion to authorise the directors to sell the lift and to wind up the company was carried (*Hastings Observer*, 2/9 December 1893).

The lift and mews were offered for sale by auction on 16 January 1894, but the outcome was not straightforward. For the lift, bidding started at £3,000 and rose to £7,450 before it was withdrawn as not having reached its reserve. The mews were withdrawn at £2,300. At this point Whiston took control and instructed the auctioneer to sell the lift without a reserve. On 1 February it was sold for £5,575 and the mews were withdrawn again (*Hastings Observer*, 20 January/3 February).

The new owner was William Plummer (1837–99), a Hastings draper who lived in Tunbridge Wells. He formed a company named the Hastings Passenger Lift Company, with himself and three others as directors. Two of them were also, with him, directors of the drapery company, one of whom had also been a Lift Company director. The capital was £6,700, £3,700 in £10 shares and the remainder in 4½% debentures. The shares were fully subscribed, and the debentures were offered to the public. Presumably Plummer would have had the majority of the shares, the remainder going to his co-directors to qualify them as directors. The debentures were probably being used to reimburse him with a portion of the purchase price but that was not spelled out (*Hastings Observer*, 10/17 February 1894/*The Times*, 27 October 1894).

On 20 February the original company's shareholders, concerned that they had lost out by not accepting the higher bid, were told that the auctioneer had doubts about its validity as he did not know the bidder's identity. Had it been valid they would not have benefited as the extra money would have gone to the creditors. They voted to have their company wound up. To rub salt into the wound, at the end of the new regime's first season, not only was a 3% interim dividend paid but 'a large balance' was carried forward (*Hastings Observer*, 24 February/8 September 1894).

At the end of the financial year enough had been made, despite the poor season and inclement weather, for another 3% dividend to be paid, and to pay for improvements to the apparatus to lessen friction on the rope, reducing wear and gas consumption (*Hastings Observer*, 16 March 1895).

The payment of 6% dividend continued until the end of the decade, then in 1900 sufficient was earned to allow the payment of 7% (*Hastings Observer*, 14 April 1900).

Plummer had not been involved with the new company after its first year; there was no published comment about his withdrawal or his replacement as a director. On 30 April 1899 his was one of the 105 lives lost when the LSWR steamship *Stella* struck rocks in fog off Guernsey. His body was recovered two months later, and he was buried with his wife at the Forest cemetery in Tunbridge Wells. His estate was insolvent (*Bexhill on Sea Observer*, 8 April/*Sussex Express*, 22 April/*Folkestone Express*, 27 May/ *Newbury Weekly News*, 1 June 1899).

The first years of the twentieth century were good for the company's shareholders, with dividends of 5 and 6%. A new initiative in August 1904 had links to the lift's earliest days, when the Hastings & St Leonard's Omnibus Company started an Albert Memorial–Henbrey Corner route, including the lift, for an inclusive 3d fare, but it was withdrawn after a few weeks for failing to attract sufficient passengers. There cannot have been much benefit to either company or the passengers in such a route (*Hastings Observer*, 6 August 1904/25 March 1905).

Some fuss was made about the rent paid for the council's land in 1905. The 1890 lease called for the Lift Company to pay an additional £10 rent for every

An exterior view of the upper station. There is an ornate arch over the top of the steps.

1% dividend paid over 5%. Although the lease had been transferred to the new company in 1894 it refused to pay an extra £20 when requested in 1895, saying the extra payment was only due on dividends paid on the original £10,920 capital, and adding that this position had been confirmed by counsel's opinion. The council saw the opinion and took no action, maintaining its position when the issue was raised again in March 1905. Two months later the local ratepayers' association took it up as though it had made a new discovery, which resulted in the council obtaining its own opinion, which confirmed the company's and the matter faded away (*Hastings Observer*, 18 October 1902/18 March/6 May/24 June 1905).

Like the Central Tramway in Scarborough, the West Hill lift was another to be affected by the introduction of electric trams. In this case the Hastings & District Electric Tramways opened its first three routes in 1905, another two in 1906 and the last, which ran along the seafront, in 1907. A decline in receipts and the need to plan for repairing the track meant that no dividend was paid for 1906. The profit in 1908 was so low that the company could neither pay debenture interest nor a dividend. A poorly attended, and unreported, meeting in November 1905 had recommended closing the lift in the winter months and taking another poll on the question of Sunday opening; a poll on this subject had been lost by a few votes in 1906. The directors thought that winter closing would be unadvisable and a poll was approved at the general meeting. Sunday working started on 22 August (*Hastings Observer*, 23 March 1907/10 April/21 August 1909).

Judging by the lack of reports, and its continued existence, the company recovered from the loss of traffic to the trams long enough to recover in a similar manner to the Central Tramway, with tourists seeing the lift as an essential quirky part of a holiday, although in this case the tramway network was closed in 1929. The gas engine had been replaced by a 32hp Tangye diesel engine in 1924.

Thomas Edward Pilbeam, the lift's foreman, died on 5 August 1938, aged 69. The *Hastings Observer* (6 August) reported that he had worked for the company for over forty years. In the 1891 and 1901 censuses he had been recorded as a gas

The West Hill's lower entrance seen from the street before the 1939–45 war. Unfortunately, the decorated window above the door has not survived. (W. J. Willmett)

lift was reported to be ready for opening, awaiting spare parts, in July 1946 but an aside referring to both of Hastings' lifts in September implies that the parts had still not arrived. The eventual reopening was not reported (*Hastings Observer*, 12 March 1938/27 July/14 September 1946).

The proposal that the council should buy the lift had been taken up, however, and a recommendation to buy it for £4,500 was put on 8 October 1946. The sum paid was £4,677, which presumably included consumables. A total of 248,673 passengers were carried during 1947, the council's first year of ownership. The company's voluntary winding up was completed on 25 March 1948 (*Hastings Observer*, 5 October 1946/24 January/22 May 1948, *London Gazette*, 27 February 1948).

The most noticeable change in council ownership has been the demolition of the upper station balustrade and the erection of a tearoom, which has been altered and extended over the years, but underground

engine driver, so he could well have been with the lift since it opened, as claimed in the paper's 13 August issue, but he was unlikely to have been engineer and manager for all of that time as the paper also claimed.

Earlier in 1938 the company had applied to the council for the fifty-year wayleaves granted in 1890 to be renewed for another fifty years on the same terms, but the parks and gardens committee recommended that they be extended for another fourteen years, with a proviso that if the council wished to purchase the lift it could do so on giving six months' notice. This must have come as no surprise to the company, as the council had taken powers to purchase the lift, or any others constructed in the borough, in the Hastings Corporation Act of 1900. No response was reported in 1938, and the lift was closed, without comment, on the outbreak of war, which obviously deferred the matter. Post-war the

An undated photograph, probably taken in the 1950s, of a car approaching the lower station. The livery is likely to be that of the Passenger Lift Company at the time the council took over in 1947. (V. C. Jones/Online Transport Archive)

1891 HASTINGS, WEST HILL LIFT • 87

The date this building was erected to surround the upper station is unknown. Although concealed from this perspective, the station remains in the open air. This picture postcard view can reasonably be ascribed to the 1960s. (Shoesmith & Etheridge)

Right: One of the cars in a lighter livery seen in May 1969.

Far right: The following series of photographs showing features of the lift was taken in 2023–24, starting with the lower station's entrance. The requirement to maintain carriage access to the Albion mews meant that it does not have the prominent street frontage that it deserves. Tunnel mouth brickwork is visible above the colonnade.

88 • CLIFF RAILWAYS: AN HISTORIC SURVEY

Lower station booking hall and entrance.

The interior of one of the cars.

1891 HASTINGS, WEST HILL LIFT • 89

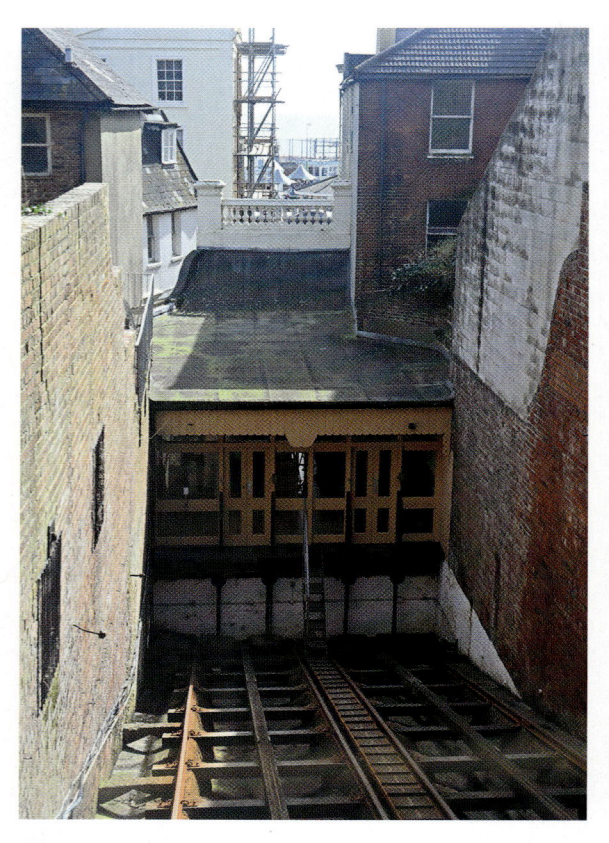

The lower station seen from a descending car.

The tunnel is partially illuminated.

the station is the same. An enquiry to the council about this work went unanswered. In 1971 the British Ropeway Engineering Company of Sevenoaks, Kent, was commissioned to modernise the system, replacing the 1924 diesel engine with a thyristor-controlled 30hp electric motor driven through a heavy-duty gearbox.

The lift was refurbished in time to celebrate its centenary in 1991, when an average of 110,000 passengers were being carried annually. The track and sleepers were replaced in 2005 and the 1971 control panels were replaced in 2010. The lift was closed for extensive maintenance in 2020–21, the reopening being delayed by the original contractor withdrawing and awaiting parts shipped from the USA (BBC, 6 September 2021).

Although the Hastings Lift Company's shareholders lost all their money, they did leave Hastings with a valuable asset that the town has benefitted from for more than 100 years.

A car emerges from the reflections to approach the upper station. During 2024, Hastings Borough Council considered seeking lottery funding for a feasibility study into making the lift more accessible (BBC, 2 September 2024).

The upper station complex looking eastwards. The open part of the station is beyond the green toilet block. The upper station of the East Hill lift is visible to the left of the flagpole.

1891 HASTINGS, WEST HILL LIFT • 91

CHAPTER 11
1892 BRIDGNORTH, CASTLE HILL RAILWAY

Opened 7 July 1892, 3ft 8½in gauge, double track, 201ft long, gradient 1 in 1.8, water balance, operational.

The Castle Hill Railway at Bridgnorth is a child of the Lynton & Lynmouth Cliff Railway, insofar as G. C. Marks was involved in its design and construction and it was chiefly financed by George Newnes.

Bridgnorth is a town on the banks of the River Severn, in Shropshire, 18 miles from the county town of Shrewsbury but only 13 from industrial Wolverhampton and the Black Country's considerable population.

The river divided the town into the Low Town, on the east bank, 155ft above sea level, and the High Town, on the west, up to 223ft and dominated by Castle Hill, a precipitous sandstone outcrop. The Stoneway Steps were the longest (197 steps) and busiest of several flights of steps constructed to aid access between the towns, the closest to the Severn crossing. The bridge, from which the town gained its name, was also a junction of several trade routes that brought many travellers to the town. There was, in the nineteenth century, some light industry and some tourism.

The railway was the idea of Robert Henry Harrison (1849–93), a man of means trained as an electrical engineer, who in 1888 wrote to the local newspaper calling for the town council to grant a concession for the construction and operation of 'an elevator', and explaining how he had conducted what is today called market research by spending two days counting the number of users of the Stoneway Steps, a perpendicular climb of 110ft to the high town. The letter attracted no attention from the council or the public, so on 4 December 1890 Harrison, then recently elected to the council, called a public meeting to promote the concept of a lift in Bridgnorth, the mayor and several councillors attending.

As well as describing his earlier research on the numbers using the steps, he also used a blackboard to explain how a hydraulic system, like the one he had seen in Scarborough, would need just over a cubic yard of water to enable a car with ten passengers weighing an average of 15st to travel from the Low Town to the High Town in less than two minutes. With his audience including several residents who thought that something should be done to make the town more attractive to visitors, a committee was formed to determine the best way forward (*Bridgnorth Journal*, 21 April 1888/13 December 1890).

When the committee realised that it would not be possible to raise the capital required locally, it recommended that the council accept Marks' offer to form a company to be called the Castle Hill Railway Company, with George Newnes underwriting £5,000 of the £6,000 capital providing the remainder was contributed locally. The route was to be from a 'handsome ornamental station and waiting room' on a site between 'Mr McMichael's shop' and the Castle Brewery on the Cartway and terminating on Castle Way in the garden of a 'house tenanted by Miss Hollick', routed past the Congregational Chapel burial ground and crossing the Stoneway Steps by an iron bridge. The top station was intended to be equipped with conveniences and designed to be in keeping with the buildings in the High Town. A pair of gas engines at the lower station would recycle the water back to the top station. Joseph Wylde McMichael (1821–95) was a stationer and grocer with premises in the High Street; the premises concerned appear to be presently known as 43 Bridgend Cottage. Hannah Hollick (1832–92) lived at 6 Castle Terrace.

Unfortunately, by the date of the meeting there was a problem with the lower station site and an alternative was found by the Stoneway Steps at the rear of the Rose & Crown Inn, which changed the angle of the climb across the cliff. The council accepted the scheme, the local shares were advertised in October and construction started without ceremony on 2 November 1891. The contractor was George Law (1838–1923) of Kidderminster (*Bridgnorth Journal*, 6 June / 10 October / 7 November 1891).

Despite the discovery of caves that required the construction of stone columns and the insertion of girders, good progress was made. At the stations, buildings were erected by Wolverhampton-based but Bridgnorth-born John Bradney (born 1850), who also acted as the clerk of works. To secure a level entrance to the lower station, the Stoneway Steps were rerouted to pass over it. The change in location meant that the upper station was built adjacent to the end of the row of houses on Castle Terrace, rather than at the end of the (now late) Miss Hollick's garden. Despite working in difficult and restricted conditions, 4,464 tons of rock were removed and no injuries were incurred by the workforce. Josiah Gimson & Company of Leicester supplied the machinery, and the cars were supplied by the Oldbury Railway Carriage & Wagon Company; one of them was still on a wagon in the GWR station less than twenty-four hours before the railway opened.

On 7 July 1892 the mayor and corporation processed through the town and after making a journey on the railway the mayor declared it open by unlocking one of the cars with a gold key presented to him by Marks. More than 2,000 journeys were made by members of the public on the first day. On 20 July the company laid on a dinner at the Swan Hotel for the construction workforce, employees and guests, sixty-five in all, and announced that the employees would be given a bonus of a day's pay. Notwithstanding his substantial contribution to the company's capital, George Newnes did not attend the opening and it seems that he never visited the town (*Birmingham Daily Post*, 8 July / *Bridgnorth Journal*, 9 / 23 July 1892).

To make the most of its property, the company built a coffee tavern at the lower station and a photographic studio at the upper. Called 'The Lift', the former provided 'hot dinners daily' and 'comfortable bedrooms'. The councillor who owned the adjacent property to the latter complained that the plans had been altered and the structure removed his view of the river; subsequently a committee visited the site and ruled that the changes did not justify any action. Soon after the opening the company published a 1d guide to the town and the railway; partially

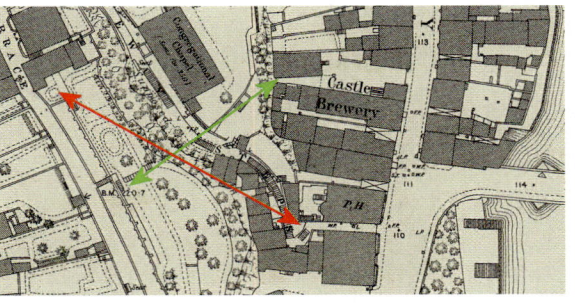

An extract from the 1:500 map surveyed in 1882 with approximations of the intended route and the constructed routes indicated. (Ordnance Survey)

A sketch of one of the cars at the time of the opening, with the location of the out-of-sight wheels indicated.

The constrained site of the lower station hides most of it from view. This image, reproduced in the railway's guide book, shows how the Stoneway steps pass over the entrance. Now rare, copies of the guide sell for between £50 and £100.

The railway in action in 1900. On the right of the cutting is evidence of one of the caves that were breached during construction. The water tank caps the upper station building. (J. Valentine)

funded by advertisements, a version with a card cover and better paper was sold for 3d. Four months after the opening, more than 80,000 passengers had been carried (*Bridgnorth Journal*, 9 April / 23 July / 17 September / 12 November 1892).

An issue for the directors was that it soon became apparent that many townspeople who needed to pass between the towns were unwilling, or unable, to pay to use the lift, which was particularly important during the winter, when there were fewer tourists. To address this, in May 1893 they announced the issue of books of twelve, thirty or sixty tickets for 1s, 2s 6d and 5s respectively, reducing the fare to 1d for a return journey. Although why anyone should want to by a 2s 6d or 5s book when there was no additional incentive remains unclear. The ordinary fare was 1d single, 1½d return. In 1896 books of eighteen single tickets were offered to residents for 1s (*Bridgnorth Journal*, 27 May 1893 / 25 April 1896).

In the first year of operation the shareholders were told that 183,494 passengers had been carried and the traffic matched that of the first days, when the lift was a novelty. It ran during the winter without interruption, and the reduced fare books had been appreciated. A 6% dividend was paid and the staff had been paid a bonus and granted a week's holiday. Marks remained in contact with the company as a director (*Bridgnorth Journal*, 26 August 1893).

Robert Henry Harrison, who had stood for the council to pursue his idea of a lift, had died on 26 June, barely a year after it had opened. His obituary said that he had made no rash promises during his election campaign but had said that he hoped to have the pleasure of getting the lift made. The town honoured him with a funeral procession led by two policemen and the major and corporation, and he was buried in the town cemetery (*Bridgnorth Journal*, 1 July 1893).

The company's unkept obligation to provide public conveniences at its stations became an issue for one of the councillors in 1898, although he failed to persuade his colleagues to take action to enforce the

94 • CLIFF RAILWAYS: AN HISTORIC SURVEY

promise. Later in the year the council had lost its copies of the plans that showed the location of the toilets and advertised for assistance in finding them, to avoid having to play for copies (*Bridgnorth Journal*, 7 May/22 October 1898).

At the annual meeting in 1898, Marks's brother, Edward Robert Charles Marks (1867–1928), who was also a director, complained that the lift had run at a loss during the winter, despite the reduced fares offered to residents. If the situation did not improve, he declared, the company would exercise its right to close the lift during the winter. He hoped that this knowledge would improve the situation but, in the meantime, the shareholders would have to make do with a 3% dividend. There was only a small increase in passengers in 1899 and the dividend remained at 3% (*Bridgnorth Journal*, 1 October 1898/30 September 1899).

The meeting report did not have the desired effect and the company announced that the lift would be closed after 17 February 1900. The notice said that the company regretted having to take this action but that it was necessary to carry out the shareholders' (unreported) instructions given at the annual meeting. Naturally this did not meet with councillors' approval and the terms of the lease were raised at their next meeting. The company was required to run during the winter unless the receipts did not cover the expenses. A councillor, who was also a director, explained that losses had been incurred in every winter since the lift had opened and that the present winter had been worse than previous ones. Normally the company had lost money, to a greater or lesser extent, twenty-eight weeks a year. Services resumed on 7 April (*Bridgnorth Journal*, 10/17 February/7 April 1900).

Any business that required its employees to handle cash was at risk of theft. Edwin Arther Walker (1870–1904), in charge of the lower station for about three months, was jailed for four weeks with hard labour after being found guilty of embezzlement in the magistrates' court on 23 July 1901. Having served his term, he obviously had nowhere to go, and no support, for later in the year he received another seven days' hard labour after having been found sleeping in a building

A 1930s view of the upper station. The car is ornately decorated and its brake wheel can be seen on the platform. (J. Valentine)

The Lift & Severn Bridge, Bridgnorth

In this undated view the livery is plain, relieved only by the railway's initials on the sides.

at the rear of Oldbury Church. He must have been in very poor condition when he died in 1904, aged 34 (*Wellington Journal*, 27 July/3 August/20 September 1901).

A 'slight accident' that occurred on 15 October 1909 failed to reach the attention of the local press until a notice was erected saying that the lift was closed for repairs and track renewals. It was reopened on 11 February 1910. No explanation was offered for the accident (*Birmingham Mail*, 19 October 1909/*Birmingham Mail*, 12 February 1910).

Two cases affecting the lift were dealt with in the magistrates' court in August 1924. Two men had burgled the lower station and stolen 4s 11½d from a hospital collecting box. It transpired that they were attempting to recoup money from losing bets placed at the station's illegal betting shop run by three employees acting as agents for a bookmaker who paid them 7½% commission. The first two were fined £2 each, with a month's hard labour in default, the ringleader of the employees was fined £5 and the other two 50s each. There is no report of whether the employees kept their jobs but in 1927 the ringleader was fined for Sunday gambling (*Birmingham Daily Post*, 12/26 August 1924/*Rugeley Times*, 9 September 1927).

A change in ownership occurred in 1929, when the Shropshire, Worcestershire & Staffordshire Electric Power Company took over. The power company was in expansionist mode at the time, buying several small power generators. The *Dudley Chronicle* (11 April 1929), in the only report found of the purchase, said that it was intended to commence using electricity to run the railway. That did not happen and the power company's time with the lift was short-lived, as it was abandoned after a breakdown in 1933. By the time the *Birmingham Daily Gazette* commented (24 June) the lift had been 'idle for some time'. The town council considered purchasing it but was deterred by the requirement for a special Act of

Parliament to do so (*Evening Despatch*, 11 September 1933).

Salvation came from a Wolverhampton brewer who owned property in Bridgnorth. John Francis Myatt (1876–1938) bought the debentures for £230 and the shares for £5,900, telling the *Birmingham Daily Gazette* (10 May 1934) that he had not bought the railway to make money, but to be of service to Bridgnorth and its visitors. Reopening was anticipated 'shortly', but no reports have been found. The *Evening Despatch*, also on 10 May, reported that the railway had been closed for twelve months.

A fatality occurred on 5 May 1943, when one of the cars ran away during maintenance and killed the foreman, Harold Augustus Howes, aged 36. The adjourned inquest appears to have gone unreported. His death certificate states that he died of 'shock and multiple injuries caused by being crushed by a car on the Castle Hill Railway, Bridgnorth, while repairs were being effected'. In 1939 he had given his occupation as 'hydraulic railway brakesman'. He was buried in an unmarked grave in the town's cemetery (*Birmingham Daily Gazette*, 7 May / *Kington Times*, 8 May 1943).

The company's response to this tragic event was to upgrade the railway's equipment, replacing the water-balanced system with one powered by electricity. How it managed to achieve this in wartime is unknown, but it obviously knew the right people and organisations to approach. The Metropolitan Vickers Electrical Company supplied the electrical equipment and Westinghouse the brake gear. Under the new system the lift was controlled from the top station and in-car illumination was powered by batteries. The mayor reopened the railway towards the end of 1944 (*Modern Transport*, 23 December 1944 / 28 July 1945).

The car involved in Howes' death was replaced with a similar vehicle in time for the reopening but in June 1955 both cars were replaced, the new bodies being made in Stourbridge by coachbuilder F. J. Fildes Ltd. That they remain in use says much for the quality of their construction. It should be mentioned, incidentally, that the date the original hydraulic brakes had been replaced by a service brake on the head wheel, rendering the drivers redundant, is unknown.

Items noted in the *Wolverhampton Express & Star* in the 1970s are an advertisement for a female lift operator, five shifts a

The electric-powered winding room in 1944.

The lower station entrance on 17 April 1959.

1892 BRIDGNORTH, CASTLE HILL RAILWAY • 97

The car did not have much time left in service when it was photographed in 1955. The livery is brighter than before, and the absence of the brake wheel from the platform indicates that the method of operating has changed. The motif includes the letters CR. The hanging board above the station's entrance promotes a 2d return fare and promises no waiting. (F. Frith)

week, part time (12 May/26 June 1972); both carriages stabled at the lower station during maintenance (11/31 January 1973); and the company's concern about the effect the town council's proposed free Low Town–High Town bus service would have on revenue (18 November 1975). Presumably the free bus service was not put into effect, although the town clerk admitted that the public would prefer to take a free bus rather than pay to use the railway. During 1977's industrial unrest and its threat of power cuts the company announced that the railway would not be run when they were expected, to avoid the risk of passengers being stranded (4 November).

In 1992 the railway's centenary was marked by the town council recreating the opening day ceremony, street performances in the town, the performance of a short commemorative play in the castle grounds and a firework display. There had been no celebrations for the diamond jubilee forty years earlier, although the newspaper did contact the company secretary about it (*Birmingham Daily Post*, 7 July 1952/6 July 1972).

On 11 January 1996 ownership passed from the Myatt family to Allan Henry and Jean Reynolds, a Bridgnorth couple. They introduced an attractive blue and cream livery for the cars and building exteriors,

One of the 1955 cars soon after it had entered service. For many years they were painted brown with yellow around the windows and a white roof.

98 • CLIFF RAILWAYS: AN HISTORIC SURVEY

Looking down the cutting and the lower station in the 1960s.

The upper station seen from below on 27 February 2022. The clean lines of the buildings erected during the Reynolds' tenure are prominent on the right, the wall that became problematic for the railway on the left. The blue and cream livery was adopted in 1996.

Seen from the far side of the river, the cars stabled out of use when the work to stabilise the wall adjacent to the railway had been started. They were moved regularly, to ensure that components did not seize up.

The reopening was marked by the erection of a banner on the upper station's gantry. This and the following photographs were taken on 5 March 2024.

100 • CLIFF RAILWAYS: AN HISTORIC SURVEY

and undertook a refurbishment programme that concentrated on the upper station, removing its water tank, and constructing another turret among other works. The braking system was modernised in 2009 and appearance of the enterprise was improved considerably during their ownership.

They sold it to an Essex-based family of developers on 19 August 2011, the new owners being descended from G. C. Marks. On 21 December 2022 they were faced with the biggest challenge in the company's history, when the Castle Walk boundary wall adjacent to the top station was found to be in danger of collapsing, forcing the railway's closure until it was repaired.

The engineers dealing with the work for the town council decreed that the work could only be carried out by making an access from the railway's property but what was expected to take three or four months took much longer and the railway was not reopened until 4 March 2024. During the closure two of the railway's employees redecorated the station interiors, the remainder of the staff having been made redundant. The works cost the council £750,000 and increased residents' council tax bills to pay for it. Four hundred passengers were carried on 4 March,

A view of the Low Town on the far side of the river with the railway in the foreground and the problematic wall behind the car. One of the disused water pipes remains in place to the left of the tracks.

The electronic control panel positioned in the driver's office.

1892 BRIDGNORTH, CASTLE HILL RAILWAY • 101

Above: A car full of passengers, and a dog. Consent was obtained for the photograph.

Above right: The pay desk/office at the upper station. There is a similar structure at the lower station.

and no fares were charged for the first two days (*Shropshire Star*, 22 December 2022/*Portsmouth News*, 9 February 2023/ *Shropshire Star*, 25 May/18 November/ *Express & Star*, 14 September/ BBC, 3 November/17 November 2023/BBC, 7 February/27 February 2024).

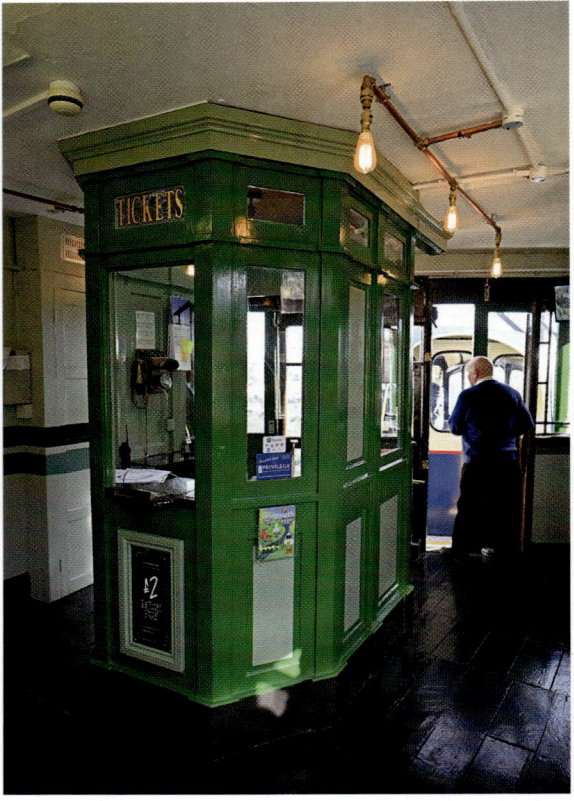

Approaching the lower station.

102 • CLIFF RAILWAYS: AN HISTORIC SURVEY

CHAPTER 12

1893 CLIFTON ROCKS RAILWAY

Opened 11 March 1893, 3ft 8in gauge, quadruple track, 450ft long, gradient 1 in 2.5, water balance, closed 29 September 1934.

Having played prominent roles in the Lynton and Bridgnorth cliff railways, George Newnes and G. C. Marks might have thought that the construction of such lines had no secrets. However, the Clifton Rocks Railway caught them out, both in the scale of the work required and in its cost. It would be a remarkable thing to be operated if it still existed but it is literally a shell of its former self, remaining an object of wonder for those who gaze upon its remains.

The Bristol Tramways Company had proposed building a lift from the Hotwells, under the Clifton Suspension Bridge, to Clifton in 1880 but had been refused permission by the site's owners, the Society of Merchant Venturers. Ten years later, when George Newnes decided that a lift would be a useful adjunct to a luxury spa that he proposed to build on a prominent plot of land on Zion Hill in Clifton, overlooking the Gorge and within sight of the suspension bridge, his influence, and the support of a high-flight firm of solicitors, was able to secure a unanimous verdict in his favour (*Bristol Mercury*, 24/28 July 1880/4 November 1890).

He had appointed Marks to deliver the lift and he produced a design completely in tunnel, effectively two lifts side-by-side to carry the anticipated numbers, for it was expected that spa users would want to experience the waters at the Hotwells, and to cover for breakdowns.

The tender of Christopher Albert Hayes (1851–1916) was accepted in January 1891 but the start of work was delayed until the first shot was fired by the mayoress, Lady Mary Anne Wathen (1849–1909), on 7 March. Two hundred labourers were soon at work (*Clifton Society*, 29 January / *Bristol Mercury*, 17 February / 19 March / *Clifton & Redland Free Press*, 10 April 1891).

It was hoped that the work would be completed by August but in July the workforce was to be increased with the intention of finishing by October. There was a setback, however, on 29 August, when James Willis, a 39-year-old quarryman, was killed by a rock fall and another man was injured, about 45ft into the tunnel. Marks showed photographs of the works at the inquest and said that the timber shoring had attracted visits from photographers. The jury returned a verdict of accidental death. It took a court hearing for Hayes's widow to be awarded £156 (*Clifton & Redland Free Press*, 24 April / 24 July / *Western Daily Press*, 31 August / 1 September 1891 / 13 January 1892).

Although the tunnel remained incomplete, the headings were connected early in September, at which point the blasting was ended, to be replaced by compressed air-driven, diamond-tipped drills. As well as the tunnel mouths, there were three intermediate shafts. By the end of the month all the plant, carriages and rails were on site and the upper waiting room was nearly complete (*Bristol Times*, 2 September / *Western Daily Press*, 23 September 1891).

Evidently, the finishing and commissioning work was more complex than anticipated and the line failed to meet its Easter and Whitsun opening target in 1892, and even after Hayes sold his surplus equipment in September there was no sign of an opening. Contributory to the delay was the discovery of clay in the rock, which increased the amount of brickwork required, but the signalling and telephone equipment was not ordered until December, when the operation of trial trips imminently and opening at Easter 1893 was expected (*Western Daily Press*, 17 March / 12 September / 10 December / *Clifton & Redland Free Press*, 30 December 1892).

The first trial trip took place on 7 February 1893, although fitting out remained incomplete. A reporter commented on daylight streaming from one end to the other and how there was no perception of movement when the cars were under way (*Western Daily Press*, 8 February 1893).

The line was opened without ceremony on 11 March. There were queues at the stations when the doors opened just after 9 am and a crush at Clifton required the services of a local police sergeant to restore order. The first passengers paid 4d, receiving a silver-gilt medal as a reward for their enthusiasm. After the supply of medals had been exhausted, fares of 2d up and 1d down were applied; the normal fares were: return, 2d; up 1½d; down 1d. First-day guests included officers of the Bristol Tramways Company, who had agreed to issue inclusive tickets to Clifton on the Hotwells route, and Hayes's wife, who were presented with a silver version of the medallion. The seven employees who ran the railway wore smart uniforms.

The equipment had been supplied by Josiah Gimson & Company of Leicester, which company had provided similar contemporaneously to the Bridgnorth Castle Hill Railway, and a pair of Crossley

A postcard view of the lower station, much more ornate than the upper station. An ice cream cart is positioned on the right.

self-starting gas engines pumped the water back to the top station. Despite the presence of a telephone installation, a signalling system enabled the number of passengers loaded to be indicated to the opposing station. Some 6,220 passenger journeys were made on the first day and most of them travelled both ways. An amateur photographer was noted photographing the railway and the cars (*Bristol Mercury*, 11/13 March/*Western Daily Press*, 11 March/ *Clifton & Redland Free Press*, 17 March 1893).

For one young man the medallions were indicative of a place of mystery and adventure that led to an encounter with the justice system and a workhouse. Henry Fellows worked in the factory where they had been made and, so fascinated by this peculiar railway, on 29 April he spent his 4s 6d wages on a day trip from Birmingham to Bristol to see it for himself. At the end of the day, and having only 2d left and unable to obtain accommodation, he gave himself up to a policeman, who took him into custody for being without visible means of support. The magistrates remanded him to the workhouse while enquiries were made. By the time he returned to court his friends had sent his train fare home and a member of the public, reading of his plight after his first appearance, had also sent him 2s. The magistrates ordered him to go home (*Birmingham Daily Post,* 2 May/*Bristol Mercury*, 4 May).

The budget for the railway and spa had been £30,000 but this amount had been expended on the railway alone. To recoup some of the expenditure, in 1894 Newnes registered the Clifton Rocks Railway Company to run the railway and a prospectus for £10,000 6% cumulative preference shares and £10,000 4½% debenture stock was issued on 28 April. A total of £10,000 in £5 ordinary shares was to be allocated to Newnes in part payment of the purchase price. Would-be investors were informed that 427,403 passengers had been carried in the first year of operating and that the receipts amounted to £2,460 11s. Working expenses of £874 5s therefore left

A posed view of one of the cars on the railway.

£1,586 6s for the payment of interest and dividends. Since the year end a contract for advertising in the stations and cars had been let for £150 but in future some of the surplus would be absorbed by rent and directors' fees. The issue closed on 3 May (*Bristol Mercury*, 28 April 1894).

The outcome of the issue was not published, and neither were the company's reports. The railway's operations rarely troubled the press. On one occasion the hydraulic brake flooded and caused the emergency brake to lock on, which took a few minutes to release before the six passengers in transit completed their journey. On another, the cars ran faster than they should have, and glass was broken when they stopped (*Clifton & Redland Press*, 11 November 1898/*Western Daily Press*, 22 February 1908).

At some point the debenture interest went unpaid and on 17 July 1908 the holders appointed a receiver, who sold the railway to the Bristol Tramways & Carriage

Clifton seen from the far side of the gorge, the location of both stations indicated. Also visible is the footpath the railway was intended to replace. (Borough Series)

Company for £1,500 in November 1912. The receiver resigned on 20 October 1914 and the company was dissolved in 1915.

The new owner promised to operate the railway in connection with its motor bus services, to operate it for longer hours, to use four cars instead of two, to replace the cars and to illuminate the tunnel when the cars were running. At Easter 1913 two of the cars were at the company's Brislington works for repair. Receipts had increased after the up fare had been reduced from 2d to 1d. The references to refurbishment and the running of four cars instead of two suggest that the railway had been allowed to run down,

The upper station is located in the centre foreground, in the junction between Sion Hill (right) and Prince's Lane. The footpath down the cliffside starts on the left. (Mitchell & Co.)

106 • CLIFF RAILWAYS: AN HISTORIC SURVEY

The ballroom entrance of the Spa Hotel with the railway's entrance indicated.

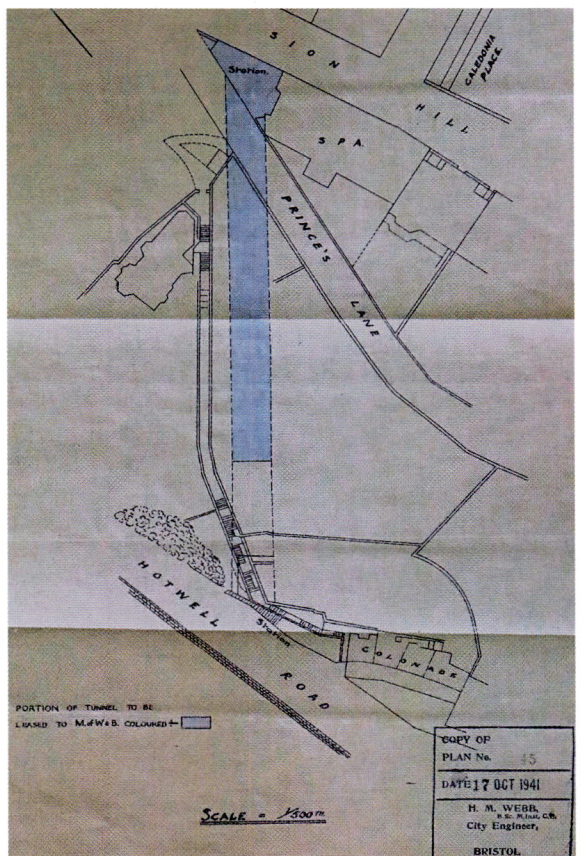

which had probably been going on for some time (*Western Daily Press*, 24 October 1912 / 12 February / 26 March 1913 / *London Gazette*, 29 June 1915 / *Bristol Times*, 26 October 1912).

There was no publicity when the railway ran for the last time on 29 September 1934. Much of the traffic had been lost to more convenient bus services and it was probably not unconnected that the council was in negotiations with the company over exercising its rights to purchase the tramway, which excluded the railway.

The Second World War led to new uses for the railway, but not carrying passengers. In 1941 part of it was used as an air raid shelter for a limited number of people and later Bristol Corporation's archives were moved in, racking and an air conditioning plant being installed. The BBC also took over the tunnel and created chambers for use as emergency studios. The site was vacated in 1960 but in 1961 the lower station's façade was found to be detaching from the cliff,

A 1941 plan of the railway with the section to be taken over by the Ministry of Works & Buildings coloured blue.

1893 CLIFTON ROCKS RAILWAY • 107

The four cars together when the track was being lifted by the BBC.

The lower station in 1942, with the BBC's entrance on the left and the air raid shelter entrance on the right. The air-handling vents are clamped to the front of the building.

requiring the structure to be stabilised. From 1996 enthusiasts have been working to make the railway accessible, and maybe even restore it. A charity was registered in 2008 but is not sufficiently active to be required to make returns to the Charity Commission. Some site surveys have been undertaken, and open days have been held (*Western Daily Express*, 21 January 1921 / 14 January / 30 April 1946 / *Bristol Evening Post*, 27 February 1996).

Like the West Hill lift at Hastings, the Clifton Rocks Railway suffered from being built in a tunnel that caused it to be saddled with excess debt. In Clifton's case, having a promoter who was keen to show off his wealth probably did not help in the longer term. Its public transport role was removed with the development of motorised transport and spa users had no use for it after the Hotwells were closed in 1913, when the water source was found to be polluted.

The upper station entrance seen on 1 August 2023, following restoration by the Clifton Rocks Railway Trust.

Also in 2023, the lower station seen between a gap in the traffic on the busy Hotwell Road. The concrete reinforcing was erected after the façade was found to be detaching from the rock due to the presence of clay in the strata in 1956.

1893 CLIFTON ROCKS RAILWAY • 109

CHAPTER 13

1896 FOLKESTONE, SANDGATE HILL LIFT

Opened 20 February 1896, 5ft 6in gauge, double track, 670ft long, gradient 1 in 4.75 at each end, 1 in 7.04 over Radnor Cliff Crescent, hydraulic, closed July 1918.
With the future and reliability of the Folkestone lifts secured with the duplication of the original lift in 1890, the forthcoming completion of development along the Leas, to the west of Folkestone, where it would overlook the coastal village of Sandgate, turned the directors' eyes westwards, probably also influenced by the opening of the Folkestone, Hythe & Sandgate Tramway between Hythe and Sandgate in 1891; the powers to extend to Folkestone were never exercised. The tramway's eastern terminus was at the bottom of the hill on the road to Folkestone and the cliff company's directors saw an opportunity for making a connection to the western end of the Leas with another lift.

To advance their plans, the Sandgate Hill Lift Company was formed in February 1892. Lord Radnor agreed to leasing a strip of land between a point on Sandgate Road, a short walk from the tram terminus, and the Napoleonic Martello tower near the western end of the Leas. The lease was for fifty years for £25 per annum plus 2½% of gross takings over £1,000, not the bargain

The complete length of the lift can be seen in this early view of the lower station.

Radnor had made for the 1885 lift. At the upper end, a plot was leased from the War Department for a station building on payment of £1 per annum. Reginald Pope was commissioned to design the works, with support from C. E. Robinson, and a prospectus was issued to raise the £6,000 capital on 22 April (*Folkestone Herald*, 6/10 February/*Folkestone Express*, 30 April).

The £5,000 capital offered to the public was fully subscribed by May. Contracted for the buildings and earthworks, John Newman soon had twenty men at work. By the end of August, the track had been laid and progress was being made with the bridge over Radnor Cliff Crescent and on the buildings. A 7hp Crossley gas engine had also been installed. On 3 September a *Folkestone Herald* contributor said that there had been no scrimping in the work, and he did not expect to see the cars running soon (*Folkestone Herald*, 7/14 May/*Folkestone Express*, 2 July 1892).

Unexplained, there had been a delay in completing the agreement with the War Department, and by the decision to lower the floor of the bottom station building to bring it closer to street level. The car bodies, built in Folkestone by Worthington Brothers, were mounted on carriages supplied by Jones Brothers of Lynton and equipped with Bob Jones' patent brake. This modification to the Folkestone system of operating had come about after the directors had visited the Lynton & Lynmouth Cliff Railway in Devon on 30 April 1892. The downhill end of the cars was provided with a platform on which the conductor rode to control the brakes and one of them was able to carry bath chairs (*Ilfracombe Chronicle*, 7 May 1892/*Folkestone Express*, 25 February 1893).

Sure enough, the lift was not ready to be inspected until 28 January 1893, although some of the directors had ridden on it during commissioning trials in December. C. S. Hutchinson, again, reported that 75lb rail had been used for the track, secured to 9in × 6in longitudinal timbers set in concrete and at intervals with 6in × 5in transoms and iron straps. The sixteen-seat cars were similar to those used on the first Folkestone lift. The installation of wedge brakes designed to act if the cable failed was incomplete, as was weather protection for the brakesman. Recommending a modification to the hydraulic brakes to ensure that they operated if the brakesman became incapacitated, and with the speed not exceeding 4mph, he thought that the lift could be used safely by passengers (*Folkestone Herald*, 26 November/24 December 1892/*Folkestone Express*, 4/15 February 1893).

Without any fuss, the Sandgate Hill Lift commenced operations on 20 February 1893, more than 400 passengers being carried on the first day. The stations were quite different to those Pope had designed for the Folkestone lift, with the large lower station having a grand entrance portico with the company's name in stone above. It accommodated a waiting room, ladies' cloak room, lavatory, and offices as well as the engine room; the refreshment room and toilets were let out to an operator on a seasonal basis. The brick-built upper station was decorated with stone around its roof and housed a waiting room. Nearly 3,000 passengers were carried on the August bank holiday (*Folkestone Express*, 25 February/22 April/12 August 1893).

Traffic levels came nowhere near the expectations of the promoters, or the Earl of Radnor, and peaked at 196,029 passengers earning £816 15s in 1900, when a 5% dividend was paid. By 1906 passengers had fallen to 130,000, influenced by the convenience offered by horse brakes and charabancs for those travelling to or from the centre of Folkestone. The only reported occurrence during the lift's history was a landslip in January 1910 that took a few weeks to repair (*Folkestone Express*, 16 May 1900/16 May 1906/22 January/5 February 1910).

Remarkably, services did continue during the First World War but the lack of resources for essential maintenance led to their withdrawal in June 1918. With repairs expected to cost at least £500 and with the company only £29 16s 6d in credit, buyers

One of the cars crossing the Radnor Cliff Crescent bridge. Behind the car can be seen the range of buildings at the lower station.

At a later date, this postcard view shows the lift in action with the upper station on the left. Sandgate Castle can be seen close to the sea. Built by Henry VIII in 1539–40, the castle's keep was turned into a Martello tower in 1805–08. (Spells Series)

112 • CLIFF RAILWAYS: AN HISTORIC SURVEY

were sought but the only offer received was £500 from Sandgate Urban District Council, which refused to consider the directors' £750 counteroffer. In 1921 the council's chairman said that if it could acquire the property the track would make a good path to the Leas and the station buildings could be converted into bungalows (*Folkestone Herald*, 16 July 1921).

However, the council did not acquire the lift and it was bought by Alfred Matthew Cawthorne (1870–1957), a London-based architect. The sale was completed for £650 in June 1923 and the company was wound up in March 1924.

Cawthorne had been in Folkestone looking for a home for his sister when he came across the lift site and thought the top station would make a suitable site for a house for himself. He submitted plans for the conversion of the upper station to a dwelling in October 1923, and built Sandgate Point there in 1924. However, he never occupied the house as his wife thought the site was too exposed (*Folkestone Express*, 13 October 1923 / *Folkestone Herald*, 24 May 1924 / 2 October 1987).

As the lift was sold complete, Cawthorne was responsible for its public liability. In July 1924 the council's surveyor reported that he had complained to him about the corrugated iron decking on the Radnor Cliff Crescent bridge that had blown on to the road after its holding-down bolts had corroded and had received a reply saying that it had been attended to. Hart (see Bibliography) says that the bridge was removed in 1924 (*Folkestone Express*, 12 July 1924).

When the council wanted 130 square yards of lower station land for its Sandgate Hill road-widening scheme during 1924, incidentally, Cawthorne attempted to recoup a good part of the price he had paid for the lift, holding out for £300 against the council's £100 offer. The outcome is not known. When Cawthorne disposed of the lower station is also unknown. At some time the street-facing section was modified with the addition of a first floor, in a manner that does not look as though it was blessed with the services of an architect (*Folkestone Herald*, 13 / 27 September / 11 October).

Sandgate High Street with the last few yards of the Folkestone, Sandgate & Hythe Tramway in the road and the Martello tower No. 4 overpowering the lift's upper station. (F. Frith)

The average passerby would have no reason to suspect that this ugly structure incorporates part of what was once an attractive cliff railway terminus.

That was the end of the Sandgate Hill Lift. Had it a lower terminus more convenient for Sandgate it probably would have had a better existence. The adoption of the Jones brakes increased operating costs by requiring two brakesmen instead of one but the only losers from that were the shareholders, whose dividends were reduced. Had the council the resources to take it over in 1923 and it had survived the Second World War then there's a possibility that it could still be running as a twenty-first-century tourist attraction. Happy dreams.

CHAPTER 14

1896 ABERYSTWYTH, CONSTITUTIONAL HILL LIFT

Opened 1 August 1896, 4ft 10in gauge, double track, 778ft long, gradient 1 in 2 variable, hydraulic, electric from 1921, operational.

Located on Cardigan Bay to the north of the mouth of the Afon Rheidol, there is evidence of human habitation around Aberystwyth for thousands of years. The castle was built in 1277 and a charter of incorporation was granted by Henry VIII. The harbour was developed from the eighteenth century and considerable development took place after the railway was opened from Borth in 1864. Ways of increasing its attractions for tourists and holidaymakers were still being sought as the nineteenth century drew to a close, attention being focused on extending the promenade northwards. With distant views to the north and south as well as locally, there was also interest in improving access to the Constitution Hill, which rises some 319ft at the northern edge of the town.

The story of the development of the Constitution Hill and its cliff railway is not as straightforward as it might appear from a chronological reading of the contemporary newspapers, and it took several years for the full story to become apparent to the public. In the summer of 1893, Thomas Davies Harries (1850–1938), an Aberystwyth GP and town councillor, opened negotiations with landowner Roderick Clement Richardes (1857–1925) to acquire 7 acres of the Constitution Hill with a view to having a hydraulic lift erected there. Elected mayor in November 1893, Harries made no attempt to 'sell' the idea to residents and there was at first some scepticism about it, but nevertheless a lease was agreed in January 1894 (*Cambrian News*, 22 September/6 October 1893/18 May 1894).

Harries was in fact acting for Thomas Barnet Grant (1862–95), who in 1891 had gone to Aberystwyth to install street lighting as a partner in the firm of electrical engineers Bourne & Grant. Much taken with the town, he bought, refurbished and reopened the promenade pier, and also started to build a steam laundry and a hotel. His plan for the Constitution Hill was to develop pleasure grounds and tea gardens accessed by a lift. With these works barely started, though, he died of typhoid on 19 January 1895 (*Cambrian News*, 4 May 1894/*Montgomery County Times*, 26 January 1895).

Grant's partner, John Bourne (1841–1923), became the figurehead for funding Grant's projects and the Aberystwyth Improvement Society was formed, taking control from 1 June 1895 with G. C. Marks as managing director. Although the local press usually referred to the society as a company, it was not registered as such on 30 September 1897, when it had capital of £52,100.

Bourne seems to have been a sleeping partner in Bourne & Grant. He lived at Hilderstone Hall, near Stone, Staffordshire, and was regarded as a person of substance but when he died, still resident at Hilderstone, his estate was worth a mere £1,255 8s 7d; Grant's estate had been valued at £10,056 14s. There is no report of him visiting Aberystwyth (*Aberystwyth Observer*, 24 September 1896/*Liverpool Mercury*, 11 October 1897).

However, Grant's and Bourne's roles as financiers of public works in Aberystwyth were a deception, for they were working for HRH Prince Arthur, the Duke of Edinburgh, otherwise known as the Duke of Saxe-Coburg & Gotha, Queen Victoria's second son. He had apparently visited Aberystwyth in his youth and when he died in 1900 the *Aberystwyth Observer* (2 August 1900) declared that his involvement in funding the schemes was 'no secret', but no contemporary report to that effect has been found.

Marks appears to have been introduced to Bourne by Henry Webster (1842–1914), a licensed victualler who in January 1897 withdrew his claim against Marks for £150 commission in respect of the introduction the day before a scheduled court hearing; he had to pay Marks' costs. On an unknown date before December 1896, Marks was appointed the Duke of Edinburgh's civil engineer (*Aberystwyth Observer*, 31 December 1896 / *Cardiff Times*, 23 January 1897).

Marks' plans were naturally adopted for the railway. Reports are contradictory about when work started, with references to construction in progress in May and June 1895 and the *Cambrian News* on 8 May

Constitution Hill Railway works in progress on 18 October 1895.

1896 saying that work was not started until 'October last'. A photograph of the works in progress reproduced in the Aberystwyth town guide is dated 18 October, however, and the works had clearly been under way for more than a couple of weeks (*Aberystwyth Observer*, 14 March / 6 June).

While the debris was being removed from the lift site a temporary track was laid, with a cable used to haul and lower wagons. On 12 November the cable snapped, and a loaded wagon ran away, narrowly missing one of the labourers. In January 1896 the formation had been completed from the top as far as the second bridge and from the bottom as far as the first bridge, with good progress being made between the bridges. The railway works were under the charge of George George (1863–1950), who had been the gang master on the Clifton Rocks tunnel (*Cambrian News*, 15 November / *Aberystwyth Observer*, 21 November 1895 / 9 January 1896).

The council approved plans for the lower station, described as a dwelling entrance, in February 1896, and by mid-March four fifths of the formation had been completed and rails were being laid but there was still a great deal of rock to be removed at the top. Some 12,000 tons were removed in total (*Aberystwyth Observer*, 12 March / *Cambrian News*, 8 May).

Despite being unfinished, the lift was inaugurated on 26 June, on the occasion that the Prince of Wales was installed as Chancellor of the University of Wales. The ceremony, such as it was, was performed by the Princess of Wales by turning an electric switch located in the rooms allocated to the royal party in the university, the building built by contractor Thomas Savin as a hotel in the 1860s. The switch was supposed to have started the lift but as there was no one there who reported seeing it move, and the trackwork was incomplete, this seems unlikely.

Public services started on 1 August. Marks had made several changes in the light of his experience at Lynton, Clifton and Bridgnorth, the most notable of them

116 • CLIFF RAILWAYS: AN HISTORIC SURVEY

Early in 1896, the cars are in situ and the rope laid out but groundworks at the lower station and the roof and other works at the upper station remain outstanding.

being the use of much longer cars capable of carrying thirty persons each, with compartments in a stepped arrangement that loaded from the side, and the water tank installed under the downhill platform. Built locally by Richard Jones, they had open sides. There was double track only where the cars passed and no provision was made for the carriage of goods (*South Wales Daily News*, 27 June).

No published comment was made about the buildings. The lower station, at the end of Queen's Road, close to the north end of the promenade, is an attractive two-storey red-brick structure decorated with stone. As built, the upper station was more basic, essentially an open-fronted shed, large enough to accommodate the cars under cover.

The *Aberystwyth Observer* (6 August) complained that the press was not invited to the 'opening' but it seems to have sent a representative anyway. 'Only a few hundred persons travelled,' it claimed, adding that it thought that the fares, 1s 2d, including admission to the grounds, reduced to 8d in the evening, were prohibitive. The charge seems to have been reduced to 5d, which the paper (13 August) still thought was too much, alleging that the railway had not been well patronised. Its opinion was vindicated, it claimed, when a large number of visitors from Newtown and elsewhere had taken advantage of an offer to travel at half fare on 29 August (3 September).

A different perspective was offered by the *Cambrian News* (18 September), which said that the railway and gardens 'continued to be well patronised' and the railway was carrying an average of 200 passengers daily. When Marks hosted a dinner for councillors and employees in October, he said that 35,725 persons had passed through the railway's turnstiles in August and September (*Aberystwyth Observer*, 22 October 1896).

By the time the railway and grounds reopened on 1 June 1897, after winter closing, the *Observer* (17 June) had forgotten its sclerotic attitude towards the admission charges and made no comment about them, even though the inclusive rate had been set at 2d. On the August bank holiday, nearly 6,900 persons passed through the railway's turnstiles (*Cambrian News*, 16 April/*Montgomery County Times*, 7 August 1897).

An accident occurred on 11 September 1903, when the cars ran away a distance of 28 yards. A cylinder that had recently been inserted in the brake circuit failed, the *Cambrian News* (18 September) alleging that the distance left was too short for the automatic brakes to work, but in fact they should have reacted instantly. The thirteen passengers were thrown about when the cars stopped and sustained various injuries, fortunately none of them life threatening or changing.

The situation regarding the ownership of the Improvement Company and its assets after the Duke of Edinburgh's death in 1900 is clouded by conflicting and incomplete reports. A single report in the *Welsh Gazette* (25 August 1904) referred to a 'report current in London', a rumour, that Marks had been contracted to purchase the company on behalf of a 'wealthy syndicate' of which he was a member. However, given that this did not happen and there are no other reports, it was obviously a figment of someone's imagination.

What actually happened was that early in 1905 Sir Thomas Henry Tacon (1838–1922), a maltster of Eye, Suffolk, who had apparently given a mortgage secured on the company in 1897, took possession of the company's assets. So, since 1893, Grant, Bourne and the Duke of Edinburgh had been successively credited with being great benefactors in Aberystwyth when for most of that time they had been spending Tacon's money. The Improvement Company was struck off on 26 February 1909 (*Aberystwyth Observer*, 23 February).

The railway in 1923, the cars at the passing place and the bridges still with rustic handrails. This appears to be the oldest dated image of the railway.

The length of time between the Duke's death and Tacon taking possession is probably connected with delays in settling the Duke's estate. In 1907, however, the council became concerned that the pier and railway weren't being properly maintained and asked Tacon for information about any work that had been carried out. He replied that, regarding the railway, the Manchester & Milford Railway had overhauled it in 1905, which had been reported in the *Aberystwyth Observer* (10 August).

Not convinced by Tacon's reply, the council copied the correspondence to the Board of Trade and asked that, if it was appropriately empowered, it would 'take such steps as [it] may deem desirable and necessary'. The Board's harbour department replied to little effect, leading the council to ask it, copy to Tacon, to nominate an engineer to inspect the pier and railway but the Board did not reply. There is no indication that Tacon took any action.

New water tanks were installed in 1907, after the council resolved that it would not supply water to the railway during July and August. In 1906 a lot of water had been wasted from leaking tanks. Informed of the renewal, the council rescinded its resolution and allowed the railway up to 500 gallons a day (9/24 May/21 June/ *Welsh Gazette*, 9/23 May).

Smoke was an issue first mentioned in June 1907, when George Tunstall Coleman (1853–1915), the Constitution Hill manager, told the council, in response to an unpublished complaint, that there had been no fire in the boiler house since 20 September the year before, and that he bought smokeless fuel to avoid complaints. His efforts were to no avail, however; a letter to the *Welsh Gazette* (1 August) saying that, having lain dormant, the boiler house had become 'a spasmodic, noisy, dirty activity' and its chimney 'belches forth a dense black smoke'. The writer seemed to think that the chimney was too low (*Welsh Gazette*, 20 June).

This image is dated 1931 and shows the car without its roof. It is not known if they both ran in this condition. The notice in the window reads, in reverse, 'Do not lean out of the cars'. (Lilywhite)

The council's sanitary inspector made observations, served an improvement notice, and saw no change, which resulted in Coleman making an appearance at the petty sessions later in August. Giving evidence that he had purchased smokeless fuel, Coleman was given seven days to abate the nuisance. Apart from a letter of complaint sent to the council by a neighbour a year later, the matter of smoke was not mentioned again (*Welsh Gazette*, 20 June/22 August/*Cambrian News*, 9/23 August 1907/21 August 1908).

This was largely because in 1909 the steam engine was replaced by an electric motor. As well as eliminating the smoke, the new equipment was expected to allow the railway to extend its operating season, as a large volume of passengers was needed to justify raising steam. Previously, the season had usually been from July until the third week in September. Allen & Company of Bedford supplied the equipment; it was installed by staff from the local Eagle Foundry.

The grounds, which were run down, received attention, too, and Tacon said that if the income from admissions covered costs then admission from October, for the winter, would probably be free (*Aberystwyth Observer*, 3 June 1909).

Earlier, in 1907, the council had been given the opportunity to manage the property itself for the season, providing it paid the ground rent and the public was allowed free admission. However, the authority thought the rent, £120, was excessive. In 1908 Tacon offered the railway, buildings, fixed and moveable plant and interest in the leases for £4,000 but the council remained unmoved (*Cambrian News*, 19 April 1907/24 April 1908).

Having improved the property and been refused by the council once again, in 1910 Tacon advertised it for sale or to let. Three Londoners formed Cliff Grounds Ltd to acquire the rights but nothing more was heard of them, and the company was struck off in 1914. In 1912 Liverpool-based solicitors acting for a Mr Myring tried to encourage the council to offer £40,000, then £30,000, but it still remained uninterested. As Tacon still owned the property, the unknown Myring must have been angling after a commission if he secured a sale (*Cambrian News*, 22 April/8 July/*Welsh*

The upper station in 1943.

The earliest known colour view of the lower station, taken by an American visitor in August 1955. The lampshade and curtains visible in the first-floor windows indicate that the space is in domestic use.

The same visitor also photographed the railway in action.

1896 ABERYSTWYTH, CONSTITUTIONAL HILL LIFT • 121

Gazette, 4 August 1910/7 March 1912/ *London Gazette*, 6 February 1914).

In 1914 tenders were sought for running the Constitution Hill grounds, and, hence, the railway, but if it was opened during that season, or during the 1914-8 war, no reports have been found. In 1915 Tacon made yet another futile attempt to sell the property to the council (*Cambrian News*, 14 April 1914/16 July 1915).

He had to wait for the war to end before he found a buyer, the details, such as they are, being contained in the report on a licensing application for the pier pavilion bar in March 1920. During the previous twelve months the pier, pavilion and Constitution Hill had been sold to a Mr Furber. Paying a deposit of £3,000, he had plans drawn up for improvements that would have cost up to £60,000 to implement but he became ill and withdrew from the contract. George Stevens, a surveyor and land agent, then paid a £2,000 deposit for the property but he also became ill. He afterwards made an agreement for auctioneer and estate agent Alfred Arthur Holroyd to take it on, on condition that he (Holroyd) commenced to put it into a proper state of repair straight away. The deposits probably represented 10% of the intended sale prices and were the only money that Talcon obtained at this time (*Welsh Gazette*, 11 March 1920).

Holroyd focused his attention on the pier and pavilion but also had the railway put back into working order in July 1921. Unreported, it had probably not been run since 1913 or 1914 (*Welsh Gazette*, 9 September 1920/21 April/7 July 1921).

Despite the energy he devoted to Aberystwyth, Holroyd turned out to be a man of little substance. In March 1919 he had registered a company called British Properties to purchase and resell property. Its nominal capital was £10,000, of which £4,000 was allotted to himself for promotion and supplying office accommodation. His impressive London address in Oxford Street was a single room. One of his creditors obtained a winding up order

A 1950s view of the upper station, by which time the mouldings on the car's front panel have been removed in favour of plywood or similar material. (J. H. Meredith)

against the company on 14 September 1921, which brought an end to his plans for Aberystwyth. The company, which had a deficiency of £28,344, appears to have been released from liquidation in 1928 and was dissolved in 1936 (*Welsh Gazette*, 13 April/28 July 1922/*John Bull*, 9 February 1924/*London Gazette*, 28 July 1928).

Immediately after Holroyd the business was transferred to Isaac Gaunt Butler (1879–1943), an engineer from Stanningley, Yorkshire, who, in 1923 registered the Aberystwyth Pier Company with a capital of £1,000, its assets including the Constitution Hill and the railway. His son, Samuel John Butler (1916–54), liquidated the company voluntarily in 1949 (*Welsh Gazette*, 6 July 1922/*Western Mail*, 1 October 1923/*London Gazette*, 7 September 1948).

At this point in time the ownership is unknown and it is likely that the pier and hill then transferred to separate owners. In 1970 the railway was bought by William George Mowbray Truman (1914–77), also an antique dealer in the town. He sold it to the Mid-Wales Mining Museum Ltd for £21,250 in June 1975 and, after some repairs, it reopened under new management on 31 July 1976, the Aberdaron-based company registering the Aberystwyth Cliff Railway Company to run the Aberystwyth segment of its enterprise (*Modern Tramway*, July 1977).

The new company sought ways of increasing visitor numbers and reducing costs, and in 1984 a Wales Tourist Board grant funded the installation of a camera obscura at the summit. Opened on 5 April

By 29 June 1964 the cars had been rebuilt with flat roofs and simple mouldings on the end panels. The car liveries have been reversed. By the early 1970s both were painted as the right-hand car here, which ran in yellow with red highlights; the left-hand car then had a red roof, a cream or yellow body and green highlights, and had the name *TED* crudely painted on the carriage underframe. The right-hand car had been painted white and fitted with a glazed panel by 1982. (J. H. Meredith)

The cars had been rebodied using fibreglass and without glazing when seen by a Dutch enthusiast on 9 September 1990. (J. C. de Jongh)

1985, it was said to be the largest in Britain, and probably contributed to the 18,695-passenger boost, to 78,069, for the year. A camera obscura had been located on the summit before the First World War. In 1985 the railway's mercury arc rectifier was replaced by a solid-state system that weighs the loaded cars, adjusting the tractive and braking forces, and making use of electricity generated by the loaded cars going down. A 75kW winding motor was installed in 1991 (*Liverpool Daily Post*, 14 August 1984/3 April 1986/*Modern Tramway*, January 1986).

A community group took possession of the railway land, its stations and the land at the summit, on a ninety-nine-year lease from Ceredigion Council in March 1998, having registered an operating company, Constitution Hill Ltd, the year before. Volunteers support the company and from 1998 it has been a charity.

As well as refurbishing the property, the company started a programme of improvements, building a toilet block at the summit, and improving or providing access for the disabled. The following information was extracted from the company's reports. In the first year of ownership, 50,000 passengers were carried. One of the cars was glazed in 1999; the similar treatment applied to its partner went unreported.

A complaint made to the Health & Safety Executive by a passenger in 2011 resulted in an inspection and a notice of works to be carried out. Successful in obtaining £50,000 of grants, the work, which included realignment of the track, fitting Pandrol

The upper station in August 1996.

For the railway's centenary in 1996 the cars were named. Seen in August that year, *The Lord Marks* was captured at the passing place, with Aberystwyth and the bay behind it. The other car was named *The Lord Geraint*.

The names, on-car advertisements and bright colours were subsequently changed for the sombre livery seen on 13 September 2023, when this photograph inside the upper station was taken. What survives of the original ironwork is enclosed in the new structure.

1896 ABERYSTWYTH, CONSTITUTIONAL HILL LIFT • 125

Constitution Hill on 12 December 2022 with the railway in the foreground and Snowdon looking deceptively close in the distance. (Scott Waby)

clips, laying ballast and improving drainage, was done before the end of the year.

The following items were also dealt with: the roof canopy at the top station was extended in 2013; the first floor of the lower station building, which had been used as student accommodation, was adapted to residential use in 2015, resulting in an increased income from that source; railway repairs in 2017 included replacement ropes and axles and track renewal; the cable rollers were renewed in 2018, when the 1970s control system was also replaced; work on a disabled access, including a lift, at the top station, was started in 2019 and completed in 2022.

The roof canopy was made in a contemporary style, clad in timber, and incorporates the structure of the original roof. The buildings on the summit complement each other too, probably for the first time since 1896.

CHAPTER 15
1898 PORT SODERICK LIFT

Opened July 1898, 4ft gauge, double track, oil engine, closed September 1939.
Port Soderick is a small cove on the east coast of the Isle of Man, about 3 miles south of Douglas and nearly ½ mile from the Isle of Man Railway's station of the same name via a road down, and up, a steep hill. Although it could be accessed by small boats, and goods were collected and delivered by carters, it was not a port in the traditional sense. The population was sparse and agricultural.

Popular with tourists, who could reach it by sea from Douglas, it was served by a hotel and restaurant that had been established there for many years. Around 1889 the hotel was taken over by Thomas Forrester (born 1858), who improved the road and built a new sea wall (*Isle of Man Times*, 21 June 1890).

The story of his cliff railway is linked to the stories of the Douglas Head Marine Drive and the Douglas Southern Electric Tramways along the impressive sea cliffs on the coastline between Douglas and Port Soderick. In 1889 the Douglas Head Marine Drive Company was launched to construct a carriage drive with promenade between these points, a venture that was inspired by the recently opened marine drive around the Great Orme at Llandudno. The work was started on 1 January 1891 and the first 2½ miles, to Wallberry, where a bridge was required, was opened on 23 July (*Isle of Man Times*, 6 July 1889/10 January/25 July 1891).

Delayed by a shareholders' rebellion over the high level of debt incurred by the original, London-based, directors, the appointment of new directors, and the raising of additional capital, the drive was not opened throughout until Easter 1895 (*Isle of Man Times*, 16 April).

Motivated by the success of the Douglas & Laxey Electric Tramway, which opened in 1893, the company awarded a concession for an electric tramway to be built on its property to the Electric & General Contract Corporation. The General Traction Company undertook to build the tramway and the Douglas Southern Electric Tramways Company was registered to acquire the concession and tramway, launching its prospectus on 14 October 1895 (*Isle of Man Times*, 19 October).

With work starting on 30 December 1895, the standard-gauge, single-track tramway, with passing loops, was completed quickly, the formal opening taking place on 16 July 1896, although trams ran for only 2 miles, to Whing. Public passenger carrying started on 7 August and services were extended to Keristal on 5 September, and to Port Soderick at Easter 1897. Tramway works included replacing three timber trestles with steel bridges; valued at £4,079, they were adopted by the company in part payment for the concession (*Leeds Mercury*, 17 July 1896, *Isle of Man Times*, 16/20 February 1897).

While the new tramway was capable of delivering large numbers of customers to Forrester's establishment on the Port Soderick beach, they were still 180ft above and a steep footpath away from it. Fortunately for Forrester, the Falcon Cliff railway became available in November 1897 (*Isle of Man Times*, 20 November).

He bought the components and constructed the island's second cliff railway. It mostly comprised a timber viaduct mounted on stone columns, not dissimilar in appearance to the bridges erected by Brunel on the Great Western

A fine view of the Port Soderick lift with the old Falcon Cliff cars in line astern on the promenade.

There are many similar views of Port Soderick. The distinctive feature of this one is that both cars are at the lower station. Whether or not this indicates that the photograph was taken when the lift was being commissioned in 1898 is not known. (H. Hough)

Railway. An oil engine and winding gear were installed at the upper station, a short walk away from the southern tramway terminus. Because the gradient was shallower than the Douglas installation, the small Falcon cars were laid aside and used as kiosks, and new longer cars were obtained from an unknown source. The government inspector approved the lift for public use in August 1898 (*Isle of Man Times*, 27 August).

The railway's operation attracted no discoverable comment during its existence, although it did feature in dozens of picture postcards. Its closure went unreported but was probably a response to the outbreak of war in September 1939. The hotel was sold in 1946 and the railway had been dismantled before 1950.

The plinths are still standing, albeit overgrown, at the time of writing, and the upper part of the railway remains in use as part of the footpath up to the marine drive.

128 • CLIFF RAILWAYS: AN HISTORIC SURVEY

By the time this photograph was taken in the inter-war years the lower station had been given a roof and the walkway to the so-called 'smugglers' caves', of which there are several in the area, had been constructed. When the tides were favourable there were often sailings to the cove from Douglas.

The classic view of the cove seen on 5 September 2023. Only the sea wall and the stone arch remain of the entertainment complex, although it is still possible to see where the lift once ran. (Barry Edwards)

1898 PORT SODERICK LIFT • 129

CHAPTER 16

1900 DOUGLAS HEAD INCLINE RAILWAY

Douglas Head, viewed from offshore at the turn of the century, with the incline railway in the centre of the picture. (J. Valentine)

Opened July 1900, 4ft gauge, double track, 450ft long, oil engine, closed 1953.
The fourth Manx cliff railway has very little recorded or reported history. Located at the Douglas end of the Marine Drive, it was first proposed during the last quarter of 1887 by Thomas Cain, the same whose son had been killed in the Falcon Cliff accident earlier in the year. In October an editorial in the *Isle of Man Times* (15 October) had bemoaned that the access to Douglas Head from the Battery Pier was 'a disgrace'. Cain's proposal was approved by the Douglas Commissioners, but it was not put into effect (*Isle of Man Times*, 5/19 November/17 December).

Ten years later, in 1897, the speaker of the House of Keys, Sir John Goldie-Taubman, notified Douglas Corporation that an application was about to be made for a tramway from the Battery Pier to Douglas Head. The council made no published comment on this, and progress was slow, the application not being approved until March 1899 (*Isle of Man Times*, 11 December 1897/25 March 1899).

The applicant on this occasion was Richard Maltby Broadbent (1850–1940), best known among railway enthusiasts for building the Groudle Glen Railway that had been opened in 1896. He undertook to pay 7½% of revenue up to £2,000 a year,

130 • CLIFF RAILWAYS: AN HISTORIC SURVEY

and 15% above that, as rent; the minimum sum to be paid annually was £80 and the concession was for nineteen years.

Despite the railway's proximity to Douglas, there is no report of its opening, which is assumed to have been in July 1900, soon after the delivery of two basic, roof but no sides, toast rack cars built by Hurst, Neilson of Motherwell. The railway was unusual in having a change in direction on the horizontal plane. Notwithstanding Broadbent's undertaking to the council not to use an oil engine at the upper station, that is just what he did, but he does not appear to have attracted any complaints.

In 1916 Broadbent wrote to the council 'with respect to the rent'. The town clerk was instructed in the reply, but the details were not reported. Presumably, during wartime, he wished to be relieved of the obligation to pay a minimum of £80 a year rent (*Isle of Man Examiner*, 15 April 1916).

Island visitors in 1933 were offered a 2s excursion that included return travel on the Douglas Head steam ferry, the railway, the Marine Drive and Port Soderick lift, a combination that would probably attract a premium if it could be offered in the twenty-first century (*Isle of Man Daily Times*, 13 June).

Broadbent had sold the railway to the Douglas Head Incline Railway Ltd in 1922, which sold it on in 1940. Closed by the war in September 1939 it changed hands again in 1947, having earned the owners nothing during their ownership, an island-based consortium taking over. It appears to have been reopened in 1948, by which

A view down the lift from the upper station, with the Battery Pier projecting into Douglas harbour. It is seen on 9 August 1947, after nearly eight years of disuse because of the war.

Services resumed in 1948 with the cars running in a plain livery, as seen on 25 May. When the tourists arrived in the summer a gaudy colourful livery had been applied to the cars. (V. Goldberg/ Online Transport Archive)

By the time the railway closed in 1953 a plainer livery had been restored. The photographer included his wife in this image of a car at the upper station. (J. H. Meredith/ Online Transport Archive)

time the demand for the attractions on Douglas Head was much reduced and Douglas Corporation had started running a more convenient bus service. The railway was closed for good at the end of the 1953 season and on 9 January 1954 the shareholders resolved that the company should be wound up voluntarily. The Manx Electric Railway recovered the rail for reuse in 1955 (*London Gazette*, 19 January 1954).

132 • CLIFF RAILWAYS: AN HISTORIC SURVEY

CHAPTER 17

1902 HASTINGS EAST HILL LIFT

Opened 16 April 1902, 5ft gauge, double track, 267ft long, gradient 1 in 1.28, hydraulic, operational.

Hastings' second lift was built by the town council and remains in local authority ownership. While it has carried numerous passengers perfectly safely, it has been beset with more than its fair share of problems, including a fire and several accidents.

The first suggestion that there should be a lift serving Hastings' East Hill was in 1889, contemporary with the development of the West Hill lift, a clergyman from York putting the idea to readers of the *Hastings Observer* (6 September). However, the town had to wait until 1903 to get its second lift.

Before then, in 1890 the council gave its approval to a proposal made by William Gray, a Hastings businessman, for a hydraulic lift on the East Hill. Poor health seems to have forced the abandonment of his scheme but in 1892 F. & J. Plowman, the West Hill's engineers, produced plans for a lift on the East Hill. However, they were unable to obtain the consent of the land's previous owner to relax the covenant that inhibited building thereon. The difficulties encountered by the West Hill lift promoters in respect of the same covenant have already been mentioned (*Hastings Observer*, 4 January 1890/18 June 1892).

The council, however, was keen that there should be a lift on the East Hill, and started discussions over the covenant, eventually being successful in August 1898. Having secured that approval, though, there was no rush to take advantage of it, and it was November 1890 before the borough engineer produced his report and estimates. He thought that the lift would attract sufficient passengers to justify year-round opening and could make an annual profit of £500. He produced three power schemes, AC current, DC current and water. Electricity, he said, would be much cleaner than water, an interesting comment made more than 100 years ago, but running costs would double. Construction, including buildings, would cost £2,940. At £2,160, the water plant was cheaper than electricity, £2,820 for DC and £2,783 for AC (*Hastings Observer*, 3 September 1898/24 November 1900).

Powers to build the lift were obtained by the Hastings Corporation Act, 1900, which also gave authority to the council to take control of the West Hill lift. In February 1901 it resolved to adopt the water-balanced system and accepted a tender to supply and fix the machinery, including mahogany-framed cars, for £2,160, requested that tenders be obtained for the buildings, and instructed the engineer to construct the gradient and the permanent track using unemployed labour (*Hastings Observer*, 16 February 1901).

West Hill engineer Frederick Plowman responded to this news with a letter to the *Hastings Observer* (23 February) saying that the plans adopted were identical to those produced by him and his brother in 1892, which he had passed to the council in support of its Parliamentary Bill, and that if the former landowner had approved them, he would have been rewarded for his efforts. In an interview with the paper, he said that the only differences between his scheme and the council's were that the upper station would be half above ground, instead of being completely subterranean, like the West Hill lift, and a different water supply being adopted. There was no published response to his assertion that his plans had been used (*Hastings Observer*, 23 March).

Work to create the slope started on 1 March 1901, twenty men being set to work. The *Hastings Observer* (9 March) said that in view of the dangerous nature of the work they were mostly skilled men, 'experienced in work of this kind', in which case they were unlikely to have been unemployed. Speaking after the lift had been opened, the borough engineer, Philip Henry Palmer (1860–1925), said that most of the work had been carried out during the winter to facilitate the use of unemployed labour, but the only work carried out during the winter of 1901–02 was building the stations, carried out by contractors (*Hastings Observer*, 12 September 1903).

There were several interruptions to construction during the first few months. In March human remains were discovered, causing much speculation about their origin; in April a few days were lost to bad weather; and in May several hundred tons of rock fell from the cliff close to the work site, presumably dislodged by the activity there. The reports did not say exactly where the bones were found, nor how the rock removal was being carried out (*Hastings Observer*, 9/30 March/13 April/25 May 1901).

The slot in the cliff was 'practically finished' in November. Arising from the excavations had been thousands of tons of sharp sand, suitable for building, which had been dumped on the foreshore, close to the lower station site. Palmer advertised it for sale at 2s per cubic yard, and an offer to take 12,000 yards at 1s 6d over twelve months was accepted (*Hastings Observer*, 17 August/2/9/30 November 1901/18 January 1902).

Before the lift was completed and afterwards, a considerable debate took place in Hastings over whether it should be allowed to be opened on Sundays. The council's parks and gardens committee's proposal to open was lost on the deputy mayor's casting vote. Supporters of Sunday opening pointed out the inconsistencies of the objectors' position. They did not object to the council employing a man to manage the deck chairs on Sundays, for example, or refuse to read Monday morning's newspaper that had been printed on Sunday (*Hastings Observer* 5/26 April/23 August 1902).

Testing started in July. Over several days the lift was run satisfactorily but on the occasion that two councillors and some workmen travelled, their car derailed on the way down, about 20 yards from the top. Testing resumed after rerailing but later it derailed again, at the same spot. The problem was deemed to be that the wheel flanges were too shallow; with the wheels replaced there were no repeats (*Hastings Observer*, 19 July).

Public operation started without ceremony on 9 August 1902, King Edward VII's coronation day. A breakdown during the afternoon closed the lift after around 600 passengers had been carried. A correspondent to the *Morning Leader* (13 August) wrote that while he had read that the lift had been opened on Saturday without ceremony, it should also be noted, he continued, that it was closed, also without ceremony, on Sunday, to the great inconvenience of the public. During the following week loadings were about 1,000 a day (*Hastings Observer*, 16 August).

The stations had been built by William Francis Ditch (upper, £655) and John Parker (lower, £265). The upper station, an imposing castellated structure appropriate for its position on the clifftop, had been built using a patent stone, and included public toilet facilities in addition to the usual accoutrements required by a lift station; its towers accommodated the water tanks. The lower station was, and remains, a more homely structure. The cars, 'very handsome in design', had garden seats with reversible backs, and were also pivoted to enable them to be turned to permit the carriage of bath chairs (*Hastings Observer*, 21 December 1901/5 April/19 July/16 August 1902).

A postcard promoting the new lift, although the image required some retouching for it to be seen. (Victoria Series)

The lift and its lower station in 1904. The structure to the left of the lift entrance encloses a water tank. To its left is an animal drinking trough. (J. Valentine)

1902 HASTINGS EAST HILL LIFT • 135

HASTINGS FROM EAST HILL, SHOWING NET HUTS. 2088.

Hastings from the East Hill, a view that happens to include most of the lift's upper station. The towers were built to accommodate the water tanks. Ladders pitched to the three roofs indicate maintenance activity in progress. Contrast the visual impact of the East Hill station with that of the West Hill lift's upper station, indicated. (Shoesmith & Etheridge)

There was a loss in confidence in the lift on 22 September, when twelve passengers in the down car were hurt when it ran away about 20 yards from the lower station. Glass was broken and a man was thrown through a window. There was no one in the up car. The council paid £231 15s 6d in compensation; the largest amounts were £111 11s and £50, the first paid to a couple who were, respectively, badly stunned, and shaken and slightly bruised; the second to a woman who sustained a badly bruised back and shoulders and shock. The man who went through the window, who sustained a deep cut to his hand and was told not to work for a week or two, either did not claim or received very little.

The parks and gardens committee's report into the accident was published in January 1903, concluding that it could have been avoided if the top station attendant had exercised more care and discretion. He had not followed instructions, and established, by phone, that the ascending car was empty, while the descending car was nearly full and its tank half full of water. Consequently, the descending car had too much impetus before the brake was applied and could not be stopped. The committee also decided that the handbrake, the speed governor and the automatic brake were all dependent on the same brake blocks and drum, and that if anything went wrong with them the brakes would fail. It had therefore commissioned an additional and independent brake and would not reopen the lift until it had been fitted. It had also insured the lift against future accident claims (*Hastings Observer*, 27 September 1902/3/17 January 1903).

Equipped with its independent brake, the lift was reopened on 9 April 1903, in time for Easter, and carried 8,239 passengers in the first week. On 11 August, no doubt anxious to assure ratepayers that the lift was paying its way, the council released Palmer's report on traffic for the period 9 April–29 July. As well as 40,968 passengers, the lift had carried eighty-four

136 • CLIFF RAILWAYS: AN HISTORIC SURVEY

bicycles, twelve bath chairs and eighty-three mailcarts, and had taken £172 4s 7d (*Hastings Observer*, 11/18 April/15 August 1903).

Sunday opening was brought before the council again on 3 June 1904, when a resolution to open the lift from 1 pm on Sundays from 12 June until 1 October, was passed on the mayor's casting vote, an action that was greeted with applause. A total of 721 passengers were carried on the first Sunday, and on 31 July, the day before the August bank holiday, 2,169 passengers were carried. By 11 September (inclusive) there had been 16,167 Sunday travellers (*Hastings Observer*, 4/18 June/6 August/17 September).

When the matter was brought back before the council in 1905, it was resolved that the lift be opened annually from the first Sunday in April until the last Sunday in October, from 1 pm until sunset on Sundays. Once again, the resolution was carried on the mayor's casting vote (*Hastings Observer*, 18 March).

For several years the lift had a quiet existence and covered its costs. The 1920s started well with profits of £366 17s 3d and £308 reported in 1922 and 1923 but losses of £178 in 1924, £478 in 1925 and £226 in 1926 before profitability resumed in 1927 (£365) and 1928 (£244).

The losses from 1924 were no doubt consequential on a fire at the lower station during the evening of 26 February. The appliance from the local fire station turned out but despite the crew's best efforts, a strong wind off the sea fanned flames up the cliff and the building was gutted. The car stabled there also sustained some damage. The cause was unknown, but decorators had been working in the building during the day, which knowledge leads the author to suspect that a cigarette end had been left smouldering.

The absence of any reports of the lift being unavailable during the summer suggests that the building was repaired quickly, but the fire must have contributed to the insurance company's demand that the lift equipment required urgent attention. The specialist lift company Waygood-Otis was commissioned to carry out the work, which included overhauling or replacing the head wheel, and replacing three wheelsets, the ropes and the rails at a total cost of £890. The work was started on 7 January 1925 with reopening at Easter anticipated. An overspend of £142 8s 3d was reported in June. The cars were expected to require replacing within five years but, again, no report of the work being carried out has been found; another £558 5s 1d was spent on 'renewal of machinery' in 1926 (*Hastings Observer*, 1/29 March 1924/17 January/6 June 1925/7 May 1927).

A serious situation arose in July 1929, when the parks and gardens committee, which 'owned' the lift, was informed that it would not be supplied with water for the lift from its usual council-owned source in August and September, increasing numbers of holidaymakers and water going to waste after it had been used by the lift putting pressure on the supply. An electric pump that cost £250 installed enabled the water to be recycled and secured the lift's ability to operate in the summer (*Hastings Observer*, 3 August 1929).

Nelson James Read, one of the lift attendants, was found drowned in one of the tanks at the lower station on 15 September 1930. The inquest found that he could not have fallen in accidentally and had no reason to go into the tank. Aged 49, he had worked on the lift for two years, was in good health and had no money or family worries. The doctor estimated that he had been dead for about an hour when found and that the post mortem had shown that his death had been caused by drowning. A verdict of accidental death was recorded (*Hastings Observer*, 20 September).

The lift took much longer to be reopened after the Second World War than the West Hill lift. It had been closed in August 1940 and the upper station was requisitioned by the military. Removal of the barbed wire that surrounded it when it was derequisitioned in 1946 left it at the mercy

The lift seen from the beach, with the distinctive tackle sheds dominant. The fishery is said to have the largest beach-launched fleet in the world. (Excel Series)

OLD TACKLE SHEDS AND THE EAST CLIFF LIFT, HASTINGS

The lower station and one of the cars on 11 August 1951, the car doors and adjacent windows having been replaced following the 1950 accident. The car also appears to have lost its clerestory. The building's tiled roof was probably replaced by corrugated iron during the post-war restoration works; the reason for doing it are unknown, but its timbers could have been weakened during the 1924 fire. The railings that once decorated the boundary wall were presumably lost to the war effort. (J. H. Meredith)

of vandals, who smashed the doors and windows, destroyed the toilets, removed the machinery cover plates, stole the building's lead pipes and smashed the car stabled there. In 1947 the council estimated that, including unspecified works at the lower station, it would cost £1,500 to repair the lift (*Hastings Observer*, 20 April 1946 / 8 March 1947).

Restoration started in 1947 and the lift was reopened without ceremony at Whitsun (15–17 May) 1948. A total of 147,246 passengers were carried before the end of the season (*Hastings Observer*, 15 May / 23 October 1948).

There was another accident on 21 June 1950, when the cars collided with the stations. The ascending car had three passengers, Edith Kate Nethersole (1897–1983) and her daughter Alma Rose, and a child who was staying with them. The descending car was empty. Alma was thrown across the car and knocked out, also sustaining a broken wrist, and was hospitalised. Edith and the boy sustained cuts and bruises and required no treatment. Alma appears not to have sustained any long-term injury from the incident as she died in 2022, aged 97. There being no reports on the cause of the accident leads to speculation that it was due to inexperienced staff. After repairs, the

138 • CLIFF RAILWAYS: AN HISTORIC SURVEY

One of the cars at the upper station in 1966.

lift was reopened on 5 August (*Hastings Observer*, 24 June/5 August 1950).

Following the failure of the electric pump in 1973, the lift was, apart from a few months in 1974, out of action until 1976. During the first closure electric winding gear and a modern control system were installed by British Ropeway Engineering Company (BRECO) of Sevenoaks. During the second, the remainder of the system, the carriages, the car bodies, the brakes, the rails and the sleepers were renewed. BRECO supplied the new undercarriages and brakes for £22,000, and the new fibreglass-clad cars were supplied by Reginald Clayton Ltd of St Leonards for £6,900.

The lift was reopened in time for the 1976 August bank holiday weekend, when 7,300 passengers were carried. The extended

One of the Clayton cars at the upper station on 27 June 2017. (Ian Boyle/simplonpc.co.uk)

1902 HASTINGS EAST HILL LIFT • 139

One of the cars introduced in 2010, seen on 27 June 2017. Supplied by Essex-based Embankment Engineering Ltd, the design of the new bodies was based on that of the cars that entered service in the 1920s. The roofs were clad in zinc.

closure appears to have been partially caused by delays in obtaining specialised components and materials, but also by the failure of anyone to make an overall assessment of the lift and its component parts when the pump failed in 1973. After the new brakes had been installed, the track was found to be out of tolerance with it, and when the new rails were first being laid it was found that the existing sleepers were incapable of holding them in alignment, so they needed replacement, too. The old timber-bodied cars had to be replaced because the insurance company refused to continue to insure them; why this arose at this time was not stated in published reports (*Kentish Express*, 4 April 1975 / *Hastings Observer*, 31 January / 5 June / 28 August / 4 September 1976).

Things ran smoothly on the East Hill lift for just over thirty years, until 27 June 2007, when the cars collided with the stations. The four passengers on the descending car were unhurt but there was much damage to the cars and stations. The lift had only been reopened the day before, following a three-week closure for the control panel to be replaced after it had been struck by lightning. It remained closed until March 2010 as the council took the opportunity to bring forward a refurbishment programme that had been due to start in 2008. The cars, track and control equipment were replaced,

The lift's upper station forms the backdrop to this colourful scene on 1 July 2012, one of the residents stringing their own bunting across the street. (Steve Sedgwick)

1902 HASTINGS EAST HILL LIFT • 141

The upper section of the lift on 6 June 2023 during the overhaul closure. Although the author did not see or hear any sign of any activity while he was in the vicinity of the lift, the temporary work platform was moved during his time in the town.

The entrance to the upper station on the same date.

142 • CLIFF RAILWAYS: AN HISTORIC SURVEY

new cars having timber bodies instead of fibreglass with space to carry pushchairs and wheelchairs (*The Argus*, 27 June / BBC 28 June 2007 / BBC, 27 March 2010).

Just when the operators and owners must have breathed a sigh of relief at the lift being returned to service, on 3 April thirteen passengers needed rescuing by the fire service after it broke down. The cause was thought to have been a fault in the new control gear (BBC, 4 April 2010).

The 2020s saw the lift beset with closures. In 2021 reopening after the winter closure was delayed until 3 September, delays caused by the contractor withdrawing and having to wait for parts to be shipped from the US. Then, in October 2022, it was closed for track renewals that lasted until 23 October 2023, when the cars were also replaced (*The Argus*, 6 September 2021 / *Sussex World*, 21 March 2023 / *Railway Magazine*, December 2023).

As if that was not enough, in January 2024 'Storm Henk' washed a gorse bush and the soil surrounding its roots on to the west track, closing the lift again. It was reopened in February 2025. (*Sussex World*, 8 January / 15 May).

The new cars that entered service in 2023 were supplied by Rotherham-based Wheel Sets (UK) Ltd. One of them was seen stabled near the upper station on 9 March 1924, with the fallen bush and associated debris that caused the lift's closure a short time after it had been reopened after a year-long closure highlighted. In October 2024 the council obtained listed building consent to repair a crack found in the upper station's wall (BBC 19/24 October).

Hastings and the East Hill lift's upper station in 2024. The location of the West Hill lift's open air section is indicated.

CHAPTER 18

1904 FOLKESTONE METROPOLE LIFT

Opened 31 March 1904, 5ft 6in gauge, double track, 96ft long, gradient unrecorded, hydraulic, closed 1940.

No doubt it was the impending completion of the Grand Hotel alongside the larger Hotel Metropole (opened in 1896) at the western end of the Leas, that motivated the Folkestone Lift Company directors in 1902 to take advantage of their agreement with Lord Radnor to build yet another lift. Once more, a separate company, the Folkestone Metropole Lift Company, was created to finance, construct and operate it; its capital was £7,500. Its architect was Reginald Pope and the engineer was John Collins, who held the same positions in the Folkestone and Sandgate companies.

The agreement with Lord Radnor, made on 20 September 1902, awarded a fifty-one-year term for £5 a year plus 1½% of the gross earnings. The site was actually closer to the Grand than the hotel from which it took its name (*Folkestone Herald*, 3 January 1903 / 3 February 1912).

Although contractor Tilden Tunbridge (1846–1920) had the site staked out by the end of 1902, active construction did not start until June, after the council had

The lower station with the lift in action.

39 FOLKESTONE. — The Cliff Lift. — LL.

144 • CLIFF RAILWAYS: AN HISTORIC SURVEY

seen the plans. Messrs Waygood & Otis supplied the machinery for a water-balanced lift. A traction engine hauling three wagons loaded with lift machinery overbalanced when the brake on one of the wagons failed as the ensemble was descending Dover Hill on 2 July 1903, fortunately without injury (*Folkestone Herald*, 3 January/6/20/27 June/4 July/ *Folkestone Express*, 6 June).

Construction was nearly completed on 20 January 1904, when the directors entertained the workforce with a celebration dinner. However, when the company asked, on 23 February, the Board of Trade for the lift to be inspected it received an unexpected reply, for it was no longer the Board's policy to inspect 'appliances of this kind' unless there was a statutory obligation. The lift had been built without powers so there was no obligation (*Folkestone Express*, 23 January 1904).

A member of the public saw the new lift on 3 March and took to the pages of the *Folkestone Herald* (26 March) to express his dissatisfaction with it. He had been strolling on the Leas, he wrote, when he had been horrified to see what appeared to be the body of a London omnibus perched upon the edge of the cliff, adding that the lift might be useful and necessary, but it had been carried out in the worst possible taste.

The shortest of the Folkestone lifts, the groundworks had included provision for a second lift if that was ever found to be necessary and the lower station buildings had clearly originated from the same drawing board that produced the earlier lifts. A cabin was provided for the brakesman at the upper station, and one of the cars was enabled to carry bath chairs. The braking systems were the same as those used on the original lifts.

No newspaper report on the opening has been found in digitised newspaper archives but it appears to have taken place on 31 March, the day before Good

The upper station, complete with flag, one of the cars visible in transit. This station was less than ¾ mile from the first Folkestone lift and less than ½ mile from the Sandgate lift. (Polden & Hogben)

Friday. The small number of reports of its passenger numbers suggest that it regularly carried one third of the number carried on the original lifts.

The £4,700 capital raised was insufficient to cover the construction and in August 1904 another 200 £5 shares were issued to pay the outstanding construction bills and provide some working capital. In 1908 a 4% dividend was paid (*Folkestone Express*, 20 August/ *Folkestone Herald*, 27 February 1908).

There were no reported incidents affecting the tramway and it was probably closed for the duration of the First World War as no report has been found about its status then. It did run in 1919 (*Folkestone Herald*, 23 August 1919).

In 1940 the military took possession of the lift but in attempting to operate it without the benefit of experience or instruction, failed to balance the cars, causing one of them to run away and inflicting considerable damage. Hart (see Bibliography) says that the top car was lowered to the bottom as a precautionary measure in the event of enemy action and that the building was rendered inaccessible. The company claimed £1,000 for its property's repair but was offered only a 'trifling sum' in settlement (*Folkestone Herald*, 20 October 1945).

By 1951 the company had given up any hope of being able to restore the lift and on 8 June resolved to enter voluntary liquidation, the winding up being completed on 25 November 1952 (*London Gazette*, 15/19 June 1951/21 October 1952). In the meantime, several correspondents to the *Folkestone Herald* (18 October/1 November/13 December 1952) suggested that the lift should be taken over by the council and restored to mark Queen Elizabeth's coronation, but the idea did not get any traction.

In due course the site was cleared and the building demolished, the council's landscaping taking over.

Looking westwards with the lift in action. On the clifftop are the Metropole and Grand hotels. The lift was actually closer to the Grand than it was to its namesake. (Hartmann)

CHAPTER 19

1908 BOURNEMOUTH, EAST LIFT

Opened 16 April 1908, 5ft 6in gauge, double track, 170ft long, gradient 1 in 1.46, electric, closed 24 April 2016.

There are three cliff railways in Bournemouth. On the West and East Cliffs, opened in 1906, and further east at Southbourne, opened in 1935. Built and operated by Bournemouth Town Council, there appears to have been very little interest in them on the part of the ratepayers and little reporting on them in consequence.

Located on the south coast between the Isle of Purbeck and the Isle of Wight, the development of Bournemouth as a health resort began in 1810. Sufficiently developed to be incorporated as a town in 1870, it experienced considerable growth following the arrival of the first railway in 1874. Administratively, it was in Hampshire but transferred to Dorset in 1974 and is now a unitary authority. Blessed with miles of beaches and cliffs, it calls itself 'Britain's coastal garden'.

Connecting the clifftops with the beach were several zig-zag paths and a flight of stairs. The first proposal for a lift was made on 18 February 1902, when John Henry Ralph Smythe (1857–1930), a town councillor and solicitor, proposed that the West Cliff should have one, saying that it would benefit invalids who could see the sea from the clifftop but were unable to reach it. One of his council colleagues added that there should also be a lift on the East Cliff. The proposal was referred to the general purposes committee, but no action was taken (*Bournemouth Daily Echo*, 19 February).

Action was taken in October 1904, however, when the council voted £10,000 to be spent on two lifts and an improved road access to the beach at Pokesdown. When the Local Government Board Inquiry was held for approval to the borrowing, the town clerk said that the landowners had given their approval to the lift proposals, James Edward Cooper Dean for the West, and Sir George Meyrick for the East (*Bournemouth Daily Echo*, 7 September / *Bournemouth Guardian*, 4 November 1904 / 14 January 1905).

Requests for tenders for the construction of both lifts were solicited on 23 September 1905 and that of R. Waygood & Company, £3,700 for both, was accepted. What the tender advertisements had not made clear was that construction of the foundations and buildings would be tendered separately. The council accepted Waygood's recommendation to power the lifts by electricity (*Bournemouth Guardian*, 30 September / *Bournemouth Daily Echo*, 31 October 1905).

Construction on the East Cliff was started during November 1905, and it was opened on 16 April 1908, Maundy Thursday, after Lady Meyrick had opened the lower station waiting room and she and her husband and council members had made a return journey on the lift. More than £100 was taken in fares over the weekend (*Bournemouth Graphic*, 23 November 1905 / *Bournemouth Graphic*, 16/23 April 1908).

The cliffs at Bournemouth are generally unstable and subject to regular falls, which explains the length of time it took to build the lifts and the scale of the concrete structures in which they were erected. The Birmingham-based contractor, Harrison & Company, was also engaged on building the first portion of the under-cliff drive and promenade, which was opened on

The east lift under construction. 6 November 1907 (*Bournemouth Graphic*, 24 January / 7 November 1907).

The cars were typical of their time and held twelve passengers each. The identity of their maker was not reported.

Notwithstanding the successful operation over Easter, a few days were lost in May while the contractors resolved a problem with the ascending car jerking as it neared the top station (*Bournemouth Graphic*, 14 May 1908).

As Bournemouth had an electric tramway system, it seemed quite appropriate that the operator should also maintain the electric lifts. In July 1909 the tramway manager asked for the arrangement to be put on a formal basis, whereby the Beach, Cliffs & Foreshore Committee, which operated the lifts, paid cost price plus 15% for overheads. He also wished to be relieved of responsibility for providing regular relief men, otherwise they would be employed by two departments, which he thought was undesirable (*Bournemouth Guardian*, 10/31 July 1909).

Since then, in common with Bournemouth's other lifts, there is little to say about it. The cars were replaced in 1960 and 2007. The track was renewed in 1987, timber track components being replaced by concrete, the same standards having been adopted in the West Cliff lift the year before. An electronic control system was installed in the 1990s and the original 500v DC system operating a 25hp motor was upgraded to a three-phase 415v supply in 2000.

The unstable cliff face brought an end, for the time being at least, to the East Cliff lift on 24 April 2016, when a slip damaged the track and lower station. One of the cars was also dislodged from the track. Council employees had noticed cracks appearing in the cliff and had the area fenced off before the slip occurred. The authority became aware that something had happened when the local CCTV cameras went off air at 5 am.

When it had been established that there would be no further ground movement, the cars were craned off the site. The council said that it was committed to the reinstatement of the cliff and lift but a year later announced that the lift would be closed for another

A view taken on the opening day and posted a mere five days later. The sender wrote: 'This is the PC of the lift. It was opened on Thursday so I thought you may be interested in it. I have just been along to see it working. Alice went up in it, but I did not. I thought I was safest climbing the steps …' The notices posted on the right contain the rules for public bathing.

Seen in 1922, one of the cars near the upper station. The platform on its roof became a popular vantage point for visitors. (J. Valentine)

1908 BOURNEMOUTH, EAST LIFT • 149

The original cars were replaced in 1960, and this photograph was taken during that year. The council's crest is barely discernible on the body sides.

New cars with stainless steel bodyshells introduced in 2007 were painted white enlivened with the leisure department's logo on the sides. (J. Salmon Ltd)

two years, then in 2018 said that it had no funds to carry out the work and was seeking external funding. Two applications were rejected but in 2023 it was announced that the Government's Levelling Up Fund was financing the cliff stabilisation and a feasibility study for the reinstatement of the lift. An illustration in the application pack, however, suggests that the lift might be reinstated, if it is, in the form of a user-worked vertical lift (*Bournemouth Daily Echo*, 25 April / 22 May / 21 June 2016 / 13 July / 11 September 2023 / BBC, 16 November 2018 / British Geological Survey, 30 September 2020).

The abandoned lift seen on 9 August 2023. The lower station was demolished when the cliff debris was cleared from the site.

CHAPTER 20

1908 BOURNEMOUTH, WEST LIFT

Opened 1 August 1908, 5ft 6in gauge, double track, 102ft long, gradient 1 in 1.42, electric, operational.

The origin of the West Cliff lift is, of course, the same as that of the East Cliff but there was a delay in starting its construction due to a legal issue with the landowner. It is generally held to have been opened on 1 August 1908, but the author has found no report to that effect (*Bournemouth Guardian*, 10 March 1906/ *Bournemouth Graphic*, 16 May 1907).

Its cars were similar to the East Cliff cars, but with a capacity of sixteen instead of twelve. Rather than being located under the upper station building, as is usually the case, its winding gear is remote from it, being located on the opposite side of the West Cliff Promenade. The lift's 25hp motor was replaced by a 28hp device in 1962, when the DC power installation was upgraded to a three-phase system. The cars were replaced in 1962 and 1975; on the second occasion the design and dimensions were the same as used on the East Cliff, theoretically making them interchangeable. The track was renewed in 1986. An electronic control system was commissioned in the 1990s.

The upper station looking eastwards, with one of the cars and the pier, circa 1930.

The Lift on the West Cliff, Bournemouth.

152 • CLIFF RAILWAYS: AN HISTORIC SURVEY

A close view of one of the cars on 22 July 1962. The aluminium-bodied cars had replaced the originals earlier in the year, at the same time as a 28hp winding motor had been installed. The livery was blue, with the council's crest on the bodysides. (J. H. Meredith)

The lower station. This and the following photographs were taken on 9 August 2023.

1908 BOURNEMOUTH, WEST LIFT • 153

The lower station from one of the cars.

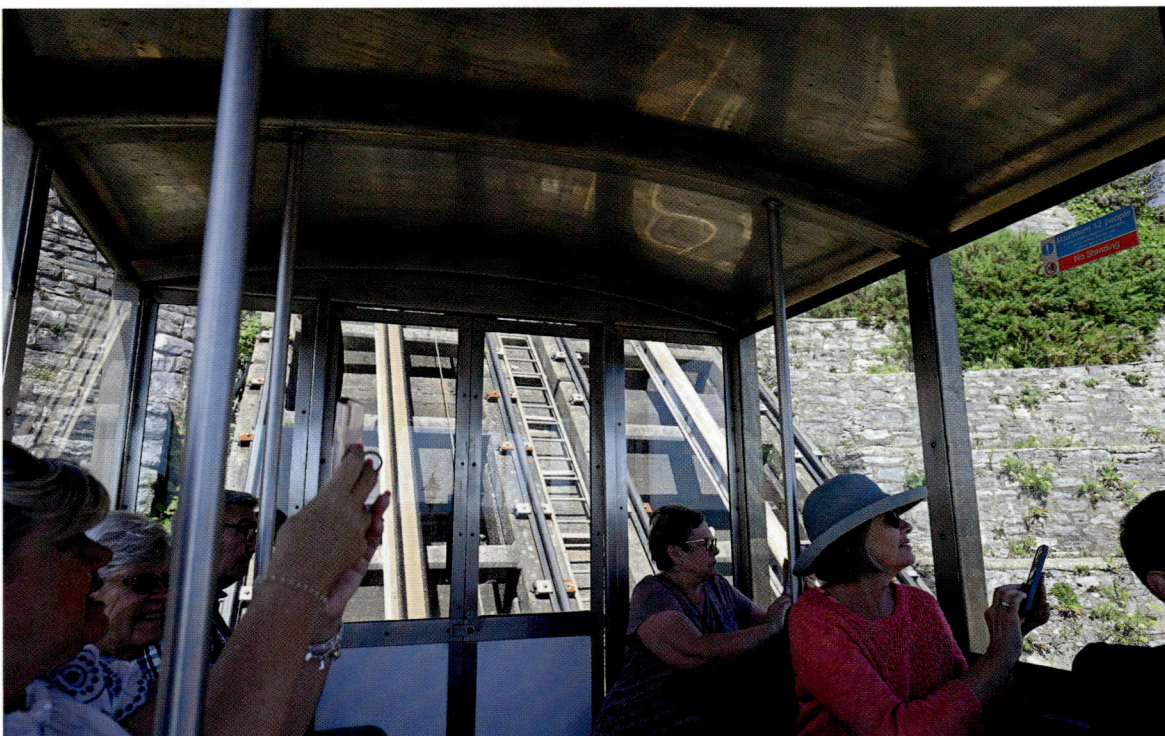

Passengers enjoying the view via their phones.

Above: Decorated with advertisements for ice cream, the cars pass each other. The yellow flags above the doors give the staff a visual cue that the doors are closed.

Below left: The upper station after the lift had been closed for the day.

Below right: The lift's winding room is located across the road from the upper station.

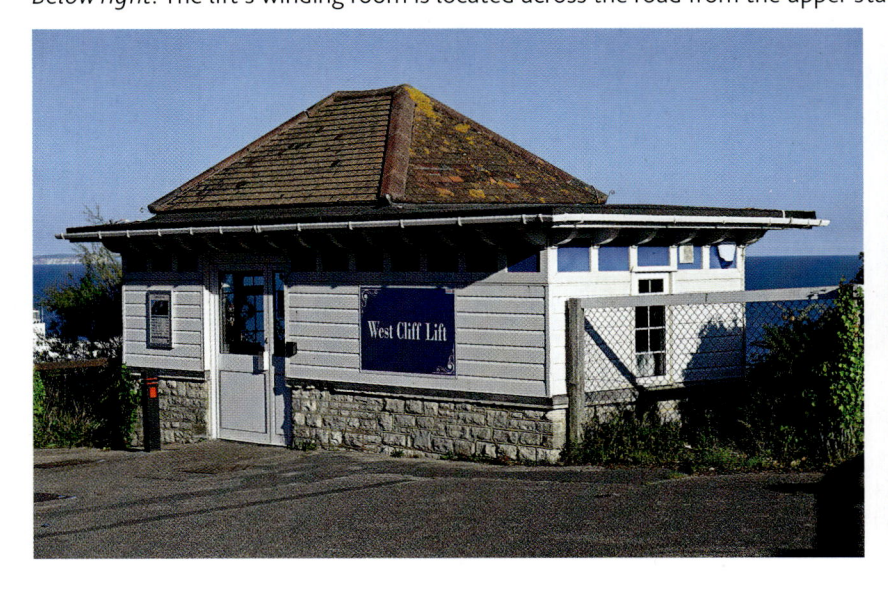

1908 BOURNEMOUTH, WEST LIFT • 155

CHAPTER 21
1910 BROADSTAIRS LIFT

Opened 12 May 1910, 5ft 3in gauge, single track, 100ft long, gradient 1 in 1.41, electric, closed 1991.

The lift at Broadstairs might not be the least publicised of them all but it is certainly among the least photographed.

A small town on Kent's North Sea coast, Broadstairs became easily accessible from London when the Kent Coast Railway opened in 1863, and attracted visitors who enjoyed its sandy beaches, especially the one in Viking Bay, overlooked by the cliff on which the town had been built. Access to the beach was via the Waterloo steps, which, of course, were not accessible to all users. What was needed was a cliff railway or a lift. Broadstairs got both, but not contemporaneously.

In 1908, George Graham Tucker (1866–1932), a Ramsgate architect, applied to the town council for permission to erect a lift. At the time he was engaged on constructing a vertical lift in Ramsgate for the lift-maker R. Waygood & Company. His first Broadstairs proposal was rejected after the council had seen the structural mock-up the town's surveyor had erected to show its potential impact on the promenade. His second was rejected after the council consulted with owners and occupiers likely to be affected; although most of them had ignored the request for observations, eight of those who replied objected and only two were in favour (*East Kent Times*, 26 February/11 March/14/28 October 1908).

Tucker's third application collapsed when the landowner changed his mind about selling the land required. These schemes appeared to have been for vertical lifts, like that at Ramsgate. For his fourth proposal, however, Tucker went underground, with a single-track inclined lift that passed under the Parade to emerge at an upper station at the rear of 14 Albion Street. The rear of the properties on one side of Albion Street backed on to the Parade, which ran along this part of the clifftop (*East Kent Times*, 28 July/15 September 1909).

Charged with the task of safeguarding the public's rights, on 21 September 1909, the surveyor reported with his requirements for reinforcing the road over the tunnel and reinstating it, protecting the utilities and constructing a concrete collar on the tunnel's brickwork where it emerged at the base of the cliff (*East Kent Times*, 29 September).

Work started in January 1910, and digging through chalk, within a week it was possible to see daylight through the tunnel. The lift was opened without ceremony, in deference to the death of King Edward VII, on 12 May. The contractor had been a local man, Walter Herbert Northover (1866–1924). The single car had a fifteen-passenger capacity, not all seated, and the lift was balanced by a concrete counterweight in a brick-lined shaft (*East Kent Times*, 26 January/18 May 1910).

During 1910 Waygood & Company registered a subsidiary, Cliff Lifts Ltd, to manage its directly owned lifts, and in 1919 this company offered to sell the lift to the council, but there was no interest. In 1920, therefore, the lease was transferred to Thomas Wilson (1856–1931), who had a refreshment room on the beach. His wife Susannah Elizabeth (1861–1921) ran the lift (*Thanet Advertiser*, 9 August/11 October 1919/13 March 1920/31 December 1921).

From this point the ownership timeline is incomplete. One source says that their daughter, Maud Alice (born 1883), took over. Presumably the family's involvement ended later in the 1920s, when the council took control of the bathing rights and Wilson moved to Teignmouth, Devon, where he traded as a 'bathing tent proprietor' until 1929. He died in Cornwall in 1931. When the brothers Arthur John (1905–57) and Frederick Benjamin Garnett (1908–75) took over is unknown but in 1946 they transferred the lease to Thanet Amusements Ltd. Closed during the war, the lift was in need of refurbishment, which the new owners carried out, before passing it on in 1951 (*Thanet Advertiser*, 11 December 1931/8 October 1946).

By 1959 it was owned by an H. E. Marshall, who lived in Broadstairs but probably was not born there and may not have died there; he has not been identified in the available records. Running the lift might have been a retirement activity for him; when he offered it for sale in 1961 and 1962, he said that it was a 'congenial and remunerative seasonal business' (*East Kent Times*, 20 March 1959/11 October 1961/30 May 1962).

Whether the lift then passed directly from Marshall to Frederick Justus Llandgrebe (1908–90) is not known but when he decided to retire in 1974, he offered the lift to Thanet Council for a reported £3,000. That council's technical director inspected it and reported that it would be expensive to repair, and the town council was unsuccessful in its effort to persuade Thanet to buy it (*Thanet Times*, 17 September).

Concerned about the possible effect of the lift's closure on the town's viability, a group of hoteliers decided that they should take it on. Despite Thanet Council refusing to buy the lift it appears to have obtained control of the lease, because it refused to allow them to operate it, declaring it to be unsafe, notwithstanding the hoteliers' insurance company being willing to offer cover. An engineering inspection removed the impasse, and the lift was opened on 19 July 1975, operated by the Broadstairs Lift Company, which the hoteliers had registered (*Thanet Times*, 3 June/22 July 1975).

Under the new regime, the only employees were the lift operators.

A busy day on the beach in 1951. The location of the lift is indicated by a sign fixed to the cliff face. (J. Valentine)

The lower station in the 1990s. The door had been sealed but it did not remain so. (Mark Hows)

The lower entrance when the lift was operating. The car was immediately behind the door.

A rare view of the car's interior, revealed after vandals broke the door down. Photographed on 29 September 2018, the track can be seen beyond the far door. How much of this, if any, survived the subsequent resealing of the site is unknown. (Canterburian)

Volunteers assisted with cleaning and other tasks to minimise costs. Despite their best efforts, the company struggled to break even; it made a £60 loss in 1978, and was unable to accumulate any reserves. Poor seasons in 1985 and 1986 worsened the situation and by December 1986 the company did not have the resources to pay its closed-season expenses, including insurance renewal and rope replacement. Fortunately, an appeal to Thanet Council bore fruit and a grant of £1,500 was awarded (*Isle of Thanet Gazette*, 24 December / *Thanet Times*, 27 January 1987).

Thanet Council helped again, with another £750, in 1989. An electrical fault had caused the loss of three weeks' traffic and while the hoteliers had raised the money to pay for the repair, and the rent had been halved, the company was still unable to balance its books at the end of the season (*Thanet Times*, 31 January 1989).

In June 1990 the company published an appeal for help to repair a mechanical fault that had caused services to be suspended. They were resumed but by August the company was negotiating with the town council to take over the lift, and giving six

158 • CLIFF RAILWAYS: AN HISTORIC SURVEY

months' notice of its intention to liquidate the company (*Isle of Thanet Gazette*, 8 June/3 August 1990).

The future looked more promising in 1991. In June, Otis Elevators (R. Waygood & Company's successors) were on site, servicing the motor, and orders worth more than £2,000 had been placed. But although the town council had given a £1,000 grant and Thanet Council £425, the company still needed another £6,000 for essential repairs, including replacing the gates and interlocks.

However, before much work could be done, the upper station was flooded during a 'ferocious storm' that hit the Isle of Thanet in July. Company members were not immediately deterred by this setback and continued their fundraising efforts, securing £2,500 from Powergen and £100 from the local branch of the South Thanet Liberal Democrats (*Isle of Thanet Gazette*, 2/23 August/1 October/29 November 1991).

The company soon realised that it needed as much as £100,000 if the lift was to be given the comprehensive overhaul that it required but applications for grants from government departments and national charities were rejected. In February 1992, it threw in the towel, and refunded the donations received (*Isle of Thanet Gazette*, 21 February/22 May 1992).

Broadstairs did not forget its lift, though, and in 1995 the town council decided to see if lottery funding could be obtained. However, Thanet Council did not share the town's enthusiasm, using £40,000 of £88,000 allocated to the lift to rewire its offices. No lottery application was made (*Isle of Thanet Gazette*, 20 January/7 April/21 July 1995).

In 2000, Thanet District Council installed a vertical lift in Broadstairs, probably in the location that Tucker had wanted to use in 1908. In 2017 the lift site and the adjacent public conveniences were included in Thanet Council's asset disposal programme and sold for £350,000 at auction, the new owners opening a coffee house named The Funicular in honour of the lift.

A restaurant's outdoor seating has been extended over the upper station site and there is no sign of it there, but the lower entrance was subject to vandalism, exposing the car to the elements until the façade was removed and access was blocked.

The lower station on 12 August 2023.

CHAPTER 22
1912 CLIFTONVILLE LIFT

The car at the lower station on 10 April 1950. Like the Broadstairs lift, the counterbalance was in a brick-lined shaft. (D. W. Winkworth/Online Transport Archive)

Opened 1912, 5ft gauge, single track, 69ft long, gradient 1 in 1.38, electric, closed 1972.

Located in the Cliftonville area of Margate, on the Kent coast, the cliff railway one of the lowest profiles of the railways in this book.

It was another Waygood venture, the company's tender to pay £10 annual rental plus 2½% of takings for thirty years being submitted to Margate Corporation in March 1910. Like the Broadstairs lift, it was single track, with a car that could accommodate fifteen passengers. Serving the beach-level Clifton Baths, it was opened in 1912 and had an apparently trouble-free existence until it was closed in 1972. The lift is quite often associated with the Lido, which was opened in the 1920s (*East Kent Times*, 13 April 1910).

An aerial view of the Lido with the lift's location indicated. (Lincoln Green Ltd)

The lift's substantial remains on 12 August 2023.

1912 CLIFTONVILLE LIFT • 161

Chapter 23
1912 SOUTHEND-ON-SEA LIFT

Opened 5 August 1912, 130ft long, single track, gradient 1 in 2.28, electric, operational.

Southend-on-Sea, a city since 2022, has developed from a small fishing community on the north bank of the Thames, in Essex. Holidaymakers and visitors were attracted to its 7 miles of beaches, and it found international fame as the home of the longest pleasure pier in the world.

Its lift came about because of the failure of an electric stairway, or escalator, that had been installed on the cliff to the west of the pier by the UK agent of the US-based Reno Inclined Elevator Construction Syndicate in 1901. Located immediately to the west of existing steps up the cliff, opposite the Jubilee Jetty on the Lower Esplanade, construction had started in July 1901, and it was opened on 3 September.

There were already Reno stairways in operation at Crystal Palace, the Earl's Court exhibition centre, Blackpool's Adelphi Hotel, and Seaforth, Liverpool, and there were to be others in Clacton and Tynemouth, and connecting the Piccadilly line with the District line at Earl's Court station. One report said that the Southend installation was different to the others in being in the open air, but the known photographs show it with a cover; what the writer probably meant was that the others were inside buildings.

In Southend, the corporation had driven a hard bargain, demanding 20% of the takings with £125 guaranteed annually, insisting that it supplied the electric power required and having the right to purchase on agreed terms. It also insisted on the agreement being made with William Henry Aston (1857–1937), Reno's agent, who was also making the stairways in the UK, probably thinking that he had more substance than the Reno organisation did in England (*Southend Standard*, 11 April / 9 May / 18 July / 5 September 1901).

Once initial problems with noise generated by the installation had been overcome, the stairway ran without comment until 29 September 1907, when it was closed on engineers' advice, citing the condition of the handrail and the chain (*Southend Standard*, 9 January / 13 March / 3 April 1902 / 17 October 1907).

By this time the corporation had come to regard the stairway as an essential part of the town's infrastructure. When, in 1908, it became apparent that not only was Aston in arrears with rent and electricity payments but also that he had no intention of reopening the stairway, the councillors decided that immediate action should be taken to take control of it under the terms of the contract. After £120 had been spent on a new rubber handrail, nothing more was said about the chain, the stairway reopened under corporation control on 4 July (*Southend Standard*, 21 May / 18 June / 23 July 1908).

How long the corporation ran the stairway is unclear, but by October 1911 discussions had been started with the Waygood company for its replacement. In February 1912 Aston and the Reno company's receiver and liquidator agreed to transfer ownership to the corporation in exchange for being relieved of responsibility for paying £450 owed by Aston.

The terms agreed with Waygood were for a thirty-year contract requiring

The Reno electric stair. This postcard view shows the beams that were reused when the lift was built. (G.D. & D. Ltd)

approximately £1,500 to be spent on a lift, and payment of £10 annual rent plus 5% of the gross receipts. The corporation had the right to buy the lift as agreed and required its electricity to be used. Waygood was given the right of first refusal if further lifts were required (*Southend Standard*, 22 February 1912).

Construction of the lift was started in May, reusing the Reno girders. The upper station was built over the Reno motor room, and the counterweight was located on a 21in-gauge track positioned between the Reno girders. The single car, reported to have a thirty-person capacity, some of whom must have been standing, and bath chair-carrying capability, was lined in oak and fitted with bench seats. The twin-cable system was powered by a 20hp motor and equipped with magnetic brakes. Its final cost was £1,700 (*Southend Standard*, 1 August/19 December 1912).

Incidentally, there is a story in circulation that the Reno stairway was put into storage and components reused in a chairlift at the Cunningham holiday camp on the Isle of Man that entered service in 1923. Given that the Reno girders were reused in Southend and the Cunningham chairs took a very different form to the Reno stairs, there would appear to have been very little of the stairway that survived First World War scrap drives available for reuse in the Isle of Man.

Opened on 5 August, bank holiday Monday, the new lift ran without reported comment or complaint. When, during the First World War, Cliff Lifts Ltd, Waygood's subsidiary operating the lift, proposed to charge half-fares to soldiers and to carry the wounded for free, the corporation's priority was to find a way to check that the half-price tickets were issued properly (*Southend Standard*, 19 August 1915).

No report has been found concerning the transfer of the lift's ownership to the corporation, but it may be relevant that from 1926 the *Chelmsford Chronicle* (28 May) included lift receipts in its reports on the level of business achieved by the

This photograph might well be a fake. The makers of 'Fairy' brand cocoa and chocolate put a working 'fairy windmill' on their stand at a food and drink exhibition held in Islington in 1908 (*Daily News*, 21 September) and McIlroy's store in Reading had one when it celebrated its fifty-sixth anniversary in 1931 (*Reading Standard*, 2 May) but neither report was illustrated or gave any indication about the windmills' size, except that they were large enough for a child to enter. And there is no report found referring to one being erected in Southend. Fake or not, the image does show the lift during the first eighteen years of its existence.

462 FAIRY WINDMILL AND LIFT, SOUTHEND-ON-SEA

corporation's revenue-earning activities for the Easter, Whitsun and August holiday weekends.

In 1930, the car was replaced when the lift was modernised by the Otis Elevator Company, which had merged with and then absorbed the Waygood company. The new installation included a 24hp 160v DC motor.

Another overhaul in 1959 also saw the car being replaced and on this occasion

The lift estate seen from below.

164 • CLIFF RAILWAYS: AN HISTORIC SURVEY

the stations were rebuilt, too. To improve access for prams and wheelchairs at the lower station the car's lower door was moved from the end to the side, the station layout being altered to suit. The car was replaced with one of a more attractive design in 1990.

When a problem with the counterweight in 2003 caused the lift to be closed, the corporation included the renewal of the station buildings in a scheme to restore the adjacent Cliff Gardens that secured £1.5 million from the Heritage Lottery Fund but in 2004 a change in European Union legislation designated the lift as a cable car, which required considerable additional work to ensure that it complied with the Cableway Directive 2004.

Presumably the directive was targeted at suspended cable cars, not those that run on rails. The stations were rebuilt in 2006 and with the additional work required costing £650,000, a fully refurbished lift was reopened on 25 May 2010 (*Daily Gazette*, 5 September 2003/*Southend Echo*, 13 May 2008/BBC, 25 May 2010).

Faced with the need to reduce costs, in 2011 the corporation developed an

The 1930 overhaul included rebuilding the foundations of the main structure.

The 1930-built car at the upper station on 8 September 1951, the image also showing the Reno girders. (D. W. Winkworth/ Online Transport Archive)

The lift seen from below on 9 February 1952. (J. H. Meredith/Online Transport Archive)

Extensive works carried out in 1959 included moving the lower station access and commissioning this new car, this view showing the doors used at both stations. (J. H. Meredith/Online Transport Archive)

166 • CLIFF RAILWAYS: AN HISTORIC SURVEY

innovative solution with regards to the lift, training volunteers to operate it. Apart from the occasional cancellation when there have been insufficient volunteers, this has worked well. From April 2023 travel has been free of charge, with volunteer numbers increasing after the Pandemic. In that year nearly 30,000 passengers donated nearly £10,000 towards the running costs.

The lift's technical significance as the only operational single-car lift with a counterweight located under the running track was recognised by the award of the National Transport Trust's Red Wheel plaque on 28 March 2023. The plaque was unveiled by Lady Judy McAlpine, widow of railway enthusiast Sir William McAlpine Bt, in the presence of Southend's mayor and the Lord Lieutenant of Essex.

This undated view shows the other side of the car and the large viewing window provided now that the lower-end door has been relocated to the side.

The lift as it was between 1990 and 2003. (E. T. W. Dennis & Sons Ltd)

The upper station on 28 May 2023. The following photographs were taken on the same date.

The car near the upper station.

168 • CLIFF RAILWAYS: AN HISTORIC SURVEY

The lift seen from the far side of the Western Esplanade.

The access to the side entrance of the car at the lower station. The lift works with a 'call attention' button to summon the car when the station is unmanned.

1912 SOUTHEND-ON-SEA LIFT • 169

CHAPTER 24

1926 BABBACOMBE CLIFF LIGHT RAILWAY

Opened 1 April 1926, 5ft 8in gauge, double track, 720ft long, gradient 1 in 2.88, electric, operational.

In the nineteenth century Babbacombe was a small fishing village on the south Devon English Channel coast, 1½ miles from the centre of Torquay, one of the resorts that the Great Western Railway called the English Riviera. The Borough of Torquay, as it became, acquired over the years the nearly 9 miles of coastline within its boundaries. It was, therefore, particularly interested in the wellbeing of the thousands of visitors who enjoyed the broad sandy Oddicombe beach. The only thing that marred the enjoyment for many was the access road from Babbacombe Down, as steep as 1 in 5 in parts. Although the first proposal that a cliff railway would benefit the beach was made in 1890, it was more than thirty years before the facility was installed. The lift that was made has the distinction of being the only one built as a light railway under the 1896 Light Railways Act.

In April 1890, as the Lynmouth & Lynton Cliff Railway was about to be opened, George Newnes, who had recently bought a house in Torquay, announced his intention to build a lift in Babbacombe, to Oddicombe beach. The idea had not originated with Newnes. The *Western Morning News* (22 April 1890) claimed that it had originated with retired cement merchant and founder member of the Metropolitan Board of Works, Charles Richardson (1819–90), who had died recently but no report of his proposal has been found. At the time of Newnes' announcement, Bob Jones and G. C. Marks had been to take the levels.

Despite objections from some residents who petitioned against it, the St Marychurch Local Board gave its approval to Newnes' scheme in October 1890 and in June 1891 obtained the Local Government Board's approval to lease the land required. However, in September 1892 Newnes asked the Local Board to 'let the matter stand over for a little while … and would write … further on a later date', but no more was heard from him on the subject. A '50 years ago' item published in 1941 claimed that the stumbling block had been Newnes' refusal to make an agreement with the landowner to fence the site. He was at that time engaged with developing the Clifton Spa and a cable tramway at Matlock, so it might be no surprise that something had to give. In 1893 it was reported that the railway had been abandoned (*Torquay Times*, 15 August / 31 October 1890 / 17 April / 12 June 1891 / 9 September 1892 / 23 June 1893 / 13 June 1941).

The opening of Torquay Tramways, which had a route passing through Babbacombe, in 1907 prompted a group of local businessmen to revive Newnes' scheme. As they acted through their solicitor, their identity is unknown. Despite the council's support, the scheme was not developed (*Torquay Times*, 5 July / 9 August 1907 / 24 July 1908).

In the following years occasional comments in the local press showed that opinion about the lift was changing. Private enterprise had failed the public need, it was felt, and it was time for the council to step in and do something. On the initiative of the Babbacombe Ratepayers Association, therefore, Torquay Town Council adopted a resolution in support of a cliff railway at Babbacombe in 1913, instructing the borough surveyor to survey the site, produce plans and invite tenders. In April 1914, with no reason given, the council deferred the issue for six months, and it was, of course, subsequently deferred more by the First World War (*Torquay Times*, 20 October 1911/*Western Times*, 9 May/*Exeter & Plymouth Gazette*, 4 July 1913/*Western Morning News*, 9 April 1914).

Interest in reviving the cliff railway proposal started with letters to the *Torquay Times* later in 1921 but the council did not respond until June the following year, asking the borough surveyor to invite the contractors who had tended in 1914 to update their prices (*Torquay Times*, 9/16 September 1921/9 June 1922).

Deciding that the railway would be run more efficiently if it were operated by an established transport operator, the council started negotiations with the Torquay Tramways Company. Whether this had any connection with the company's manager also being the chairman of the council's finance committee was never explained, although there were some objections because of the link. To obtain the required powers, an application was made for an order under the Light Railways Act of 1896 (*Torquay Times*, 13 July/3 August/*London Gazette*, 24 July 1923).

When the town clerk, Herbert Adamson Hield (1882–1957), had enquired of the Light Railway Commissioners if an application for an order for a cliff railway would be accepted, his attention was drawn to the Ventnor and Malvern Orders of 1898 and 1911 respectively, and it was noted that as he had previously been Swansea's assistant town clerk, he could be expected to be familiar with the procedure; he had been involved with the applications for orders made in 1914 and 1918. He had been appointed to Torquay in 1920 (*Torquay Times*, 14 January 1921).

At an inquiry held in Torquay's Town Hall on 18 September 1923, the town clerk explained that the intention was for the council and the tramway company to make an agreement for what these days would be called a build and operate contract. The

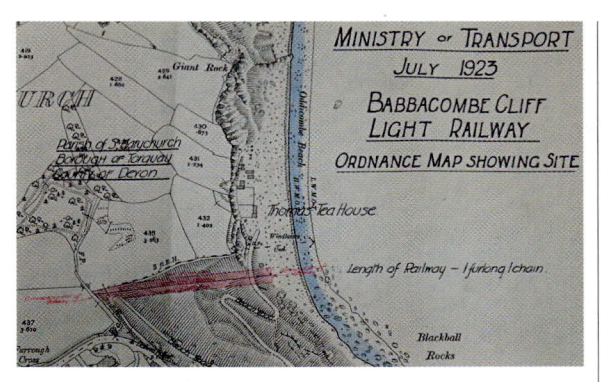

The plan of the railway submitted with the Light Railway Order application. (National Archives)

company would build the railway to the council's, and the Ministry of Transport's, requirements and then lease it for forty-two years, paying £25 a year rent for the first fourteen years and £50 a year thereafter. The council could also take control of the railway at the fourteenth year and at seven-year intervals thereafter, on giving six months' notice, on terms to be agreed, except that if the council bought the tramway at any time the purchase would include the railway. The company would also reimburse the council the estimated £300 cost of obtaining the order.

The borough engineer, who designed the railway, was Henry Augustus Garrett (1861–1934). At the age of 15 he had been articled to the Bournemouth Commissioners' engineer and surveyor, staying in the town and holding various posts there until he became assistant surveyor in 1884. He moved to Torquay as surveyor of the Local Board in 1890. In response to an objection about the railway crossing the road, he said that was to enable the lower station to be closer to the beach.

One objector complained that the railway would destroy some of the area's natural beauties before asserting that 'motor cars suitably constructed, and not allowed to be overcrowded', could supply the necessary service and a light railway would be a waste of money. He had read in the press, he said, that 'light railways will soon be a thing of the past'. Other objections questioned whether the tramway company was an appropriate body to run the railway and whether it would not be preferable for

1926 BABBACOMBE CLIFF LIGHT RAILWAY • 171

it to be run by the council (*Torquay Times*, 31 August/21 September 1923)

The Babbacombe Cliff Light Railway Order was made on 22 December 1923, but more than two years were to pass before Oddicombe beach got its railway, much of the delay taken in completing the agreement with the tramways company and obtaining the Ministry of Transport's agreement to the same. The council was able to seal the agreement at a special meeting on 2 September, the company on 12 November, both dates in 1924 (*Torquay Times*, 5 September/24 October).

Notwithstanding the agreement with the tramway company, the railway was constructed by the National Electrical Construction Company, its parent. How much of Garrett's design survived NEC's involvement is not known. Neither is it known if the alignment was the same as that proposed by Newnes.

Work on site was reported in progress during November 1924, an avenue soon being cut through the trees, but further progress was hampered by heavy rain aggravated by a spring flooding the works (*Torquay Times*, 21 November/*Western Morning News*, 4 December 1924/*Torbay Express*, 11 February 1925).

Construction took another year before the railway was ready to be inspected, Major G. L. Hall (1882–1947) performing that duty on 25 February and 25 March 1926 and reporting on 27 March. The cars were loaded with concrete blocks to simulate the weight of passengers during braking tests.

Where the railway runs above ground level a reinforced concrete viaduct was constructed. The viaduct, and 2ft 6in square × 9in deep concrete blocks used elsewhere, carry concrete stringers 10in wide and 17in deep that run the full length. On to these 9 × 5in creosoted pitch pine longitudinal beams were bolted, cross-braced with similar beams at 3ft 6in centres. A 30ft, 35lb/yd Vignoles (flat bottom) rail was fixed to the longitudinal beams. The safety gear made use of a continuous pitch pine stringer mounted in the centre of each track.

The lower station was 30ft above the beach, built on a reinforced concrete structure, and its pedestrian access was by a ramp with a 1 in 9 gradient. At the upper station the motor room was located under the floor, accessed by a ladder. Power for the 500v DC installation was taken from the council's supply.

Safety gear fitted under the cars was operated by an independent safety rope that would grip on the centre rail in the event of the failure of the suspension ropes. A slowing-down mechanism reduced speed automatically as the cars approached the stations. Electric brakes would act if the power was lost.

Car capacity was twelve passengers seated and eight standing. The bodies were timber with fixed windows in the sides. Ventilation was by flap vents above the windows and shuttered vents in the roof clerestory. The end doors were locked from the outside.

The winding gear was driven by 'standard Waygood-Otis elevator equipment', using a 45hp lift motor. The drive between the motor and the winding sheaves was of the worm type used in elevators. The controller was located in the upper station. The safety gear was of 'the ordinary elevator type', an auxiliary rope running free between the cars, so that if the distance between the cars altered it would be tensioned and trigger the gear mounted under the cars and force it to jam into the safety beam between the rails, holding the cars stationary.

Operation was controlled by a single-stroke bell at each station. The bells were wired in series with the door locks at the opposite end to ensure that the starting signal could not be given unless the doors were closed properly. Car travel was designed so that the short-stroke hydraulic buffers positioned in the centre of each track at the lower station were just touched by the descending car, the protection provided by their full strokes remaining as a safeguard against incorrect rope adjustment.

Hall had noted some cracks in the structure under the lower station and required that they be both monitored for movement and repaired to prevent water access to the reinforcing. He also required the haulage cables be shortened by 2ft to ensure that the cars stopped in the correct place at the lower station. The Ministry of Transport certificates authorising the railway's use by the public were issued on 31 March.

The cars and the lift equipment were supplied by Waygood-Otis Ltd, the cars unpainted. With them freshly painted in Torquay Tramways livery, the railway was opened by the mayor of Torquay on 1 April 1926, Maundy Thursday, in time for the Easter weekend. During the speeches, the mayor, J. Taylor, said that 'seven or eight years' previously he had been involved in a scheme to build a vertical lift; no contemporary reports have been found but it is probably the proposal referred to in a 1945 news review, which said it was an initiative of the Babbacombe & St Marychurch Ratepayers' Association, that a company had been formed and that permission had been refused. Speaking at the opening, a Torquay Tramways director made much of the use of British labour and materials in the railway's construction. It would have been cheaper to have used Belgian cement and ironwork, he claimed. About a thousand tickets were issued on the first day and twice as many on the second, Good Friday (*Torquay Times*, 3/9 April 1926/2 November 1945).

The objectors who had complained about Torquay Tramways Company's participation in the railway's operation must have felt their positions justified by an editorial and a letter that appeared in local papers a few weeks after services had started. The first noted that it was a great asset to the borough but 'unfortunately the Torquay Tramways Company is not always noted for meeting the wishes of the travelling public in the matter of timetables and in their management of the Cliff Railway they appear to have forgotten that

Despite the concrete already looking rather weather worn, this view shows the lower station before the railway was opened, and before the cars were painted. (National Archives)

The substantial crowd that gathered to see the railway's inauguration. The cars were painted in tramway company livery.

Summer Time is in existence', adding that the last cars ran soon after 7 pm, catching visitors unaware who had intended spending the evening on the beach. In the letter, 'Observer' sought to remind the company that the railway was for the convenience of the public and not to be run at times that suited it, particularly in the height of the season. He had, he wrote, seen many of these lifts and railways but not one that started so late and finished so early. The company made no public response (*Torquay Times*, 11 June/*Torbay Express*, 21 June).

On 8 September 1926, apparently without any consultation, the Ministry of Transport issued regulations 'for securing to the public and to passengers all reasonable protection against danger' from the railway. Copies were to be displayed in each car. Torquay Corporation, or any person using the railway, were subject to a penalty of up to £10 for any breach of the regulations and up to £5 for each day a breach continued after conviction.

Despite the complaints about operating times, more than 400,000 passengers were carried in 1926, generating a profit of £1,947 17s. Thereafter, the profit was reduced each year to 1929, £1,666 19s 9d in 1927, £1,332 in 1928 and £1,327 in 1929. Initially this was attributed to the novelty value having worn off and to the railway not being able to accommodate everyone who wanted to travel at peak times, but of course they were also the years of the Great Depression. No explanation was offered for 'considerable reconstruction work' being required on the track during 1927 but the cost was applied to the renewals account (*Torbay Express*, 2 February 1927/5 March 1930/*Torquay Times*, 24 February 1928/ *Western Morning News*, 28 February 1929).

This view of one of the cars near the road bridge is a rare pre-war example of a visitor's photograph of a cliff railway.

The closure of the Torquay tramways on 31 January 1934 was accompanied by much discussion on the benefit of the council buying the railway but in April 1934 the councillors voted against the idea, despite the legal obligation to buy it on the termination of the lease (*Torquay Times*, 3 November 1933/*Western Morning News*, 12 April 1934).

Liquidation of the company rather forced the council's hand, though, but the road to taking ownership was indirect. In May, a letter from the liquidator was discussed, wherein he said that the railway had cost £15,648 to build and had carried 2,550,384 passengers since, making an average annual gross profit of £1,153. He thought that ownership by the council, which could operate it along with its other activities, would be more economical than letting it go to a third party, and that it would be improper to abandon it. However, his proposal that the tramway company's shareholders should form a company to be assigned the railway's lease was accepted by the council (*Torquay Times*, 11 May 1934).

This never came to be because within a few weeks the council had agreed to purchase the railway, along with the tramway sheds, bus garage, offices and six cottages, all in St Marychurch, for £10,000. The council's earlier refusal might have been because of works being undertaken to repair the concrete structure carrying the track, but they had been completed and the railway was operational again. The buildings cost £7,500 so the railway was a bargain at £2,500 (*Torbay Express*, 6 June 1934/*Torquay Times*, 11 January 1935).

Exactly when the council took control of the railway is not known. Sources give 13 March and April 1935, but no news reports have been found. During the first year an estimated £850 profit was made. It appears that the council made its mark on the railway by eliminating the tramway livery and painting the cars white, which resulted in criticism by an observer who thought that they should be green, 'nature's livery' (*Torquay Times*, 6 December 1935/1 March 1936).

1926 BABBACOMBE CLIFF LIGHT RAILWAY • 175

In addition to repainting the cars, the council also put in hand 'extensive renovations' and upgraded the electrical installation, changing from DC to AC. No details were given as to what the former involved, while the report on the latter said that the change had 'considerably reduced' the car speed, 'with consequent loss of time and money'. It was anticipated that normal speed would be restored when a new sub-station was installed in St Marychurch. It could be that the electrical installation had been altered during the renovations, although the comment about its effect on speed was not made until October, when the railway had ceased running for the winter. The sub-station tender, with a five-week build time, had been accepted in May (*Torquay Times*, 27 March/8 May/9 October 1936).

Further works were required in 1937, when more cracks were found in the lower station structure, delaying the start of the operating season. A total of £2,000 was borrowed to pay for the works, which were expected to include piling to stabilise the ground (*Torquay Times*, 8 January/23 March/7 May 1937).

Torquay's tourist attractions, including the railway, remained open for business after the war started. In 1941 one of the councillors was puzzled by the highways committee's report that the railway had had a record year while the Oddicombe beach café had made a loss of £351, presumably expecting that if the railway had been busy then the café should have been busy enough not to make a loss (*Torquay Times*, 7 November 1941).

The railway, and the beach, were closed after the end of the 1941 season, however, and the stations were taken over by the Home Guard. By 1945 the railway was in a very poor state, damaged by ground movement, not just neglect. A 1948 report described its condition: the upper station and the cars looked to be in a fair condition, the track reminded the observer of a carnival switchback, while the concrete viaduct had splits caused by subsidence and bases as much as 6in out of line; the lower station had broken windows and patched-up doors (*Torquay Times*, 4 May 1945/28 January 1948/27 June 1951).

Restoring the railway to use at a time of inflation and shortage of materials was going to take time and strategic vision, as well as funding, if it was to be reopened at all. In 1945 the council started by appointing Oscar Faber (1886–1956), a cliff works specialist, as consulting engineer to prepare alternative schemes to restore the railway and increase its capacity. His £22,000 scheme to stabilise the structure, increase the speed from 400 to 600ft per minute and increase car capacity from twenty to thirty was accepted but approval was needed to borrow the money, increased to £25,000 when Faber's fee and expenses were taken into account, and to obtain the required materials (*Torquay Times*, 8 June 1945/3 April/1 July 1946).

By mid-1948 the estimated cost had nearly doubled, to £45,000, but by the end of the year it had reached £60,000, a sum that clearly frightened the councillors, who rejected a proposal to borrow it and decided to examine alternatives. Schemes considered included escalators; a vertical lift in the cliff, as at Whitby; making the beach road suitable for buses; and extending it through to Babbacombe beach to create a circular route for use by trolleybuses. Advised that the escalator and the road schemes were impractical, and that a lift would cost £71,000, the councillors decided to spend £60,000 on restoring the railway (*Torbay Express*, 3 November/8 December 1948/1 January/8 April/28 July 1949).

That decision did not signify that work would be started anytime soon, and by January 1950 the council was engaged in finding ways of reducing the cost. This was as well, as in April Faber reported that authority for the £60,000 scheme had been refused due to 'austerity restrictions'. He proposed carrying out the work in stages, with a £12,000 first phase that would allow the railway to be opened sooner. Drawing attention to his earlier report, that the lower section of the cliff on which the railway had been built was moving at the rate of 1in per year, he proposed rebuilding the lower 100ft of the viaduct, including the road bridge; above that, sleepers needed resetting, reinforced concrete required reconstructing, and rails needed realigning (*Torquay Times*, 13 January 1950).

With approval in hand, the work started with the demolition of the road bridge in September 1950. Twenty men were working up to twelve hours a day by March 1951, the cars and machinery had been overhauled, and mass concrete buttresses were being built to support the bridge and prevent the railway sliding towards the sea. One of the bridge buttresses required excavating 32ft to reach the bedrock. To save money the

Photographed on 26 March 1951, this image shows the cars as they were stabled during the war. (D. W. Winkworth/Online Transport Archive)

Looking downhill on the same occasion, it can be seen that the track really was like a 'carnival switchback'. (D. W. Winkworth/Online Transport Archive)

rails were turned round, so the cars ran on the unworn edges (*Torquay Times*, 1 September / 20 October 1950 / 2 March 1951 / *Torbay Express*, 2 December 1991).

A few weeks later than planned, the railway was reopened on 29 June 1951. In charge of its operation was Reginald 'Reg' Russell Tonkin (1905–65), who had worked on it since it opened in 1926. He and the two men who opened and closed the doors at each station were joined by two female ticket collectors, described as an innovation; they would have been cheaper to employ as the council had advertised for 20-year-olds.

Among the first passengers were Elsie Kate Richman (1892–1991) and her daughter, Jenny Channon Richman (1920–2018), local residents who said that they had travelled on the railway when it had opened in 1926. They would have found that the cars were unaltered, apart from being painted in the council's green and cream livery with its crest on the side panels (*Torbay Express*, 29 June / *Torquay Times*, 22 / 27 / 29 June).

Nearly 20,000 passengers were carried in the first four days, 11,061 up and 8,375 down, four times greater than equivalent pre-war figures, the highways committee chairman informed the council. The numbers held up and 371,000 journeys had been made by the time the season ended on 14 October. Explaining the increase in numbers, Tonkin said that pre-war people had been wary about using the railway, whereas post-war they were blasé about it. They were also prepared to pay the increased fares applied, 3d down, 4d up, 6d return. The pre-war fares had been 2d up or down and 3d return, unaltered since 1926; the changes had required the Ministry of Transport's approval, in the form of the Babbacombe Light Railway (Increase of Charges) Order, made on 25 May (*Torbay Express*, 4 July / 8 August / 21 September / 12 October 1951 / 9 May 1952 / *Torquay Times*, 8 December 1950 / *London Gazette*, 5 June 1951).

There were two setbacks when the council tried to put the second phase of the railway's renovation into effect later in 1951.

The lower station with its plinth encased in stone and the new road bridge. Painted green and cream for the reopening, the cars were replaced in 1955. (Wholesale Stationers (Devon) Ltd)

178 • CLIFF RAILWAYS: AN HISTORIC SURVEY

Firstly, the tender returned from the firm that had done the first phase exceeded the estimate and then the borrowing approval was denied on the basis that its purpose was not 'exceptionally urgent or in the national interest' (*Torquay Times*, 9 November 1951/ *Torbay Express*, 5 January 1952).

The way ahead was agreed in July 1953, after Faber had reported that as it would take fourteen months to obtain new machinery, an allowance for erection and testing could have it in use from the start of the 1955 season. A £12,234 tender for supplying and installing the equipment plus approval for £3,750 for ancillary works and contingencies was sanctioned in October (*Torbay Express*, 28 July/31 October 1953).

Work on the upgrade started twelve months later. By the time the railway reopened on 21 May 1955, once again a few weeks later than planned, the car bodies and undercarriages, the motor and control equipment had all been replaced. With the new equipment, the railway ran at 500ft per minute, up from 320ft. AC power from the mains was converted to DC to drive the new 100hp motor. The cars could carry forty passengers (fourteen seated, twenty-six standing), double the number of the old ones. The work was overseen by J. & E. Hall Ltd of Dartford, Kent, who employed local company Hilary Hurtley & Company to supply additional labour (*Torbay Express*, 12 October 1954/18 January 1955/*Torquay Times*, 18 March 1955).

Nothing else was reported about any further work, so the council delivered what had started off as a £60,000 scheme for less than half that. During the post-war British seaside holiday boom more than half a million passengers were regularly carried each year. The capital debt was repaid during the 1960s, enabling surpluses to be transferred to the rates fund, more than £9,000 in 1966 and 1967. A total of £4,000 was allocated for unspecified repairs in 1967 and £15,000 for track renewal in 1972 (*Torbay Express*, 6 October 1958/18 August 1961/23 January 1964/7 March/13 June 1967/19 January 1972).

A few weeks after services had been resumed in 1955 an accident that could have had serious consequences occurred, when William Arthur Barnett (1920–87), one of the lift's employees, broke his knee when he slipped, fell through the upper station's machine room trapdoor and fell 20ft. He had to go to court before the council agreed to award him £225 in damages (*Torbay Express*, 15 June/*Torquay Times*, 28 September 1955).

A development that took place a long way from Babbacombe occurred on 14 July 1971 that had a minor impact on the railway's legal status. On that date, the Torbay Corporation Act, 1971, received royal assent and by article 161 thereof, the 1923 and 1951 Light Railway Orders were re-enacted and references to the former town council became references to the corporation. (Torbay had been created by the amalgamation of Torquay, Paignton, Brixham and other areas in 1968. The purpose of the Act was to re-enact local enactments in force within the enlarged authority and to confirm that the new authority had the various powers held by its predecessors.)

In 1983, a tenacious local resident brought the railway into line with other forms of transport when it came to using the council-issued tokens that could be used on buses and trains, but it took some effort. Asking in June 1982, John Lambert, barely able to walk following a stroke, was told that his request had merit but that it was too late in the season to be introduced immediately. But the tokens were still not accepted when the railway reopened in 1983. Asking again, he was told that tokens could not be accepted. The correspondence had been lost, he was told when seeking an explanation. A further appeal produced the desired result, though, the council replying that the tokens could be accepted, with immediate effect. Tenacity pays (*Torbay Express*, 1 June 1983).

More than thirty years after the railway's post-war restoration it started to become clear that it required more than routine maintenance. In August 1988 passengers

The cars that entered service in 1955 did so in the council's maroon livery, with its crest on the sides. This livery was short-lived and was soon replaced by an attractive blue scheme that was also applied to the station buildings. (J. Salmon Ltd)

had to be evacuated when the cars jammed near the halfway point. A sudden stop in June 1990 was resolved after twenty minutes but it had followed a breakdown the week before. In October, £40,000 was budgeted for emergency repairs but it was November 1991 before Hocking & Company, track specialist of Cardiff, started work to renew the track and the car wheels. The 1951 economy measure of turning the rails had given them another forty years of life. The work eventually cost £60,000 (*Torbay Express*, 25 August 1988/1 June/17 October 1990/15 April 1992/2 December 1991/*South Wales Echo*, 12 November 1991).

Also replaced after forty years were the 1955 cars and carriages, with new vehicles made by H. H. Martyn & Company in Cheltenham in 1995 and costing £35,000. The builder was more accustomed to making architectural lift cages. For Babbacombe, they had designed cars with more glass and non-slip floors and had applied the council's turquoise and gold livery externally. The railway was reopened on 12 April (*Torbay Express*, 29/30 March/13 April 1995).

A sudden-stop incident in 2003, in which passengers were stranded for two hours and one of them was injured, ultimately caused the railway to be overhauled and transferred to new management. It ran for the remainder of the 2003 season but became very unreliable during 2004. In November 2005 a £571,000 refurbishment programme was started, replacing the track and the cars and installing a new control system. One of the undercarriages was damaged when it was being reinstalled and had to be replaced, delaying the reopening (*WalesOnLine*, 30 June 2003/*Funimag photoblog*, 27 November 2005).

Local uncertainty about the railway's future earlier in 2005 had led to the formation of the Friends of Babbacombe Cliff Railway to promote it and encourage its use. It soon had more than 400 members. As the council wished to be relieved of responsibility for running the railway, the friends registered the

One of the 1995-built cars photographed in this teal and yellow livery on 19 May 2004. (Tony Martin)

The upper station. This and the following photographs were taken on 10 August 2023.

1926 BABBACOMBE CLIFF LIGHT RAILWAY • 181

Babbacombe Cliff Railway Community Interest Company, and took a forty-year lease on it, a development authorised by the Babbacombe Cliff Railway Order, made on 15 April 2009. The Ministry of Transport Regulations of 1926 and 1955 were revoked and the CIC was authorised to charge fares.

The change of management took effect on 1 August 2009, when a symbolic handover took place, the 'grand reopening' taking place on 6 March 2010. Under the new regime, the season was extended and a Heritage Lottery Fund grant was obtained to establish a visitor centre on the beach. The company changed its status to that of Charitable Incorporated Organisation in 2019 (*Herald Express*, 30 July 2009).

A tragedy occurred on 4 September 2022, when the railway's 79-year-old engineer, retired lift engineer Cyril David Smith, was killed when he was on the track during maintenance and the cars were set in motion. At the time of writing, in 2024, the inquest has not been held and the result of the Health & Safety Executive's investigation into the accident has not been published. However, a month after the accident the HSE did serve two improvement notices on the operator, having found shortcomings in the railway's communications systems and in its maintenance (*itvX*, 5 September / *New Civil Engineer*, 13 September 2022 / *DevonLive*, 11 May 2023 / 24 April 2024).

As well as bringing the subjects of the HSE's notices into compliance, a refurbishment programme was put in place, which included replacing rail and sleepers. The railway reopened on 16 July 2023 (*DevonLive*, 28 June / 18 August).

The upper station interior, also providing a glimpse of a car interior.

The profile of the lower station with a car on the road bridge.

Seen from a descending car, the lower station at high tide.

1926 BABBACOMBE CLIFF LIGHT RAILWAY • 183

Unloading at the lower station.

A car near the upper station.

184 • CLIFF RAILWAYS: AN HISTORIC SURVEY

CHAPTER 25

1927 FALCON CLIFF HOTEL LIFT II, DOUGLAS

Opened 1927, 5ft gauge, single track, 129ft long, gradient 1 in 1.15, electric, closed 1990.

Thirty years after the Falcon Cliff lift was dismantled and sold, a new Falcon Cliff lift was installed on a different site, to the south of the first one, accessed from Palace View Terrace, use of the original site having been blocked by later development.

As a private venture it attracted no press attention. The equipment was supplied by Messrs Wadsworth & Sons of Bolton, who supplied goods lifts to the GWR and probably other railway companies. A single-car system, it was erected by a Jack Morgan of Croydon and was in use by April 1927, when the hotel's advertisements mentioned that there was an 'electric lift from Prom'. The car carried six passengers. The controller was upgraded in 1934 and in 1950 the power supply was upgraded. In the early 1960s more than 2,000 passengers a day were carried at peak times. But times were changing and when the hotel was sold in 1990, and later converted to offices, the lift was taken out of use and abandoned.

Below left: A view of the lift soon after it had entered service, before nature had started to assert its dominance on the locality.

Below right: Seen on 13 August 1965, the hotel had erected an illuminated sign to draw attention to its lift. (Alan Bowler)

Above left: The car at the lower station, also in 1965. (Alan Bowler)

Above right: When the author visited in 1975 the upper station was hidden from view from below.

In April 1993 it was possible to place the lift in context with the hotel.

186 • CLIFF RAILWAYS: AN HISTORIC SURVEY

The entrance to the upper station on 26 August 1995.

The motor and winding gear at the upper station in 1995.

1927 FALCON CLIFF HOTEL LIFT II, DOUGLAS • 187

CHAPTER 26

1929 SCARBOROUGH, ST NICHOLAS LIFT

Opened 5 August 1929, gauge 7ft 6in, double track, gradient 1 in 1.33, electric, closed February 2007.

Scarborough's fourth and fifth cliff railways were late on the cliff railway scene and came about because the council wished to improve the town's facilities for tourists. The St Nicholas lift also resulted in a stand-off between the council and the Ministry of Health, which had taken over the Local Government Board's function of approving local authority borrowing.

Council approval was given to the lift in January 1927, with a rider that its cost was not to exceed £5,500, which required borrowing approval. After an inquiry in March, permission was refused on the basis that it was unjustified by the traffic, which might seem to be a reasonable conclusion as the proposed location was at the other end of the Grand Hotel from the existing Central Tramway (*Yorkshire Post*, 25 January/5 March/22 April 1927).

The council was not to be deterred, though, and made another application in 1928, ensuring that the Ministry's inquiry was held in the summer as it was certain that the larger crowds would persuade the inspector. But once again, the application was refused, because 'the need for an additional lift at this particular spot has not been established' (*Yorkshire Evening Post*, 14 August/*Leeds Mercury*, 26 September 1928).

Furious at what he perceived as the Ministry overreaching its authority and imposing its will on the town, the mayor arranged for a company to be formed that would lease the relevant land and build and operate the lift while agreeing not to make a profit and to sell the undertaking to the council at cost price after three years. This would 'convey to the Ministry evidence of the determination of the Council', he declared.

The St Nicholas Cliff Lift Company commissioned Medway's Safety Lift Company to build its lift. This was a constituent of J. & E. Hall Ltd, a Kent-based company that had previously done work in the Grand Hotel. Opening on the August bank holiday, during its first full week of operation, it carried 41,000 passengers (*Leeds Mercury*, 13 January 1923/*Yorkshire Post*, 3/8 January/*Leeds Mercury*, 16 August 1929).

The 1939 25in Survey of the area with the Grand Hotel in the centre, the Central Tramway on one side and the St Nicholas lift on the other. It is no wonder that the Central Tramway Company objected. (Ordnance Survey)

Far left: The lift being operated soon after it had been opened; the postcard was published in 1930. The track was laid on a concrete structure connected to the platform constructed to create the space required for the upper station. (J. Valentine)

Left: The lift from street level in 1963. The attendant had the benefit of a small kiosk but little protection was provided for passengers. Some art deco features were included in the gates and panels. (J. H. Meredith)

The lift in operation with the South Bay sands and the harbour in the background. Pelmets had been mounted over the door mechanism, presumably to protect it from the weather. (Photo Precision Ltd)

1929 SCARBOROUGH, ST NICHOLAS LIFT • 189

Right: A view from across the road in August 1982. The image shows one of the 1975-built cars; they had a different window layout and were painted a different shade of green.

Far right: Cars stabled at the lower station after the lift's closure. By this time the cars had been painted blue.

Below: The entrance to the upper station, also in August 1982. The date that the cover was erected to connect the kiosk with the lift platform and improve, slightly, passenger facilities, is unknown. The location of the South Cliff Tramway is indicated.

190 • CLIFF RAILWAYS: AN HISTORIC SURVEY

The upper station repurposed as a café, including both cars, on 23 June 2024. Also shown is the concrete structure on which the upper station was built and how the space for the station was achieved.

The lift being purchased by the council in 1945, the cars were replaced in 1975 and removed for overhaul in 2000. Otherwise, the lift ran without reported issues until 2007, when it required £445,000 expenditure. Following the precedent set at the North Bay in 1997, it was closed, but it was not demolished. The track and cars were left in situ, and the station sites were leased as refreshment outlets, the upper station site incorporating the cars into its seating area. Since 2015 the council has earned £6,000 a year from the lower station lease (*Scarborough Evening News*, 11 April 2000/CPH Property brochure, 2023).

The view offered to customers seated in one of the repurposed cars.

The lower station façade and the cars incorporated into a café at the upper station, seen on 23 June 2024. In 2015–16 the façade had been incorporated into a retail outlet with a roof terrace. The façade had lost the charm of its art deco features when the steelwork was replaced on an unknown date before closure. A new tenant is, at the time of writing, being sought for the lower station.

CHAPTER 27

1930 SCARBOROUGH, NORTH BAY LIFT

Opened 21 July 1930, gauge 6ft 6in, double track, 166ft long, gradient 1 in 2, electric, closed 1996.

Scarborough Town Council agreed to consider the construction of a cliff railway on the North Cliff in 1928. It was at the time developing the area, extending the promenade, and building new attractions, including an open-air swimming pool and the North Bay Railway.

Two years later, the estimate was £6,467 9s 6d for the lift and £554 11 6d for the shelters proposed to be built with the lower station. Unlike the St Nicholas lift, the Ministry of Health approved the borrowing. The Medway's Safety Lift division of J. & E. Hall & Company received the contract, and the lift was opened on 21 July 1930 (*Yorkshire Post*, 20 February / *Leeds Mercury*, 22 July 1930).

The stations and shelters were built of concrete in the art deco style. The cars, similar to those on the St Nicholas lift, were painted red and had the council crest on the sides. They could carry up to thirty passengers. The cars were replaced circa 1975.

No reported incidents affecting the lift have been found and its end came in 1997, when a government-induced spending

The lift soon after it had been opened in 1930. The cars were painted red, with the council's crest applied to the sides. There is a short queue of prospective patrons but there was no undercover accommodation for them while they waited. (J. Valentine)

1930 SCARBOROUGH, NORTH BAY LIFT • 193

The lift in action on 11 August 1963, by which time the cars had been painted green. (J. H. Meredith)

The lower station is seen from the upper station in this postcard view. (Bamforth & Company)

194 • CLIFF RAILWAYS: AN HISTORIC SURVEY

reduction left the council £566,000 short of its budget projections. To meet the shortfall, it had to cut services or increase charges, or both. The lift was in the firing line as not only was it being run at a loss, but the cars required £15,000 expenditure immediately and the lift required £45,000 spending on it in 1998. That it had been becoming run down is indicated by a 1993 report that planning approval for a nearby golf course included a requirement to renovate the lift. Letters in the press during 1997 also complained that the area around the lift and other North Bay attractions were run down. So, the lift did not reopen for 1997 and by June was looking 'tatty and desperately forlorn', the cars stabled halfway up the slope with their doors removed (*Modern Tramway*, May 1993 / *Scarborough Evening News*, 18 January / 11 June / 31 July 1997).

Launceston Civic Society came up with the idea of finding a new home for the lift, saying that it could be used to improve access to the Cornish town's Norman castle. The council agreed and donated it to the society, which paid the £6,000 cost of demolition, so it was a donation with a sting in the tail. At the same time that it donated the lift, the council declined two local cash offers for it, one of them for £2,000 made by Yorkshire businessman Simon Boak, who thought that a new use could be found for it within the county. The components were removed in February 1998. Subsequently, the buildings were demolished, and the area landscaped. Launceston still awaits its functioning lift (*Scarborough Evening News*, 11 January / 9 July / *Western Morning News*, 25 February 1998).

The cars were replaced in the 1970s, the new bodies having a flat roof, unlike those introduced on the St Nicholas lift at the same time. By 1982 this rather plain livery had been adopted but the cars had been painted red again before the line was closed.

CHAPTER 28

1935 BOURNEMOUTH, SOUTHBOURNE (FISHERMAN'S WALK) LIFT

Opened 8 June 1935, gauge 5ft 8in, double track, 128ft long, gradient 1 in 1.49, electric, operational.

Located 2 miles to the east of Bournemouth's former East Cliff lift, the Southbourne lift was the third built by Bournemouth Town Council. There had been calls for a lift to be provided at this end of the borough when the East and West Cliff lifts were proposed but they were rejected in favour of improving a road to the beach (*Bournemouth Daily Echo*, 4 November 1904).

The council's beach committee's proposal for plans and estimates for a lift to be prepared for consideration was accepted in May 1931 but it was not until June 1934 that the borough engineer was instructed to proceed with its construction, with a view to it entering service in 1935. The estimated cost was £7,000 (*Bournemouth Graphic*, 8 May 1931 / 9 June 1934).

The lift under construction.

Above left: The lift in operation. The splendid station windows have not survived.

Above right: The lift in operation on 16 September 1959. (J. H. Meredith)

One of the cars at the upper station in the later 1930s. The lift had been opened without ceremony but the local councillor made sure that she was the first in the queue for tickets. (Sun Ray Series)

1935 BOURNEMOUTH, SOUTHBOURNE (FISHERMAN'S WALK) LIFT • 197

The lift on 9 August 2023. The following photographs were taken on the same date.

The cars crossing.

198 • CLIFF RAILWAYS: AN HISTORIC SURVEY

Construction was carried out by the council's own labour and the lift was opened as intended in 1935. Connecting Fisherman's Walk with the Southbourne and Boscombe promenades, in use it has become known as the Fisherman's Walk lift. Once again, no account of the opening has been found. The Express Lift Company provided the equipment, including a 21hp 500v DC winding motor that was replaced by a three-phase system in the 1960s. 'Standard' cars, the same as those used on the other Bournemouth lifts, were installed in 1978. The track was replaced in 1993.

Looking down on the lower station.

The east-track car at the upper station.

1935 BOURNEMOUTH, SOUTHBOURNE (FISHERMAN'S WALK) LIFT • 199

CHAPTER 29

1979 LLECHWEDD SLATE CAVERNS

Opened 22 August 1979, gauge 3ft, 366ft long, gradient 1 in 2.79, electric, operational.

The lift at Llechwedd Slate Caverns, near Blaenau Ffestiniog, was the first to be built in Wales in the twentieth century. In 1972 Quarry Tours Ltd had commenced operating tours into some of the worked-out slate caverns using a short 2ft gauge railway and small carriages hauled by battery-powered locomotives. The venture was so successful that in 1979 the long queues at peak times were addressed by opening another tour into a deeper section of the mine. To do so they repurposed one of the quarry's underground inclines as a passenger

The manrider unloading at the upper station in 1980. The removable side panels, which prevented passengers from extending their limbs while in motion, were not an original feature. The quarry's former engineer says that while the installation was a very good piece of equipment, with many safety features, it was built for the world of coal mining and clearly installed by people used to that environment. To ensure the best alignment, the platforms were built after the car had been placed on the rails. The guard's compartment, at the lower end, is left open, so that he can operate a pull cable that runs along the side of the tunnel and stop the winder if anything should happen.

200 • CLIFF RAILWAYS: AN HISTORIC SURVEY

lift, using a purpose-built stepped, four-compartment, 'manrider' built by Tredomen Engineering Ltd, a subsidiary of the National Coal Board based in South Wales that supplied the coal industry. In 2017 the vehicle was overhauled by Clayton Equipment Ltd and returned with a new superstructure on 5 February the following year. (Manrider is the term used by personnel at Llechwedd to refer to the passenger car.)

The manrider about to be loaded at the upper station. By this time it had been painted blue and the method of securing the passengers had been altered. (J. Arthur Dixon)

The manrider being lifted out for overhaul and rebodying at the Burton upon Trent works of Clayton Equipment Ltd on 6 November 2017. It had been painted yellow since around 1990. (Jon Knowles)

1979 LLECHWEDD SLATE CAVERNS • 201

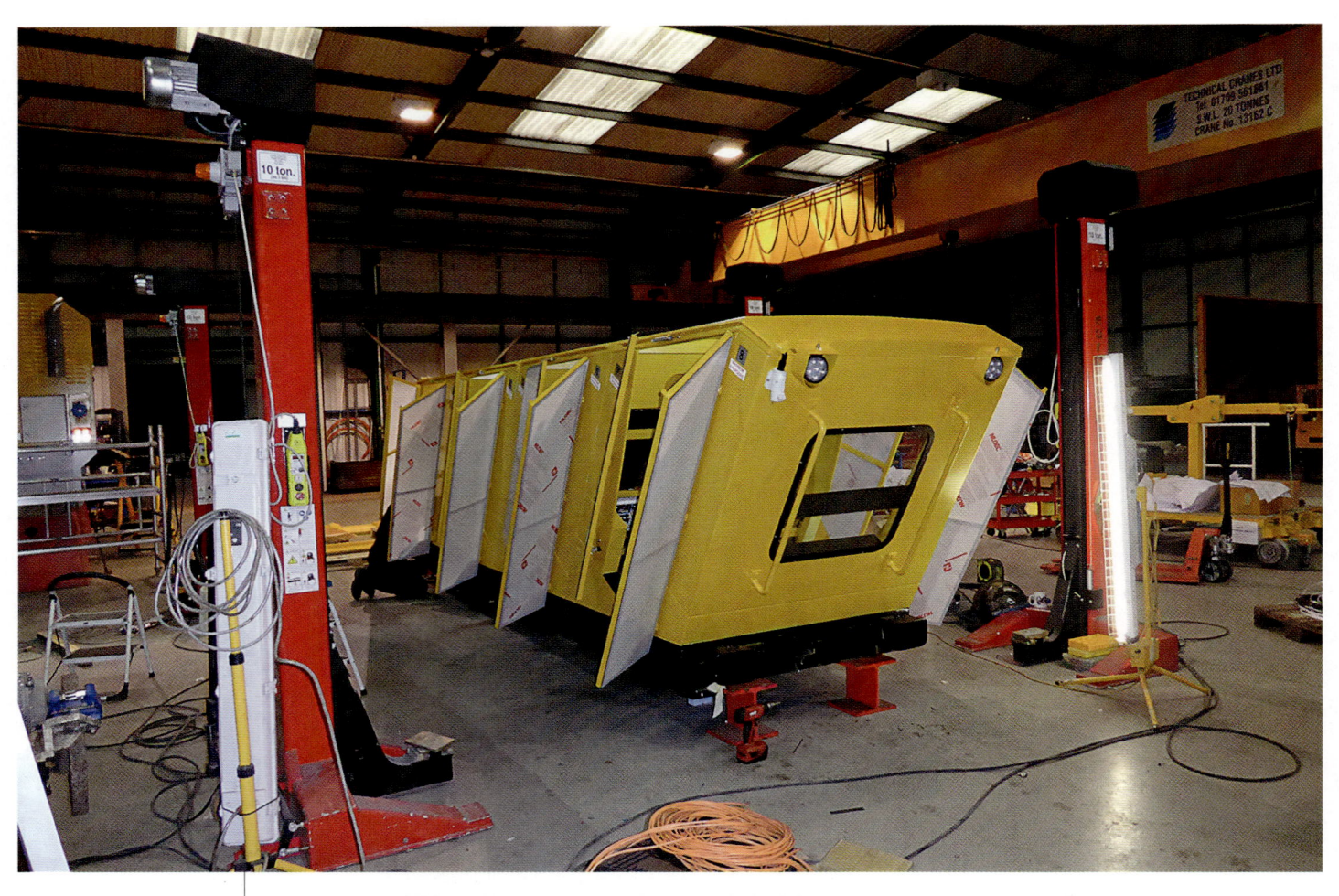

The refurbished manrider at Clayton Equipment on 3 February 2018, when the final pre-delivery inspection was made. (Jon Knowles)

Named *Y Ddraig Llechi* (*The Slate Dragon*), the manrider arrives at the upper station on 5 October 2023.

202 • CLIFF RAILWAYS: AN HISTORIC SURVEY

CHAPTER 30

1992 CENTRE FOR ALTERNATIVE TECHNOLOGY LIFT, LLWYNGWERN

Opened 7 July 1992, 5ft 6in gauge, double track, 197ft long, gradient 1 in 1.81, water balance, operational. Closed 9 November 2023.

The Centre for Alternative Technology was opened on a 7-acre site in the former Llwyngwern slate quarry in 1973, devoted to demonstrating and teaching sustainable development. The quarry is located in the Dulas valley about 3 miles from Machynlleth, and was once served by the Corris Railway.

Wishing to improve its access for visitors, the water-balanced lift was provided to provide a link with the car park. In 1990 the centre had launched a £1 million share issue to raise funding for the lift and other developments. Opened in 1992, it was the first water-balanced lift built in Britain since the Metropole lift at Folkestone in 1904. The cars were built by the Lancastrian Carriage & Wagon Company in Heysham. With visitor numbers failing to return to pre-pandemic levels, the centre was closed to day visitors on 9 November 2023 (*Liverpool Daily Post*, 4 January 1990/8 July 1992/BBC, 9 November 2023).

One weekend in April 1992 the author visited the Centre for Alternative Technology to see how the new lift was developing. The stations were unfinished and one of the cars had still to be delivered.

As built, the cars were quite stylish. Another view in April 1992.

The lift a few days after it had been opened, although the upper station was still incomplete.

Cars passing, seen from the viewing platform that is no longer accessible to the public.

The interior during an ascent on 13 September 2023.

1992 CENTRE FOR ALTERNATIVE TECHNOLOGY LIFT, LLWYNGWERN • **205**

One of the cars close to the upper station in 2023. The secondary roof, which will reduce the noise slightly when operating in the rain, had been added by 2007. The cars were also painted all-over green for a while.

The cars passing, seen from below. Named *Annie* and *Martha*, the cars are named after the first person to travel on the railway.

206 • CLIFF RAILWAYS: AN HISTORIC SURVEY

APPENDICES

Cars crossing on the upper section of the Great Orme Tramway on 5 July 1913. See Page 212.

APPENDIX 1
UNBUILT CLIFF RAILWAYS

From time to time various newspapers made a single reference to a proposed cliff railway that was not taken forward. Two unfulfilled proposals that obtained powers were for lines at Malvern (Malvern [Funicular] Light Railway Order, 1911), and Ventnor (Ventnor Inclined Light Railway Order, 1898). In November 1891 the Folkestone, Sandgate & Hythe Tramway Company deposited a Bill that included a clause authorising the construction of a cliff railway between Sandgate and Shorncliffe camp, but that clause was not included in the company's 1892 Act.

The summit of the 1,394ft Worcestershire Beacon was the target of two 3ft 6in-gauge railways authorised by the Malvern (Funicular) Light Railway Order. The longer would have been on this, the Malvern side, 670 yards long, and it would have been joined by a line from West Malvern, on the far side, 440 yards long. No details have been found of a scheme said to have been proposed in the 1880s. Another one put forward in 1900 quickly petered out.

The 1910 proposal was the initiative of the Malvern Improvement Association, but it was developed by Charles Cecil Broad (1869–1941), a local contractor, who also made the Light Railway Order application. No action was taken once the order had been made and an application to revive the powers in 1919 seems to have fizzled out. (Tilley & Son)

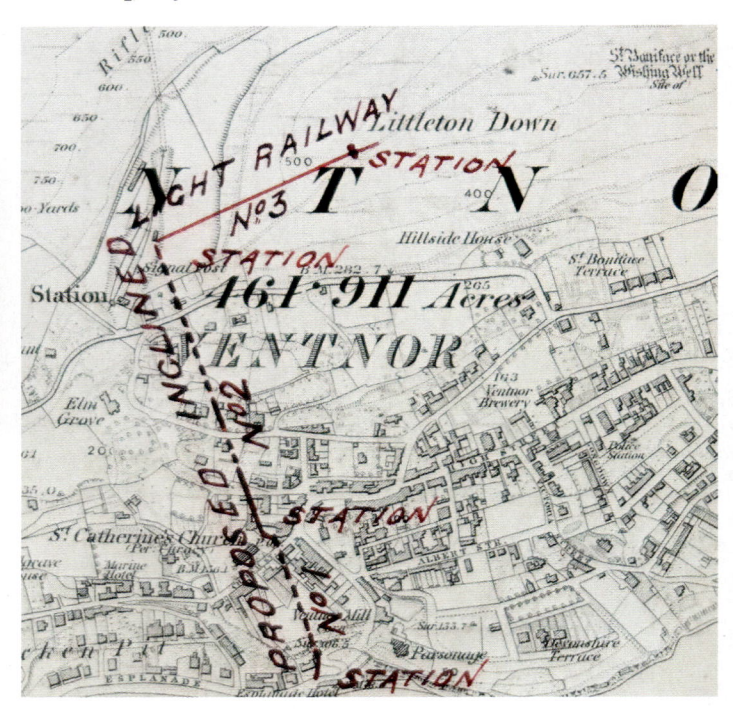

The application for Ventnor Inclined Light Railway Order was made by Ernest George Henry Wetherick (1857–1928) and John George Sinclair Coghill (1834–99) acting on a suggestion made by a W. C. Mallaby. The gauge would have been 5ft 9in and the three railways would have been water-balanced systems. (National Archives)

Ventnor looking westwards with the site of the lower station of Railway No. 1 indicated. It would have run in tunnel to a central station near St Catherine's churchyard and been 172 yards long. Railway No. 2 would have started 50ft away and would have been 385 yards long, on a viaduct for 63 yards and in tunnel for 325 yards before terminating in the yard of the Isle of Wight Railway station. (F. Frith)

St Boniface Down viewed from Ventnor pier with the site of the proposed lower station indicated. (J. Welch & Sons)

Railway No. 3 was intended to start close to the point indicated and run for 290 yards on a gradient of 1 in 2.5. Railway No. 3 was withdrawn when the order was submitted to the Board of Trade for confirmation over a disagreement with the landowner over whether it should be permitted to be built before the landowner had reached agreement with Ventnor Town Council to convey the Down as a public recreation ground. No action was taken to put the order into effect after it had been made.

APPENDIX 2

BABBACOMBE CLIFF LIGHT RAILWAY ESTIMATE OF EXPENSES 1923

Babbacombe Cliff Light Railway
Estimate of Expenses

							£ s d
1	Preliminary expenses						200
2	Length of railway	1 furlong 1 chain					
	Gauge	5 feet 10 inches					
	Construction of Line		Cubic Yards	Price per yard	£ s d	£ s d	
	Clearing site of trees				50		
	Cuttings	Rock					
		Soft soil	2,182	5/-	545 10		
		Roads					
		Total			**595 10**		**595 10**
	Embankments including roads	– cubic yards					
	Bridges	– Public roads	– Number			101	
	Accommodation bridges and works						
	Viaducts					1,178	
	Culverts and drains					119	
	Metalling of roads and approach road, and level crossing					200	
	Gatekeeper's house at level crossing						
	Permanent way including fencing					1,180	
	(1 furlong 1 chain, cost per mile £13,091)						
	Permanent way foundations					1,790	
	Permanent way for sidings and cost of junctions						
	Stations and buildings					1,246	
	Plant including signalling and telegraph apparatus						
	Electrical equipment (including posts cables wires &c. but not including rolling stock)					119	

		£ s d
		6,553
		7,348 10
	Contingencies at 10 per cent	734 1 7
	Total for construction of railway	8,083 7
	Total cost of construction an of acquisition of land and buildings	
3	Rolling stock	1,551
4	Equipment for operating railway and house for same	3,630
5	Generating stations or sub-stations	
6	General charges	
7	Interest on capital during construction	
8	Sundries	
Total amount to be charged to capital		£13,354 7 0

DATED this 27th day of July 1923
Henry A. Garrett
Borough Surveyor
[Standard form used, not all fields applicable or used]

Oddicombe Bay with the lift station as first constructed.

APPENDIX 3

CABLE TRAMWAYS

Before electric traction became capable of dealing with steeper gradients, cable-hauled tramways were built in several towns and cities, of which only the Great Orme Tramway survives. Of particular interest in the context of this book is the Matlock undertaking, which was a Newnes/Marks venture. Glasgow was notable for having a cable-hauled subway.

Edinburgh

Above: The first cable trams in Edinburgh, which had the most extensive network of such trams in Britain, were operated by Edinburgh Northern Tramways from 1888. Edinburgh Corporation took over all the networks in 1919 and electrified the remaining cable routes by 1923. The Portobello route, seen here in 1913, had been opened in 1898 and was one of the routes converted to electric operation in 1923. (J. Valentine)

Great Orme Tramway

The only cable tramway still operating in Britain, the Great Orme Tramway, was opened in two sections, each about ½ mile long, in 1902 and 1903. The undertaking was founded by the Great Orme Tramways Company and passed to the Great Orme Railway Ltd in 1935, after the first had been unable to meet the liabilities arising from a fatal accident in 1932. The local authority took it over in 1939. The photograph shows one of the cars on the lower section. (Carl Newman)

This posed view shows one of the cars on the upper section in 1903, probably before the line was opened.

212 • CLIFF RAILWAYS: AN HISTORIC SURVEY

London

London had two cable tram routes, one north of the Thames, at Highgate, and one south of the river, at Brixton. The first operated from 1884 to 1909, the second from 1892 to 1904. This is one of the Highgate trams. In Brixton, below, four-wheeled 'tractors' hauled the old horse tram trailers.

Matlock Cable Tramway

Opened in 1893, the Matlock Cable Tramway was a mere ½ mile long, its prime function to carry the infirm from the centre of the Derbyshire town to Matlock Bank, on its edge, where a number of health establishments had been opened. The idea had been suggested in the 1860s but it required the drive, and capital, of publisher George Newnes, who had been born in the town, and the engineer G. C. Marks, to bring it into effect. However, it was not profitable, so in 1896 Newnes bought out the other shareholders and donated it to the council. It ran it until 1927, when it was closed and replaced by a bus service. The 3ft 6in gauge tramway had three cars, two in use and one spare. The photograph shows one of the cars at the Crown Square terminus in 1912. (J. Valentine)

Swansea Constitution Hill

Very little is known about the short-lived Swansea Constitution Hill Incline Tramway but access to digitised newspapers has uncovered more.

Its promoter was William Bonfield Westlake (1838–1909), a Swansea businessman. The contractors were Thomas Oliver Dixon and his brother Walter John Dixon, of Woody Bay, Devon, who failed to complete the contract despite having been paid, forcing Westlake to finish it himself. The flotation of a company to run the tramway failed, both events contributing to Westlake's bankruptcy in 1900.

The engineer was Charles Tamlin Ruthen (1871–1926), an architect who moved from South Shields to Swansea to be assistant surveyor in 1890; he subsequently designed many of Swansea's more notable buildings. In private practice from 1896, he worked with Westlake on several projects and had married one of his daughters in 1894. He had been a member of the Institution of Mechanical Engineers from 1897.

The tramway failed its Board of Trade inspection and required alterations to its brakes and a further inspection before it could be opened on 27 August 1898. Then it enjoyed a few hours of operation, carrying many passengers, before a clutch failed and services had to be suspended for several days. The resumption of services was not reported, and it was several months before the *Herald of Wales* (12 November 1898) could report that it was running reliably.

Less than ¼ mile long, the 3ft 6in-gauge line was always going to be a struggle to cover its costs, its 1 in 5 gradient notwithstanding. In 1903 Swansea Corporation's £150 offer to buy it was refused in favour of one that resulted in it being dismantled for scrap. The winding house was demolished in June, and the rails lifted three years later. The 'last balance sheet', presumably for 1902, estimated the number of passengers carried at 170,000, receipts £423 15s and expenses £466. A short-lived and painful existence for a short line (*South Wales Daily News*, 29 August/3 September 1898/*Cambria Daily Leader*, 19 October 1900/22 June 1903/30 August 1906/*Herald of Wales*, 13 June 1903/*South Wales Daily Post*, 2 May 1911).

CABLE TRAMWAYS • 213

Upper Douglas Tramway

Opened in 1896, the Upper Douglas Tramway was the work of the Isle of Man Tramways & Electric Power Company, which then also owned the horse tramway and the Manx Electric Railway. With cable haulage adopted to overcome the gradients, the 1.57 mile-long, 3ft-gauge route looped around Douglas from Loch Promenade, seen here, to the Broadway, although the latter connection went unmade. Following the company's failure in 1900 the Douglas lines were acquired by Douglas Corporation and when the cable route required a structural overhaul in 1929 the council preferred to close it and substitute buses. (G. & Company)

The late Keith Pearson, an enthusiast for trams and tramways but particularly those on the Isle of Man, discovered the derelict remains of two Upper Douglas cable cars and used the best of both to create one restored vehicle. It has been demonstrated on the horse tramway several times, and was photographed here at its junction with Victoria Street, along which it once ran, on 9 July 1998.

APPENDIX 4

ELECTRIC STAIRWAYS

From 1901 the UK agent of the US-based Reno Inclined Elevator Construction Syndicate installed several electric stairways around Britain, mainly in seaside resorts. They were not railways, of course, but one of them was a precursor to a cliff railway. They had all fallen out of use by 1910, the cost of repairs not being justified. Illustrated here are those installed at seaside resorts.

Clacton

The Clacton stairway was first proposed in 1901 and it was opened on 28 June 1902. In September a 7-year-old girl got her hand trapped in the handrail and lost a portion of the third finger of her left hand. It had gone out of use by February 1908, when the town's improvement committee proposed removing it and selling its components. (Raphael Tuck & Sons)

Southend-on-Sea

The Reno stairway at Southend. Its outline history is to be found in Chapter 22. (J. Valentine)

Seen on the left of this 1907 image, a small queue is gathered at the Reno entrance, a board asking 'Why walk? Quickest way to the railway station and the cliff band'. (J. Valentine)

Tynemouth

The Reno stairway at Tynemouth was opened on 19 May 1902. Unlike the other seaside stairways that were installed by agreement with the local authorities, that at Tynemouth was installed for the operator of the Palace entertainment complex, John Harper Graham (1839–1923). No report has been found of it being taken out of use but there is no reason to expect that it lasted longer than any of the others. (B. Graham)

APPENDIX 5
STEEP-GRADE RAILWAYS

Systems that are not located on cliffs, but which share characteristics with cliff railways in their operation, are included here.

Cairngorm Mountain Railway

The Cairngorm Mountain Railway is a 1¼ mile-long balanced lift that opened in 2001, replacing an earlier chairlift, and carrying passengers from Cairngorm base, 8 miles from Aviemore, altitude 2,083ft, to the plateau at 3,599ft. Single track with a passing place, its track gauge is 2m and its maximum gradient is 1 in 2.5. Its structure comprises ninety-four linked bridges of varying height. During the winter sport season, the single-car trains run twice the speed that they run during the rest of the year, 11mph. This view is of the track just above base station.

An investigation in 2019 found that the structure's condition was 'disappointing' for its age and that it needed strengthening. The original contractor and designer paid £11 million compensation and £25 million of repairs were carried out before it reopened on 26 January 2023. On 25 August 2023, however, would-be passengers, including the author, were told that having failed its routine daily safety checks the railway had been closed. It was subsequently announced that many of the scarf joints installed during the repair programme were out of tolerance. At the time of writing, in June 2024, no date had been set for the railway's reopening.

The railway's two cars and its operating system were supplied by the Austrian Doppelmayr company. One of the cars is seen confined to the base station after the railway had been closed on 25 August 2023.

Devil's Dyke Railway

The South Downs to the north of Brighton, a National Park since 2010, became popular with sightseers during the eighteenth century; it is claimed that the wealds of Surrey, Sussex, Hampshire, Kent, Berkshire and Oxfordshire are visible from its highest point. A change in ownership of the land around the Devil's Dyke, a 300ft-deep dry gully 5 miles from the coast, in 1882 saw increased efforts made to attract visitors. The Brighton & Dyke Railway was opened in 1887 and James Henry Hubbard, a Canadian born in 1847, the proprietor of the Dyke Park Hotel since 1892, installed attractions, a switchback railway, a bicycle railway and an 'aerial flight' across the Dyke, to encourage them. With the branch railway, access from the south was easily achieved but access from villages to the north was circuitous. Hence the steep-grade railway that was opened by Sir Henry Howorth, the local MP, on 24 July 1897.

The twin-track, 3ft-gauge line was 840ft long with gradients varying from 1 in 8 through to 1 in 5 in the middle and 1 in 2.9 at the top, and the cars were quite unlike any others used in Britain. The winding house was at the upper station, along with two raised platforms. No facilities were provided at the lower station, less than ½ mile from Poynings. A 24hp Hornsby oil engine powered the system. The contractors were Messrs Courtney & Brewer, the engineer Charles Oliver Blaber (1837–1912), who had also been responsible for the branch line (*Morning Post*, 26 July 1897).

The railway had been built by the Pyramidical Syndicate Ltd on land leased for £100 a year. It sold the railway, which had cost £3,400 to build, to a company that it had formed, the Brighton Steep Grade Railway Company, for £9,000. The company was one of several floated by the Syndicate, the only one that survived being the Southend Kursaal amusement park (*London Evening Standard*, 14 March 1899).

The postcard view shows the upper station with one of the cars. (Mezzotint Company)

The railway was clearly no great success, for on 13 December 1900 it was, by order of the Court of Chancery, put up for sale as a going concern by auction but withdrawn when it failed to reach its reserve, bidding having stopped at £390 (*Southern Weekly News*, 15 December 1900).

In November 1901, one of the shareholders sued the directors, claiming that they were liable under the Directors' Liability Act, 1890, for misstatements contained in the prospectus issued in April 1897, wherein a photograph showed the railway fenced in and with ornamental stations, implying that they existed when they did not, claiming also that the debentures were a first charge on the undertaking, when an unpaid vendors' lien existed, and that construction was nearly complete, which it was not.

Ruling that one of the directors, the only one represented in court, a retired general, was not guilty of any intention to mislead as he had relied on others for information and had believed the prospectus to be true, the judge ruled that he was liable for £300 plus interest under the terms of the Act. The other directors being undefended, the shareholder was informed that he could apply the judgment against them if he wished (*Tonbridge Free Press*, 9 November 1901).

This view of Poyning's Holy Trinity church and the Dyke hill also shows the upper section of the tramway and the cars passing each other. (Palace Series)

The railway company was struck off and dissolved in 1902. The Dyke estate, including the railway, changed hands in 1904 and in 1906 they were leased to Maud Barrasford (1871–1925). She ran the railway until 1908, when she was advised that the cable required replacing. It was not run again (*London Gazette*, 18 November 1902/*Brighton Gazette*, 18 December 1912).

In 1912, despite her lease requiring her to keep the railway in good condition, Mrs Barrasford sold its components for £64. The claim against her and the purchaser, and his counter-claim against her, at Brighton Assizes took two days and resulted in what could be called a perverse verdict by the jury, which awarded only £5 and 3 farthings. The purchaser was awarded damages and costs but she was on the verge of bankruptcy; a receiving order was made against her in 1913 and she subsequently emigrated to Australia (*Brighton Gazette*, 18/20 December 1912).

This 1919 view of Poynings and the South Downs captured a part of the upper station. Its foundation slab remains in situ and the route of the short-lived tramway remains visible from the air, although partially obscured by subsequent tree planting. (J. Valentine)

Garden Festival Wales

The 1992 Garden Festival Wales was held on a former steel works site in Ebbw Vale, Gwent. As a part of the transport provision on the steeply graded site, WGH Transportation Engineering Ltd was commissioned to provide and build a 3ft 6in-gauge funicular on which ran two three-car trains. The single line, with passing place, was 920m long with a maximum gradient of 1 in 5 on the lower section easing to 1 in 8 on the upper. Its operation was contiguous with the festival, from 1 May to 4 October, during which more than 250,000 passengers were carried. After the festival ended the railway was dismantled.

Shipley Glen Tramway

To the north of the Yorkshire town of Saltaire, the area known as Shipley Glen became popular with visitors enjoying their increased leisure time there, particularly after a number of attractions were opened from the 1870s. In 1894 former publican Samuel Wilson (1856–1940) obtained permission to build a cable-worked railway into the glen. Mostly running parallel with an existing footpath, it was 386 yards long, the twin tracks 20in gauge. To compensate for the gradient, 1 in 12 at the lower end, easing to 1 in 20, the four cars were 9in higher at the rear, as shown in this postcard image. The line was opened on 18 May. At peak times it was so busy that the takings, all in coins and mostly in copper, had to be carried away in buckets (*Shipley Times*, 1 December 1894/20 April 1895). (Sun Series)

In 1905–07, the cars were rebuilt, the opportunity being taken to increase their capacity; one source gives 1912 for the rebuilding but a postcard photograph exists dated 1908. The wheelsets were also altered so that the cars ran parallel to the gradient. In this photograph the nearest car is advertising Bradford's Alhambra Theatre and the seatbacks on the further car the Princes Theatre. A gas lamp is suspended from the gantry.

Wilson retired in 1919 and the tramway was sold to John Edward Woodhead (1876-1955), who had experience with colliery winding engines. When he retired in 1928, it was taken over by two of his employees, Herbert and Patti Parr. They were noted for living in a caravan at the upper station and keeping chickens. They replaced the gas engine with an electric motor and rebuilt the platforms with stone and concrete, as seen in this 1950s photograph taken at the lower station. The tramway changed hands again in 1943, when a consortium of five Bradford businessmen formed Glen Tramway Ltd to run it, saying that they intended to develop it and celebrate its fiftieth anniversary in 1945 by floodlighting the track and decorating the cars with fairy lights. They appointed George Rushton (1888–1968) to run the tramway for them. There are no reports of any anniversary celebrations but the arrival of royal babies in the 1950s was marked by repainting the cars and naming them *Charles* and *Anne*, although this development probably followed the reconstruction of the cars with steel underframes in 1955/6. (R. B. Parr)

Several passengers were injured when the operator lost control when the cars were about 20 yards from the stations on 31 May 1966. The car that collided with the lower station was badly damaged and an axle was bent. The tramway was not operated for the remainder of the year, and by the time it was reopened on 5 June 1969 it had new owners, Glen Enterprises Ltd, another consortium. The upper station was rebuilt, the sleepers replaced, buffers installed at the lower station, the braking system improved, and the cable replaced. This green and yellow livery was adopted at the same time.

The new operator struggled to maintain the tramway and brought in Keighley & Worth Valley Railway volunteers to relay 200m of track in 1977 but much more was required. The landlord, now Bradford Metropolitan Council, was also pushing for the fence along the footpath boundary to be repaired. The company gave up in 1981 and surrendered its lease to the council. Faced with an estimated £10,000 cost to dismantle the tramway, the council instead took the imaginative step of offering the same amount as a grant towards its restoration to a new operator. The Bradford Trolleybus Association's offer, which included the use of volunteers, was accepted and after a great deal of work the tramway was reopened under the new management at Easter 1982. During its tenure, the BTA rebuilt and extended the stations, refurbished the winding equipment and built a new fence. It also strung bunting out on the cars, seen here in 1983.

The BTA, however, found it increasingly difficult to maintain the level of the volunteer support needed and in 1994 the lease was transferred to Michael J. Leak (born 1948), a Bradford man who had effectively managed the tramway for the BTA for several years. He ran the tramway with his wife and the support of volunteers until 31 December 2002. Under their management, the tramway's centenary was celebrated in 1995; one car on each track had been running with a roof since 1992. (N. Clifton)

STEEP-GRADE RAILWAYS • 219

The Glen Tramway Preservation Company, which had been registered in 2001 and become a charity in 2002, took over on 1 January 2003, Mr Leak training the volunteers in its maintenance and operation. The charity pays £10 a year for its 125-year repair-and-maintenance lease from Bradford Metropolitan District Council. The authority made a £25,000 grant for tramway purposes in 2003.

The first decade of the twenty-first century proved to be a difficult one for the tramway. A visit by the Health & Safety Executive on 21 August 2006 resulted in it being closed until the track spikes had been replaced by rail clips and coach bolts, which took until 7 January 2007. A report on requirements to make the tramway compliant with modern standards cost £2,473 and itemised work totalling £250,000. The clips and bolts, valued at £7,000, were donated by their manufacturer and supplier. A further three months of operations were lost in 2007 implementing HSE requirements. In September 2008 the insurance company gave three months' notice to equip each tram with a self-braking system, which resulted in the tramway being closed from January 2009 until July 2011. A Sheffield company rebuilt one car on each track and grants covered the £25,000 cost. Henceforth the tramway has operated with just a single car on each track.

The tramway survived a further year's closure because of the Covid pandemic. It has also survived without having to make a £250,000 investment in its infrastructure. The company runs many events to raise awareness of, and funds for, the tramway. It is indicative of the changed times in the Glen that in 2024 the tramway operates on Sunday afternoons during the winter and on Saturday and Sunday afternoons during the summer.

One of the five Victorian street lamps installed between the tracks in 2015 was seen between the cars on 27 May 2023.

APPENDIX 6

AUTOMATED PEOPLE MOVERS

These airport automated people movers are rope-hauled systems. Heathrow Terminal 5, Gatwick and Stansted have third-rail electric or guided systems. The latter is to be closed in the spring of 2026.

Birmingham International

Birmingham Airport's Air-Rail link connects the airport with Birmingham International Station and the National Exhibition Centre. It was opened in 2003, replacing the maglev system that ran between 1984 and 1995, although it used the maglev structure. It is 585m (1,919ft) long; the maglev had been 600m (1,969ft) long. The cable system was provided by Doppelmayr Cable Car GmbH, an Austrian company. The Birmingham system was the company's first airport installation in the UK. One two-car train runs on each track. Running at 22mph, the journey time is ninety seconds. At off-peak times trains run on demand.

Luton DART

Luton's DART (Direct-Air Rail Transit) was opened fully on 27 March 2023. It had previously been opened for trials and part-time operation. Connecting the Midland Main Line at Luton Airport Parkway station with the airport, it is 2.1km (1.3 miles) long. The single-car trains, one on each track, make the journey in about four minutes. They run every four minutes during the day, and between four and nine times an hour at other times. The route includes an 80m-long (260ft) bridge crossing the A1081 road, shown in the photograph, and a cut-and-cover tunnel under the airport apron. It is another Doppelmayr Cable Car GmbH system. Consultation has taken place about expanding airport capacity with a second terminal, which would include the DART being extended if it goes ahead.

APPENDIX 7
VERTICAL LIFTS

Several resorts found a solution to the requirement to transport visitors between one level and another in vertical lifts. Two of them have been demolished, three have been accorded the accolade of an English Heritage listing but only three of them were in working order at the time of writing.

Saltburn Hoist

In place from 1870 to 1883, the story of the Saltburn hoist was outlined in Chapter 4. There were no published complaints about its stability, but it did require several guy ropes to keep it upright. If it was run at the speeds used by underground lifts in coal mines then using it would have been quite an exhilarating experience for the Victorian visitor.

Brighton

Brighton's three-level lift was constructed as a part of the unique ½ mile-long cast iron promenade and terrace and opened in 1890. The ensemble was the work of the borough surveyor, Phillip C. Lockwood. It was Grade II* listed on 19 August 1971. The lift was water balanced when built but converted to electric working on an unrecorded date. It was refurbished between 2007–09 and further work was undertaken on it in 2013. Some 10 tons of lead was stolen from the lift roof and the promenade shelters in December 2019.

In March 2023 Brighton & Hove City Council announced that the lift would not be reopened after the winter closure and that its structure had deteriorated to such an extent as to be unrepairable. The closure of the terrace in 2014–15 had limited its usefulness and it could not at any event accommodate mobility scooters. Therefore, a new accessible lift to be constructed at the Royal Crescent steps is expected, at the time of writing, to be opened in 2025. The picture, taken in 2024, shows the relationship between the lift and the beach, including the route of the Volks Electric Railway. The council now no doubt expects that the fence erected on Marine Parade will protect the lift from lead thieves.

222 • CLIFF RAILWAYS: AN HISTORIC SURVEY

Shanklin I

The Shanklin Passenger Lift Company was incorporated on 10 March 1882, with £3,000 capital and the intention of constructing and operating a lift on Shanklin's sea front. Three of the signatories to the articles being Scarborough residents, it might be imagined that they wished to spread the benefits of cliff lifts to other seaside resorts. Indeed, one of them was Robert Mitchell, the former manager of the South Cliff Tramway. However, beyond a meeting with the local board, the landowner and the engineer, a Mr Thurston, in June 1882 nothing more was heard of the proposal.

Little was reported about the lift that was opened in 1891. Its engineers were John Holmes Blakesley (1853–1943) and Charles Edward Robinson (1863–1912), the latter having worked on the Folkestone lifts. In 1890 they submitted details of the proposed hydraulic lift to the local board and in July 1891 the structure was reported to have reached the clifftop. It was opened without published comment, so presumably also without ceremony. George Newnes was one of its promoters and in 1893 he transferred his interest to the Shanklin Lift Company. The company ran the lift with very little reported comment until 1940, when it sustained damage of unspecified cause or nature that rendered it unusable. The enterprise was sold to the local authority by means of powers contained in the Sandown-Shanklin Urban District Council Act, 1955, and the company was wound up in 1956.

Located near the junction of East Cliff Promenade with Palmerston Road, the upper level of the lift is accessed by a bridge, as shown in this view soon after it had been opened.

Ramsgate East Cliff

The first of three lifts built in Ramsgate was on the East Cliff. In 1902 the town had been an unfulfilled target for a Reno electric stairway installation. Lift makers R. Waygood & Company approached the town council about installing a lift on the East Cliff in 1907. In return for paying 2½% of the takings, the company obtained a thirty-year licence to build and operate the lift and had first refusal on building any other lifts on the town's cliffs. The architect was George Graham Tucker (1866–1932), already encountered in connection with the Broadstairs tunnel lift, who decorated the tower with ornate art nouveau features. The contractor was Grummant Brothers of Ramsgate. The lift was opened by the town's mayor in August 1908. Purchased by the Council in 1919, it was replaced in 1970, its successor opening on 1 August. It was closed when requiring £16,500 of repairs in 1996 and demolished in 1998. (Photochrom)

One of the postcards produced by Cliff Lifts Ltd to promote its enterprise.

VERTICAL LIFTS • 223

Ramsgate Harbour

Ramsgate's second lift was another Tucker–Waygood collaboration, proposed by the company in May 1909 to target users of the South Eastern & Chatham Railway's Ramsgate Harbour station. With features similar to those in the first lift, it was opened without ceremony in August 1910. For a few years a clock was mounted on the upper front-right corner as viewed from the Pavilion, with its numerals replaced by the letters of 'WAYGOODS LIFT'; presumably its mounting was insufficient to cope with the gales encountered in a seafront location. Both lifts were operated by Cliff Lifts Ltd, the Waygood subsidiary, and in 1919 the council agreed to buy them for £2,000, payable over three years in six-monthly instalments. The motor was replaced in 1938. The boundary of the railway station is on the lower left of this postcard view. (J. Valentine)

The lower station seen on 10 August 2024. It was excluded from the listing as it was deemed to have no architectural merit; although its roof has been replaced at some time, most of the structure appears to date from 1910.

In the 1950s cracks developing in the structure were addressed by strengthening the tower with an internal steel frame and installing a smaller passenger car, reducing capacity from twenty to sixteen. The lift was taken out of use in 1995 and fell into disrepair but funding from a seafront regeneration scheme enabled it to be restored and reopened on 23 April 1999. It was given a Grade II listing on 31 May 2007 but following the theft of the lead from the roof in 2021 it has been out of use. Although the roof has been repaired, the upper doors require replacing and other work will be required before the lift can be reopened.

Ramsgate West Cliff

In 1923 Ramsgate Town Council purchased the Murray-Smith Estate on the town's West Cliff and set about developing it for housing and leisure amenities and extending the town's seafront. A competition for the development saw the contract awarded to Franklin & Deacon, a Luton partnership that had been placed third, but whose scheme was considered to be the most practical and economical. Their plan included a lift on the adjoining Government Acre site, which had been in the council's possession 'for many years'. Architect Basil Charlton Deacon (1879–1959) managed the scheme's fulfilment. The first phase of the project, the West Cliff promenade and footpaths, was opened by the Prince of Wales on 24 November 1926. The £3,328 contract for building the lift was awarded to a local company, W. W. Martin, and it was probably opened on 2 August 1929, the date that the bandstand and pavilions were opened, although no report about the lift has been found. This postcard view was taken in 1929. (J. Valentine)

Another 1929 view shows the upper station. (J. Valentine)

Below: The date that the 'wings' were added to the lift is unknown, but cliff stabilisation work was carried out in 1952. Quotes for replacing the lift equipment obtained in 1972 would have entailed raising the top of the structure. Although one of the tenders was approved, the structural work was obviously not carried out so another solution must have been found to keeping the lift running. The date the lift was closed has gone unrecorded and unremarked. Thanet Council did not run its lifts in 1995 and 1996, on economy grounds, and it was probably never reopened. Construction of a new road to serve the port in 2000 has, in any event, separated the lift from the beach and deprived it of its purpose. It was given a Grade II listing on 31 May 2007.

Blackpool

'Famous for fresh air and fun.' So said Stanley Holloway in the voice of Albert Ramsbottom about Blackpool. The lift on the North Cliff at Queen's Promenade was built to the design of the borough architect John Charles Robinson in 1930. Designed to facilitate the transfer of passengers between the nearby tram stop and the beach, the basic design is of classical revival style. It was accessed by a bridge, seen here, at the upper level, and by a tunnel though false cliffs at the lower.

Blackpool's North Cliff lift seen in 2024. Cliff subsidence in 1979 affected the lift structure and it was closed until March 1991, when it was reopened with only one of the cars in service and the upper waiting room removed. Listed Grade II on 8 March 2010, it has not been used for several years. The concrete portal on the lower promenade indicates the position of the lower entrance; its doors remain in situ. The doors to an intermediate access have been bricked up.

Whitby West Cliff

Being in Yorkshire and having a sandy beach and cliffs it can be no surprise that there was interest in improving access to Whitby's beach by means of a lift. The *Yorkshire Post* mentioned the idea in 1911. The town council acquired most of the West Cliff and seashore in 1913 and in 1914 the Local Government Board's Provisional Order authorising, inter alia, construction and operation of a cliff lift, was confirmed by Parliament. Progress was then delayed until 1925, when the sand approach sub-committee and the surveyor were instructed to investigate the cost of building and operating a 'cliff tramway'. When the council's chairman reviewed outstanding capital projects in 1928 the lift was one that he thought could be deferred for a year or two. However, an inquiry into the borrowing required was held in 1929 and Newcastle-based W. G. Armstrong's tender was accepted before the end of the year. With construction carried out during 1930, the lift was opened by Mabel Sawdon (1888–1965), wife of the council's chairman, on 20 May 1931. Its upper station, which contains the motor room, was photographed in 1933. (J. Valentine)

The lower level of the lift is accessed by a 221ft-long tunnel from the beach promenade, the entrance to which was seen in 2024. One of the lift's cars was taken out of service in 2003 and was subsequently removed. Some 3,000 bolts were replaced at a cost of £85,000 in 2013.

In April 2022 water damage and corrosion caused the lift to be closed and a 'lift replacement' bus service substituted. The lift shaft was dug through boulder clay and water ingress has been a problem for many years, not helped by the lack of ventilation when the lift is closed. A report on the *Scarborough News* website (10 January 2024) quoted council members saying that the council was undecided about whether it should replace the lift or repair it regardless of the cost.

The pick-up point for the replacement bus service can be seen in this 2024 photograph of the upper-level building.

Margate Cliftonville

Margate Chamber of Commerce called upon the town council to provide a lift giving access to the sands at Cliftonville in 1905. In 1910 the council did discuss with R. Waygood & company its terms for permitting a lift to be constructed opposite Second Avenue, but nothing came of the proposal until March 1934. Then a £989 tender for construction of a lift tower and Waygood-Otis Ltd's £1,185 tender for the necessary equipment were accepted. The site chosen, however, was nearer to Third Avenue. Opened later in 1934, it was refurbished in the 1990s. Despite being the most used of the four lifts then owned by Thanet Council, the others being in Ramsgate, in 1992, insufficient use caused it to be closed in 2009. It was Grade II listed, with an acknowledgment of its art deco style with egyptian influences, on 5 November 2014.

The photographs were taken on 8 June 2024.

Marsden Bay

The lift at Marsden Bay is unique in that it was built by a brewery and serves a pub/restaurant and hotel. The bay is on the Northumbrian coast, just south of South Shields, the outcrops in the sea adding to its allure. The business has its origins in a smugglers' cave that was adapted for residential use and much extended by one of its occupants in the nineteenth century. The Newcastle brewer Charles Vaux & Sons Ltd bought the property circa 1900 and, encouraged by improved access following the opening of the coast road in 1935, in March 1937 started a £12,000 scheme to refurbish and extend the premises, including provision of an electric lift. With visitor accommodation, as well as four bars and a restaurant, and the lift, the Marsden Grotto Inn was reopened in May 1938. The contractor was R. W. Bell & Company (Builders) Ltd of Newcastle. Reports on the refurbishment did not identify the architect responsible. The lift shaft is 110ft high.

This view was first published in 1948. (J. Valentine)

In 1972 a further refurbishment saw the lift and its tower replaced. The property is now owned by a hotel group. The beach, which was once noted for its sand, is now one of pebbles. Photographed on 23 June 2023.

Shanklin II

Sandown Shanklin council obtained tenders for erecting a new lift on the site of the first in 1956. Substantially built of concrete, the lower entrance is twisted from the lift to face the access road. This lift had two cars, as opposed to the single car of the first. The lettering on the roof must have succumbed to the weather. The lift was opened with great ceremony, with a message from the former Prime Minister, Sir Winston Churchill, on 14 May 1958. (Nigh's)

The upper section of Shanklin's lift in 2024. The beach is on the lower right and Sandown is across the bay. The lift underwent a thorough overhaul in 2016, only the guide rails and counterweights remaining from the 1958 installation. Maintaining the bridge has not been without difficulty, aggravated by the instability of the cliff and the restricted access. After a period with a temporary structure, it was most recently replaced in 2017. Only one car was in use at the time of writing. Operation is supervised, the attendant collecting the fares. The author can attest that the ride is extremely smooth and quiet, with no sensation of movement.

Broadstairs Viking Bay

Thanet District Council opened the stylish 53ft-high Viking Bay lift in Broadstairs in 2000, just a short distance away from the abandoned underground cliff railway. Despite its recent construction, when replacement components are required for repairs, they have long lead times because they need to be manufactured to order.

Southend Pier Hill

The Pier Hill lift at Southend certainly makes an architectural statement. It was opened by Southend Borough Council in 2004 as the centrepiece of a £5.8 million development, connecting the town with the seafront and the pier. Part of the cost was contributed by the European Union. The lift has two cars.

APPENDIX 8

OTHER LIFTS

There are several locations around the country where companies, institutions and individuals have found or find a cliff railway or lift to be advantageous. Most of them are on private sites but a few are accessible from public vantage points. The sale of a house in Dawlish that has a 50ft long single-track cliff railway was mentioned in the January 2025 issue of *Railway Magazine*. They are represented here by images of RNLI sites.

In other circumstances that in earlier times might have called for a cliff railway, modern technology allows for new solutions to achieve the same objective. Illustrated here are examples at Ebbw Vale and on the Elizabeth Line.

In 1960 the RNLI built a new lifeboat station at Kilcobben Cove in Cornwall. To deliver crew and supplies to and from the station, a cliff railway was built at the inland end. It also carries rescued persons to the clifftop. (T. P. Roskrow)

The cliff railway at the St Davids lifeboat station in Wales, seen in 2007. (Steve Sedgwick)

Ebbw Vale Cableway

In South Wales, Blaenau Gwent Council built the Ebbw Vale Cableway as part of a scheme to regenerate the town's steelworks site, linking it with the town square. At the lower level it serves the railway station, Gwent Archives and Coleg Gwent's Parth Dysgu Blaenau Gwent (Blaenau Gwent Learning Zone), an 'A' level college. Its £2.3 million cost was supported by the European Union. Originally referred to as 'the mechanical link', it is 47m long and has a rise of 23m. The equipment was supplied by ABS Transportbahnen of Austria. Free to use and user operated, it was opened on 17 June 2015.

Unfortunately, it was immediately beset by vandalism, which contributed to its closure on 252 occasions during its first two years of operation, a figure much quoted by the press without explaining that there was nothing inherently wrong with the lift. Since November 2017 interruptions to service were minimised by the employment of security personnel. In April 2023 Blaenau Gwent Council announced that it could no longer afford the £52,000 annual running cost and would close the lift at the end of the month, but a few weeks later it announced that £41,000 a year had been secured from the Shared Prosperity Fund to run the lift until 31 March 2025, so it remains in operation at the time of writing.

Elizabeth Line

The engineers who designed and built London's Elizabeth Line adopted many innovative features, among them the lifts at Farringdon and Liverpool Street stations. Required to provide accessible lifts in places where the station layouts did not permit the construction of a vertical shaft, they inclined two lifts and placed them in escalator shafts. There are two at Farringdon and one at Liverpool Street. They are user worked and travel at the same speed as the adjacent escalator. It is said that these lifts are cheaper to run than an equivalent vertical lift. The photograph shows the lower level of the lift at the Barbican end of Farringdon station.

The interior of the lift.

PHOTOGRAPHIC ADDENDUM

The upper station of the Constitution Hill Lift, Aberystwyth, in the 1970s. (Graham Holt)

The upper station of Hastings' West Hill Lift seen on 15 May 1948. (J. H. Meredith/Online Transport Archive)

The entrance to the West Hill lift's upper station at Hastings after the cafe and toilets had been built, 23 May 1977. (Online Transport Archive)

The lower station of Scarborough's North Bay Lift as seen on 26 July 1985. In 1997 there were complaints in the press about the area being run down, as illustrated by the removal of the roofs of the waiting shelters. (Online Transport Archive)

One of the Bridgnorth Castle Hill Tramway's cars at the upper station in 1994. Concerned about the railway's shabby appearance and realising that its owners were not interested in addressing the issue, Bridgnorth Town Council had commenced negotiating its purchase in 1991, going so far as issuing a prospectus in 1994 and appointing John Edwards, a garage owner, to operate it in 1995. However, before the council had completed the purchase, Allan Reynolds acquired 90% of the operating company's shareholding and took control in 1996. (T. P. Cooper)

Reynolds and his wife soon stamped their mark on the railway, as shown in this 1998 photograph. (T. P. Cooper)

PHOTOGRAPHIC ADDENDUM • 235

Folkestone's Leas, looking westwards, with the roofs of cars on both 1885 and 1890 lifts visible. The Longford Hotel, on the right, was replaced by an apartment block in the 1960s.

The upper station of the Metropole lift, also looking westwards, in 1901; the Sandgate lift's upper station was half a mile beyond. On the right is the Grand Hotel, with the larger Metropole Hotel beyond it. The Grand was built by a builder aggrieved at not being given the contract to build the Metropole. Both are Grade II listed. (J. Valentine)

236 • CLIFF RAILWAYS: AN HISTORIC SURVEY

BIBLIOGRAPHY

Aberystwyth Cliff Railway, *Souvenir Guide*, Aberystwyth Cliff Railway, 1996

Bartle, Amy, *An Illustrated Guide to the Funicular Railways of Great Britain*, Heritage Railway Association, 2014

Bartle, Amy, *Souvenir History & Miscellany of the Central Tramway Company Scarborough*, Central Tramway Company

Body, Geoffrey & Eastleigh, Robert L., *Cliff Railways*, David & Charles, 1964

Bridgnorth and its Castle Hill Railway, Castle Hill Railway Co., 1892, reissued by the Bridgnorth Initiative, 1992

Brown, Fay, *Ups and Downs – titbits of information on proposals for funicular railways and lifts in Ventnor*, Ventnor & District History Society, 1999

Burrell, Michael J., *Cliff Hangers*, Pear Tree Cottage Publications, 2000

Cooper, David & Ayres, John, Babbacombe Cliff Railway to the seaside & back since 1926, Babbacombe Cliff Railway CIC, 2013

Easdown, Martin, *Cliff Railways, lifts and funiculars*, Amberley, 2018

Farrell, F. K., The Shipley Glen Tramway, *Modern Tramway*, October 1965

Foxall, F. B., The Bridgnorth Castle Hill Railway, Bridgnorth Historical Publications

Gwilt, *A History of Castle Hill Railway*, author, 1990

Hart, Brian, *Folkestone's Cliff Lifts*, Millgate Publishing, 1985

Lane, Michael. R., *Baron Marks of Woolwich*, Quiller Press, 1986

Leak, M. J., *The Shipley Glen Tramway – Its social history since 1865 and its mechanics*, Shipley Glen Preservation Co., 2016

Lynmouth & Lynton Lift Company, *Lynton & Lynmouth Cliff Railway – one of the world's most unusual railways*, Lynmouth & Lynton Lift Company, various editions

Lynmouth & Lynton Lift Company, *Lynton & Lynmouth Cliff Railway – centenary year*, Lynmouth & Lynton Lift Company, 1990

Lynmouth & Lynton Lift Company, *Lynton & Lynmouth Cliff Railway – established in 1888*, Lynmouth & Lynton Lift Company, various editions

Scarffe, Andrew, *The Railways and Tramways of Laxey*, manninmedia [2014]

Shapland, Maggie, The Ups and Downs of the Clifton Rocks Railway and the Clifton Spa, Bristol Industrial Archaeological Society, 2017

Turner, Keith, *Cliff Railways of the British Isles*, Oakwood Press, 2002

Turner, Keith, The Directory of British Tramways, Patrick Stephens Ltd, 1996

Voice, David, *The Definitive Guide to Trams (including funiculars) in the British Isles*, Adam Gordon, 3rd edition, 2005

Waite, Glynn, *The Matlock Cable Tramway*, Pynot Publishing, 2012

West Hill Cliff Railway Hastings Centenary Celebrations 1891–1991, Hastings Borough Council, 1991

Whitrick, Alan & Leak, Michael J., *1d Up – ½d Down – The Story of Shipley Glen and its tramway*, Bradford Trolleybus Association, 1982

INDEX

Aberystwyth Constitution Hill lift, 115-125, 233
Aberystwyth Cliff Railway Company, 123
Aberystwyth Improvement Company, 115, 118/9
Aberystwyth Pier Company, 123
Accidents, 11/2, 15, 26, 28, 45/6, 51-3, 61, 70, 83, 96, 103, 118, 130, 136-8, 179/80, 182, 212
Act of Parliament, 6, 39, 47, 61/2, 96/7, 133, 226
Air-Rail link, Birmingham Airport, 221
Automated People Movers, 221

Babbacombe Cliff Light Railway, 170-84
Estimate, 1923, 210
Babbacombe Cliff Railway CIC/CIO, 182
Babbacombe Cliff Railway Order, 182
BBC, 107/8
British Ropeway Engineering Company, 139
Birmingham Carriage & Wagon Company, 82
Blackpool Lift, 226
Board of Trade, 8, 11-3, 21/2, 25, 47, 61/2, 67/8, 70, 119, 145, 209, 213
Bourne & Grant, 115/6, 118
Bournemouth, 53, 147-55, 171, 196-99
East Lift, 147-51
Southbourne (Fisherman's Walk) Lift, 196-9
West Lift, 152-5
Bradford Metropolitan Council, 219
Bradford Trolleybus Association, 219
Brakes, 12, 21/2, 24/5, 30/1, 45-55, 62, 65, 67-9, 73, 77, 82, 95, 97/8, 105, 111, 114, 118, 136, 139/40, 145, 163, 172, 213
Bridgnorth, 92-102
Brighton, 34/5, 222
Bristol Tramways Company, 103-5, 109
Brixton, 213
Broadstairs Lift Company, 157/6
Broadstairs Lifts, 156-159, 229
Browside Tramway, 77-9

Cable Tramways, 212-4
Cableway Directive, 2004, 165
Cairngorm Mountain Railway, 216

Castle Hill Railway, 92-102, 103/4, 116
Central Tramway, Scarborough, 24-33
Centre for Alternative Technology Lift, 203-6
Clacton electric stairway, 162, 215
Clayton Equipment Ltd, 201
Clayton, Reginald, Ltd, 139
Cliff Bridge Company, 9, 11, 13, 25
Cliff Grounds Ltd, 120
Cliff Lifts Ltd, 156, 163, 223/4
Clifton Rocks Railway, 103-9
Cliftonville Lifts, 160-1, 227
Constitution Hill Lift, 8, 115-126
Constitution Hill Ltd, 124-6
Covid Pandemic, 39, 167, 203, 220
Crossley gas engine, 9, 38, 104, 111
Cunningham holiday camp, Isle of Man, 163

Devil's Dyke Railway, 217/8
Direct-Air Rail Transit (DART), Luton, 221
Douglas Head Incline Railway Ltd, 191
Douglas Head Lift, 130-2
Douglas Head Marine Drive, 127-9
Duke of Edinburgh, 116, 118/9
Duke of Edinburgh, visit, 73

East Hill Lift, Hastings, 133-43
Ebbw Vale Cableway, 232
Edinburgh cable tramways, 212
Electric & General Contract Corporation, 127
Elizabeth Line, 232
Electric Stairways, 162-3, 215
Engineer, 11, 14, 24, 45, 62, 70, 73, 87, 116, 123, 133, 144, 171, 196, 200, 213, 217
Express Lift Company, 199

Falcon Cliff Hotel Lift I, 45-6, 127-9
Falcon Cliff Hotel Lift II, 185-7
Fildes, F. J., Ltd. 97
Folkestone Cliff Tramway, the Leas, 47-59
Folkestone, Metropole Lift, 144-6
Folkestone, Promenade & Pier Company, 47
Folkestone, Sandgate & Hythe Tramway, 208
Friends of Babbacombe Cliff Railway, 181

Garden Festival Wales, Ebbw Vale, 218
General Traction Company, 127
Gimson, Josiah, & Company, 93, 104
Glen Tramway Preservation Company, 220
Great Orme Tramway, 212/3

Hall, G. L., Major, 172
Hall, J. & E., Ltd, 179, 188, 193
Hastings Corporation Act, 1900, 133
Hastings East Hill Lift, 133-43
Hastings Lift Company, 80-5
Hastings Passenger Lift Company, 85-7
Hastings West Hill Lift, 80-91, 233/4
Health & Safety Executive, 7, 54, 124, 220
Health, Ministry of, 188, 193
Heritage England listing, 25, 222, 226, 227
Heritage Railways Association, 7
Highgate, 213
Hocking & Company, 180
Holme & King, contractors, 81, 85
Hudswell, Clarke, 18, 29
Hutchinson, Charles Scrope, 11-3, 21-4, 47/8, 50, 63, 82/3, 111

Inspection, 11-3, 21/2, 54, 63, 82, 124, 157, 202, 213

Jones, Bob, 60-3, 65, 68, 68, 70, 73/4, 111, 114, 170
Jones Brothers, 60, 63, 65, 70, 111

Lancastrian Carriage & Wagon Company, 203
Laxey, 77-9
Lifting Operations Equipment & Lift Regulations, 1998, 7
Light Railway Order, 6, 53, 170-2, 178/9, 208
Llechwedd Slate Caverns, 200-2
Local Government Board, 60, 170/1, 188
London cable tramways 313
Lynmouth Pier Order, 60
Lynton & Lynmouth Lift, 6/7, 60-76, 92, 170
Lynton & Lynmouth Lift Act, 61-3

Malvern Funicular Light Railway, 171, 208
Manager, 14, 25/6, 74, 87, 119, 148, 171, 223
Margate Lift, 227
Marks, George Croydon, 6/7, 37, 62, 68, 92-5, 101, 103, 115/6, 118, 170, 212/3
Marsden Bay Lift, 228
Matlock Cable Tramway, 213
Medway's Safety Lift Company, 188, 193
Metropole Lift, Folkestone, 144-6

Metropolitan Railway & Carriage Company, 9, 22, 38
Metropolitan Vickers Electrical Company, 97
Mid Wales Mining Museum Ltd, 123
Middlesbrough Owners, 37/8

National Coal Board, 201
National Lottery Heritage Fund, 56, 159, 165, 182
National Transport Trust, 43, 75, 167
Neville, George, Truck Equipment Ltd, 29
Newnes, George, 6/7, 60-3, 65-7, 70/1, 74, 92/3, 103, 105, 170, 172, 212/3/ 223
North Bay Lift, Scarborough, 193-5, 234

Oddicombe beach, 175
Otis Elevator Company, 6, 145, 159, 164, 172/3, 227
Otto gas engine, 38, 39, 45, 83

Paston Place Lift, 34
Patent, 12/3, 24, 62, 65, 111
Plaxton, F. W. Ltd, 28/9
Port Soderick Lift, 127-9
Princess of Wales, 116

Quarry Tours Ltd, 200
Queen's Parade Tramway, 20-3

Ramsgate lifts, 223-5
Ramsgate Town Council, 223-5
Red Wheel award, 43, 75, 167
Reno Inclined Elevator Construction Syndicate, 162
Reno stairways, 162/3, 165, 176, 178, 215, 223
RNLI lifts, 231

Saltburn Hoist, 36, 222
Saltburn Improvement Company, 36/7
Saltburn Incline Tramway, 36-44
St Nicholas Cliff Lift Company, 188, 191
St Nicholas Lift, Scarborough, 188-92
Sandgate Hill Lift, 110-4
Scarborough Spa, 9-11, 14-6, 25
Scarborough, North Bay Lift, 193-5, 234
Scarborough, St Nicholas Lift, 188-92
Scarborough, South Cliff Tramway, 9-19
Secretary, 14, 25, 51, 70, 82, 98
Shanklin Lifts, 223, 229
Shipley Glen Tramway, 218-20
South Cliff Tramway, Scarborough, 9-19
Southend on Sea Electric stairway, 162/3, 215
Southend on Sea Lifts, 162-9, 230
Stanegate Restorations and Replicas, 39, 41

Steep grade railways, 216-20
Sunday operating, 15, 54, 81, 84, 96, 96, 134, 137, 220
Swansea, Constitution Hill, 213/4

Tangye & Company, 24, 37/8, 62, 86
Thanet Amusements Ltd, 157
Thanet Council, 157-9, 225, 227, 229
Torquay Tramways, 170-5
Transport, Ministry of, 53, 171-4, 178, 182
Tredomen Engineering Ltd, 201
Tynemouth electric stairway, 215

Unbuilt cliff railways, 208/9
Upper Douglas Tramway, 214

Ventnor Inclined Light Railway, 171-208/9
Vertical lifts, 222-30
Volk, Magnus, 34/5

Wales Tourist Board, 123
Wadsworth & Sons, 185
War Department, 111
Waygood, R. & Company, 6, 47, 49, 81, 137, 145, 147, 156, 159, 160, 162-4, 172/3, 223/4, 227
Waygood Richard, 6
West Hill Lift, Hastings, 80-91, 233/4
Wheel Sets (UK) Ltd, 31, 143
Whitby West Cliff Lift, 226/7
Works & Buildings, Ministry of, 107

Yorkshire's fourth cliff railway, the Saltburn line is in the minority of lifts that have retained their use of water power. It also remains an essential part of Saltburn's infrastructure.